RIGHTS, BODIES AND RECOGNITION

Rights, Bodies and Recognition

New Essays on Fichte's *Foundations of Natural Right*

Edited by

TOM ROCKMORE
Duquesne University, USA

DANIEL BREAZEALE
University of Kentucky, USA

Routledge
Taylor & Francis Group
LONDON AND NEW YORK

First published 2006 by Ashgate Publishing

Published 2018 by Routledge
2 Park Square, Milton Park, Abingdon, Oxon OX14 4RN
52 Vanderbilt Avenue, New York, NY 10017

First issued in paperback 2018

Routledge is an imprint of the Taylor & Francis Group, an informa business

British Library Cataloguing in Publication Data
Rights, bodies and recognition : new essays on Fichte's
Foundations of natural right
1. Fichte, Johann Gottlieb, 1762–1814. Grundlage des
Naturrechts 2. Natural law 3. State, The 4. Political science
– Philosophy
I. Breazeale, Daniel II. Rockmore, Tom, 1942–
320'.01

Library of Congress Cataloging-in-Publication Data
Rights, bodies and recognition : new essays on Fichte's Foundations of natural right
/ edited by Daniel Breazeale and Tom Rockmore.
p. cm.
Includes bibliographical references.
ISBN 0-7546-5502-4 (hardcover : alk. paper)
1. Fichte, Johann Gottlieb, 1762–1814. 2. Natural law. 3. Political science.
4. State, The. I. Breazeale, Daniel II. Rockmore, Tom, 1942–

JC181.R53 2005
323'.01—dc22

2005018589

ISBN 13: 978-1-138-25225-7 (pbk)
ISBN 13: 978-0-7546-5502-2 (hbk)

Contents

List of Contributors

Michael Baur, Associate Professor of Philosophy, Fordham University.

Daniel Breazeale, Professor of Philosophy, University of Kentucky.

Yolanda Estes, Associate Professor of Philosophy, Mississippi State University

Arnold Farr, Associate Professor of Philosophy and Africana Studies, St Joseph's University.

Bärbel Frischmann, Scientific Assistant, Department of Philosophy, University of Bremen.

Steven Hoeltzel, Assistant Professor of Philosophy, James Madison University.

Jeffery Kinlaw, Associate Professor of Philosophy, McMurry University.

Hans Georg von Manz, Lecturer, Department of Philosophy, University of Munich and Associate Editor, Bavarian Academy of Sciences Edition of the Complete Works of J.G. Fichte.

Wayne M. Martin, Professor of Philosophy, University of California – San Diego.

Bruce Merrill, independent scholar.

Angelica Nuzzo, Associate Professor, Brooklyn College CUNY.

Tom Rockmore, Professor of Philosophy, Duquesne University.

F. Scott Scribner, Assistant Professor of Philosophy, Hillyer College, University of Hartford.

Violetta L. Waibel, Assistant Professor, Institute for Philosophy, University of Vienna.

Robert R. Williams, Professor of German and Religious Studies, University of Illinois at Chicago.

Michael G. Vater, Associate Professor of Philosophy, Marquette University.

Günter Zöller, Professor of Philosophy, University of Munich.

List of Abbreviations

APT	*Annalen des philosophischen Tons* (1797)
BWL	*Ueber den Begriff der Wissenschaftslehre* (1794)
EPW	*Fichte: Early Philosophical Writings*, ed. and trans. Daniel Breazeale (Ithaca, NY: Cornell University Press, 1988)
FNR	*Foundations of Natural Right*, ed. Frederick Neuhouser, trans. Michael Baur (Cambridge: Cambridge University Press, 2000)
FTP	*Fichte: Foundations of Transcendental Philosophy (Wissenschaftslehre) nova methodo*, ed. and trans. Daniel Breazeale (Ithaca, NY: Cornell University Press, 1992)
GA	*J.G. Fichte-Gesamtausgabe der Bayerischen Akademie der Wissenschaften*, ed. Reinhard Lauth, Hans Gliwitzky, and Erich Fuchs (Stuttgart-Bad Cannstatt: Frommann-Holzboog, 1964ff.)
GNR	*Grundlage des Naturrechts* (1796/97)
GWL	*Grundlage der gesammten Wissenschaftslehre* (1794/95)
IWL	*Introductions to the Wissenschaftslehre and Other Writings*, ed. and trans. Daniel Breazeale (Indianapolis: Hackett, 1994)
KA	Friedrich Schlegel, *Kritische Ausgabe*, ed. von Ernst Behler et al., Paderborn, 1958 ff.
NDN	Friedrich Wilhelm Joseph Schelling, *Neue Deduktion des Naturrechts* (W, I: 247–80; UHK: 221–47).
SS	*System der Sittenlehre* (1798)
SW	*Johann Gottlieb Fichtes sämmtliche Werke*, ed. I.H. Fichte, 8 vols (Berlin: Viet and Co., 1845–46); rpt, along with the three volumes of *Johann Gottlieb Fichtes nachgelassene Werke* (Bonn: Adolphus-Marcus, 1834–35), as *Fichtes Werke* (Berlin: de Gruyter, 1971)
UHK	Friedrich Wilhelm Joseph Schelling, *The Unconditional in Human Knowledge: Four Early Essays (1794–1796)*, trans. and ed. Fritz Marti (Lewisburg: Bucknell University Press, 1980).
W	Friedrich Wilhelm Joseph Schelling, *Sämmtliche Werke*, ed. K.F.A. Schelling (Stuttgart/Augsburg: J.G. Cotta, 1856–61).
WLnm[H]	*Wissenschaftslehre nova methodo* ("Halle Nachshrift," 1796/97)
WLnm[K]	*Wissenschaftslehre nova methodo* ("Krause Nachschrift," 1798/99)

Introduction
On the Origin and the Originality of Fichte's *Foundations of Natural Right*

When he arrived in Jena for the summer semester of 1794, Fichte had already made a name for himself, not only for his strikingly "Kantian" (which is to say, moral) interpretation of the concept of divine revelation, in his 1792 *Attempt at a Critique of all Revelation*, but also for his enthusiastic support for the principles and aims of the French revolution, in his anonymously published *Contribution toward Correcting the Public's Judgment of the French Revolution* (1793 and 1794). Indeed, it was largely on the basis of his advanced social and political views that he was, on the one hand, warmly welcomed by a portion of the students and faculty at his new institution, while on the other he was suspected and vilified by another portion of the same, as well as by many of the officials of the court at Weimar, which was ultimately responsible for his appointment. It thus comes as no surprise that when he began developing, in his lectures at Jena, his new system of philosophy (the so-called *Wissenschaftslehre*) the first systematic branch or subdivision of the same to which he turned his attention was precisely social and political philosophy – or, as he generally called it, the "theory of right" (*Rechtslehre*) or "doctrine of natural right" (*Naturrechtslehre*) – a topic that remained very close indeed to his own heart and at the center of his own, practically oriented view not only of philosophy but of human life itself.

In his earliest remarks concerning the structure of his new system, in a letter to F.I. Niethammer (6 December 1793), Fichte indicated that his new (and still unwritten) philosophy would have a tripartite structure, consisting of a first or "general" portion, augmented by two "branches," theoretical and practical philosophy. This schema is reflected in the brief "hypothetical" sketch of the contours of the new system contained in Part III of his first official prospectus for the same, *Concerning the Concept of the Wissenschaftslehre* (1794), though this theoretical/practical division had now become somewhat complicated by the fact that the foundational portion (as represented by the lectures on *The Foundations of the Entire Wissenschaftslehre*, which Fichte would begin delivering almost immediately after arriving in Jena) was itself divided into "theoretical" and "practical" portions. Nevertheless, he concluded his preview of his new system by promising his readers and prospective students that the *Wissenschaftslehre* would by no means be limited to the first, "general" or foundational portion of the same, but that the latter would in turn serve as the basis for "new and thoroughly elaborated theories of the pleasant, the beautiful and sublime, the free obedience of nature to its own laws, God, so-called common sense or the natural sense of truth, and finally, for new theories of natural right and ethics."[1]

During his first year at Jena Fichte devoted himself to a series of well-attended public lectures on *Morality for Scholars*, as well as to two semesters of much more demanding private lectures on transcendental philosophy, in which he developed the foundational portion of his new system.[2] He was, however, unable to complete his lectures during the winter semester of 1794/95 because of student unrest and turmoil in Jena, which included violence directed against his own house.[3] Consequently, he took refuge with his family in the nearby village of Osmannstädt, where he remained throughout the spring and fall, having cancelled his classes for the summer semester of 1795. Fichte devoted most of his time at Osmannstädt to the task of elaborating a new social and political theory "in accord with the principles of the *Wissenschaftslehre*" and working on a new series of lectures on natural right, which he began delivering upon his return to Jena for the winter semester of 1795/96.

Fichte's inaugural lectures on natural right extended over the course of two semesters (the winter semester of 1795/96 and the summer semester of 1796). These lectures formed the basis of the treatise, *Foundations of Natural Right*, which he published in two parts in 1796 and 1797. In fact, the first public hint concerning the radically novel and distinctive character of Fichte's new theory of natural right appeared a few months prior to the publication of Part One of the *Foundations of Natural Right*, namely, in Fichte's lengthy review of Kant's *Perpetual Peace*,[4] in which Fichte indirectly called attention to some of the more salient differences between his own political philosophy and the views expressed by Kant in *Perpetual Peace*. (This was, of course, a year prior to the publication of Kant's own *Doctrine of Right* in 1797.)

In its own way, Fichte's new theory of natural right proved to be just as original and influential as the new theory of the self-consciousness upon which it was nominally based. Of the innovative features of this work, four deserve special mention: First of all, there is the rather sharp distinction which Fichte, in explicit contrast with Kant, introduces between question of morality and questions of law or right (*Recht*), a distinction which allies Fichte's theory with earlier strands of liberal political theory and sharply distinguishes it not only from Kant's, but also from later philosophies of right, such as Hegel's.

Second, Fichte introduces a powerful and striking argument for the necessity of the individual I's being "summoned" by another free I to limit its own freedom out of respect for the freedom of the other. What this account purports to show is that there cannot be just one finite self; instead, in order for a free, finite subject to become conscious of itself – and hence to "posit" itself as an I – it must first recognize *another* such subject. This argument for the profoundly "social" character of human consciousness exercised a direct influence upon Hegel, who provided his own version of such a doctrine in Ch. IV of the *Phenomenology of Spirit*, where he purports to show that intersubjectivity is a condition for the possibility of subjective self-consciousness. But the credit for devising such a deductive strategy belongs to Fichte.

Third, the *Foundations of Natural Right* includes something that may come as a surprise to many readers: namely, a "deduction" of the necessity of an articulate body for the possibility of finite selfhood. Only by means of such a body – as an instrument of its will and a medium of recognition – can a free, individual I express itself as such and thus be recognized by another free individual. Since such recognition is a condition for the possibility of self-consciousness, there can be no individual self-consciousness without a body. The Fichtean I is an *embodied* individual.

Finally, Fichte claims that his new theory of natural right, in contradistinction to many others (including, presumably the still unfinished Kantian theory) is a "material" as well as a formal doctrine (or, as he often puts it, is a "real philosophical science"). What this means, he explains, is that his theory possess *real content* as well as universal form. It possesses such content, moreover, by virtue of its distinctive method: namely, that it *observes* and *describes* a series of "real acts." The foundational portion of the entire *Wissenschaftslehre*, which is also a "real" philosophical science in its own right, describes the most basic self-constitutive acts of the I and thus establishes the "reality" of the I itself, along with that of the world(s) of experience, both theoretical and practical; and the special philosophical sciences obtain their "reality" or material content from those additional, necessary and determinate acts of the I which they observe and describe. Hence the "real content" of the philosophical science of natural right is provided by the concept of right itself, which must therefore be deduced along with its necessary "object" or content: a community of free, embodied individuals, each of whom must limit his or her external freedom and constrain his or her efficacy (*Wirksamkeit*) in specific ways in order to posit himself or herself as one among many, and, ultimately, in order to be able to posit himself or herself (as an individual) at all.

The importance and originality of Fichte's *Foundations of Natural Right* was by no means lost on Fichte's contemporaries, for whom this new treatise became an immediate object of intense and sometimes bitter debate. Meanwhile, however, Fichte was busy revising his original conception of the overall structure of his system (the *Wissenschaftslehre*) and his understanding of the precise place therein of the doctrine of natural right. This revised system conception is evident at the end of his lectures on *Foundations of Transcendental Philosophy (Wissenschaftslehre) nova methodo*, which almost immediately replaced the old lectures on the *Foundations of the Entire Wissenschaftslehre* as his official presentation of the first or foundational portion of his overall system.[5] These new lectures were first delivered the semester following the completion of Fichte's lectures on natural right, that is, during the winter semester of 1796/97, and they were repeated each winter semester thereafter for as long as Fichte remained in Jena. They thus contain his most considered views concerning the overall structure of his own philosophy and the place therein of the doctrine of natural right.

The "Deduction of the Subdivisions of the *Wissenschaftslehre*" which concludes the lectures on *Wissenschaftslehre nova methodo* divides philosophy as a whole not into three but into four (or perhaps five) systematic subdivisions: a first or foundational part of the entire system, theoretical philosophy, practical philosophy, and "philosophy of the postulates," the latter of which is divided, in turn, into philosophy of right and philosophy of religion. The foundational portion of the system is expounded in the lectures on *Wissenschaftslehre nova methodo*. Its task is to derive only the most basic concepts (and objects) of transcendental philosophy, the further analysis and determination of which is the subject of the "special philosophical sciences," each of which has the further task of exhaustively determining the particular concepts (and objects) that constitute its distinctive sphere.

The first of these special philosophical sciences is the "specifically theoretical *Wissenschaftslehre*, or the *Wissenschaftslehre* of cognition (in the Kantian sense)"[6] and deals with everything that we simply *discover* within consciousness whenever we *discover ourselves*: i.e., nature or the world, considered as an object of objective cognition, both as a mechanical system and as a system subject to organic laws. Such a "theory of the world" establishes "how the world is," and thus stipulates what we necessarily can and cannot experience when we discover the world. To be sure, the world in question (nature) is an object of transcendental interest and inquiry only to the extent that it is determined a priori by the laws of thinking, a limitation that prevented Fichte from taking seriously the project of *Naturphilosophie* as developed by Schelling and others. Fichte himself never published a separate treatise on "theoretical philosophy" or "philosophy of nature," perhaps because – as his account of this science suggests – he thought that the basic features of such a science were already implicit in his systematic presentation of the first principles or foundations of the entire system.

The second special philosophical science is "the practical *Wissenschaftslehre*, which becomes the particular science of ethics."[7] If, of course, as Fichte notes, the domain of "the practical" is taken to be congruent with that of acting as such, then the entire system of the *Wissenschaftslehre* is shot through with "practical" elements. As a "particular science," however, "practical philosophy" or ethics deals specifically with those universal laws of reason which determine how every rational person, irrespective of his or her individual circumstances or nature, must limit his or her actions and must always act in a determinate manner. Such a practical philosophical science tells us "how the world ought be made by rational beings;" and, as such, it deals not with individuals, but with "reason itself, in its individuality," inasmuch as individuality is itself a universal condition for the possibility of reason. Viewed in this manner, ethics can be characterized as "the highest abstraction in thinking, which involves an ascent from the level of what is to the pure concept as a motive [for action]."[8] This is the philosophical science that Fichte would definitively explicate near the end of this Jena period, in his *System of Ethics* (1798).[9]

The third special philosophical science or systematic subdivision of the entire *Wissenschaftslehre* is called "the philosophy of the postulates," because it deals with the objects of both theoretical and practical philosophy (nature and freedom), but it deals with them not in isolation or individually, but rather, in their *relation* to each other; more specifically, this subdivision of the system is concerned with the specific *demands* that practical and theoretical philosophy each make upon the realm of the other, and hence with what each specifically "postulates" with respect to the other.

The postulate that theory addresses to the practical realm, that is to pure freedom as embodied in finite rational individuals, is the subject of the first systematic subdivision of the philosophy of the postulates: "the theory of right or natural law" [*die Rechtslehre oder Naturrecht*]. The theory of natural right is the special science that demonstrates how each individual must limit his or her individual freedom within the context of a "juridical world" and subject himself or herself to a "legal constitution," in accordance with a certain mechanical and externally enforceable connection, in order to advance toward the universal goal of reason itself. Since the latter is, properly speaking, the goal of morality, Fichte concludes that this "juridical world must precede the moral world."[10] This new theory of natural right is thus equally theoretical and practical, since it deals with the *world* not as it is, but rather, "as it ought to be found." It is up to us to *produce* such a social world by means of our free activity: that is, it is up to us to establish a civil society and a just state. The "postulate" addressed by theory to practice, and hence the postulate that provides Fichte's theory of right with its starting point is thus as follows: "that many free individuals ought to maintain a certain order and enter into peaceful relations with one another."[11] The *Foundations of Natural Right* (1796/97) examines and "deduces" (from this postulate and from the general nature of consciousness itself, as previously established in the "foundational" portion of the system) what must be presupposed for the possibility or realizing such a postulate and in order to construct a just social-political order.

There is also a postulate addressed by practical to theoretical reason and to the realm of the latter, that is, to nature: namely, "that the sensible world ought to accommodate itself to the goal of reason."[12] This second postulate indicates the distinctive object of the other subdivision of Fichte's philosophy of the postulates, the philosophy of religion. The distinctive task of a transcendental philosophy of religion is to describe and to deduce how nature, in accordance with a supersensible law, is supposed to accommodate itself to the goal of morality. Fichte, of course, never had the opportunity to develop adequately this subdivision of the *Wissenschaftslehre* during his tenure at Jena, though strong hints concerning the probable contents of such a "special science" may be gathered from his notorious 1798 essay, "On the Basis of our Belief in a Divine Government of the World," as well as from portions of his lectures on "Logic and Metaphysics."[13] Though he announced lectures on the philosophy of religion for the summer semester of 1799, Fichte had by then been dismissed from his position in the wake of the atheism controversy.

When one compares this extraordinarily lucid statement of the overall systematic structure of the Jena *Wissenschaftslehre* with what Fichte was actually able to accomplish during this same period one will note that he was able to publish full, scientific presentations of only two of the various "subdivisions of the *Wissenschaftslehre*": namely, a treatise on ethics and another on natural right, which Reinhold accurately described, in an Open Letter to Fichte, as "the two pillars of your philosophy."[14] Indeed, Fichte himself was well aware that his treatise on natural right, along with the one on ethics, was valuable not merely for what it had to say about its ostensible subject, but also as a clear presentation of the basic outlines of the foundational portion of his system, and hence as a serviceable introduction to this *philosophy as a whole*. The *Foundations of Natural Right* and *System of Ethics* thus do much more than simply *extend* the principles of Fichte's previously developed system to new domains; they also provide a clear and much-needed restatement and amplification of these same foundational principles. Thus, both in public announcements and in his private correspondence, Fichte unhesitatingly recommended these two works to anyone seeking a clear presentation of his "philosophy as such."[15] Thus he wrote to Friedrich Johannsen on 31 January 1801: "My published *Wissenschaftslehre* bears too many traces of the period in which it was written and of the manner of philosophizing that then prevailed. For this reason it is less clear than a presentation of transcendental idealism needs to be. Much more to be recommended are the first chapters of my *Natural Right* and my *Ethics* (particularly the latter)."[16]

Given the extraordinary interest and importance of the *Foundations of Natural Right* both for students of social and political philosophy and for anyone interested in the interpretation of Fichte's philosophy in general, a new and accurate English translation of this important work has been long overdue, and thus the appearance of an excellent new translation of the same by Michael Bauer, edited by Frederick Neuhouser and published by Cambridge University Press is a genuine cause for rejoicing.[17] Accordingly and in honor of the appearance of this new translation, the North American Fichte Society devoted its Sixth Bicentennial Meeting to Fichte's *Foundations of Natural Right*. The conference in question was held in La Jolla, California, in the Spring of 1991, under the local auspices of the University of California – San Diego and the North American Fichte Society, with support from the University of California at San Diego Center for the Humanities and the University of California at San Diego German Studies Program. All but one of the papers included in this volume were originally presented at that event, and the ones selected for publication were chosen in order to provide readers with a clear sense both of the extraordinary originality and of the astonishing breadth of Fichte's philosophy of right.

One of the more interesting and disputed issues concerning Fichte's social and political philosophy is the question of the relationship of the same to other, better known approaches to such questions, including the "social contract" tradition and the "natural law" tradition. There are elements of the *Foundations of Natural Right* which strongly suggest an affinity on Fichte's part to one or another of these traditions, but there are also other elements that appear to be incompatible with one or both of these traditional approaches. For detailed discussions of the issues involved in this debate, as well as for helpful exegeses of Fichte's own, distinctive position, the reader is referred to the contributions to this volume by Wayne Martin ("Is Fichte a Social Contract Theorist?"), Michael Baur ("Fichte's Impossible Contract") and Robert R. Williams ("Recognition, Right, and Social Contract").

Another important issue raised by Fichte's theory of natural right is the relation between legality and morality, between "natural law" and "moral law." Unlike, for example, Kant, Fichte tries to distinguish as sharply as possible between these domains. This is the topic of contributions by Violetta Waibel ("On the Fundamental Connection between Natural Right and the Moral Law in Fichte's *Contribution* [1793] and *Foundations* [1796/97])" and Yolanda Estes, "Fichte's Hypothetical Imperative." One of the more striking and original features of Fichte's *Foundations of Natural Right*, particularly within the context of early German idealism, is his "deduction" of the necessity of human embodiment, not only for the possibility of moral action (as in the *System of Ethics*), but also for the possibility of mutual recognition by free agents of one another's freedom, and hence for the possibility of civil and legal relations. This is the topic of the contributions by Angelica Nuzzo ("The Role of the Human Body in Fichte's *Grundlage des Naturrecths*") and Günter Zöller ("Fichte's *Foundations of Natural Right* and the Mind–Body Problem"). Additional aspects of this same general issue – that is, the importance of having a *material* medium of spiritual action, recognition, and influence – are explored in the papers by Bruce Merrill ("Fichte's Materialism") and Scott Scribner ("The Aesthetics of Influence: Fichte's *Grundlage des Naturrechts* in view of Kant's Third *Critique*"). Mention of the role of the human body in Fichte's theory of right suggests another topic that is also discussed at some length by Fichte, particular in the second half of the *Foundations of Natural Right*: namely, the place of sex and gender in his theory of natural right. This controversial topic is the focus of Bäbel Frischmann's paper ("Fichte's Theory of Gender-Relation in his *Foundations of Natural Right*).

The relationship between the *Foundations of Natural Right* and Fichte's other writings of the Jena period, and more specifically between the overall transcendental method of Fichte's early writings and the specific (and somewhat idiosyncratic) method he seems to employ in his treatise on natural right is the topic of Daniel Breazeale's rather critical essay ("The 'Mixed Method' of Fichte's *Grundlage des Naturrechts* and the Limits of Transcendental *Reelephilosophie*"). Perhaps the most innovative feature of Fichte's argument in the *Foundations of Natural Right* is, as indicated above, his effort to show that recognition of the freedom of another finite individual is a condition necessary for the possibility of explicitly positing one's own freedom, and hence that the self-positing "I" which was the focus of his investigation in the *Foundations of the Entire Wissenschaftslehre* must always be understood and must always understand itself as one among many such finite, individual I's. This argument forms the theoretical basis for Fichte's new theory not just of natural law and natural rights, but of civil law as well, and hence of the legitimacy of the political state. This topic is explored in the contributions by Jeffery Kinlaw ("Political Obligation and the Imagination in Fichte's *Naturrecht*") and Hans Georg von Manz ("The Universality of Human Rights and the Sovereignty of the State in Fichte's *Doctrine of Right*").

Despite the originality of his social and political philosophy, Fichte was not the only thinker working on this topic in the immediate aftermath of Kant. In fact, Schelling published his own "Aphorisms on Natural Rights" immediately prior to the appearance of Fichte's treatise on the same subject. Thus it is appropriate that two of the contributions to this volume should examine the relationship between Fichte's and Schelling's early accounts of natural right. These are the essays by Michael Vater ("Schelling's Aphorisms on Natural Right (1796/97): a Comparison with Fichte's *Grundlage des Naturrechts*") and Steven Hoeltzel ("Transcendental Conditions and the Transcendence of Conditions. Fichte and Schelling on the Foundations of Natural Right"). Rounding out the present volume is an essay by Tom Rockmore, which examines the relationship between Fichte and Heidegger and the relation of both to Nazism ("Fichte, Heidegger and the Nazis"), and another by Arnold Farr, which situates Fichte's theory of right in a more contemporary contest and examines the parallels between his theory and the views of recent philosophers of liberation ("Rights, Recognition, and Regulative Ideas: On the Relationship between Fichte's Theory of Rights and Contemporary Liberation Philosophies").

For all the interest and quality of these 16 chapters, one hopes that this collection will mark only the first step toward an appreciation on the part of Anglophone philosophers of a neglected but genuine masterpiece of the philosophical literature, one with striking relevance to a number of contemporary debates. Fichte has for too long been the exclusive property of "Fichte scholars." It is high time that his distinctive voice become more widely heard, and it is difficult to think of a text better suited to this end than the *Foundations of Natural Right*.

Notes

1 See *EPW*: 135.

2 The first five lectures on morality for scholars were published in 1794 as *Some Lectures Concerning the Scholar's Vocation* (in *EPW*: 144–84). The more technical (or "scientific") lectures on philosophy were published as *Foundations of the Entire Wissenschaftslehre* (1794/95; in Fichte, *Science of Knowledge*, ed. and trans. Peter Heath and John Lachs [Cambridge: Cambridge University Press, 1982]: 89–286) and *Outline of the Distinctive*

Character of the Wissenschaftslehre with respect to the Theoretical Faculty (1795; in *EPW*: 243–306),

3 For details of these events and Fichte's role in them, see *EPW*: 26–30.

4 This review appeared in February 1796 in the *Philosophisches Journals einer Gesellschaft Teutscher Gelehrten*. For an English translation, see Daniel Breazeale, "Annotated translation of J.G. Fichte's Review of Kant's *Perpetual Peace* (1796)," *Philosophical Forum*, 32 (2001): 311–21.

5 For a discussion of the differences between the *Foundations of the Entire Wissenschaftslehre* and the lectures on *Wissenschaftslehre nova methodo*, see the editor's introduction to *FTP*.

6 *FTP*: 467.

7 *FTP*: 469.

8 *FTP*: 470.

9 See Fichte, *System of Ethics*, ed. and trans. Daniel Breazeale and Günter Zöller (Cambridge: Cambridge University Press, 1996).

10 *FTP*: 470–71. Note, however, the passage in the *Foundations of Natural Right*, where Fichte says that the rule of right obtains a new sanction from moral conscience, which provides us a moral obligation to live in a human community and thus in the juridical world (*FNR*: 10–12).

11 *FTP*: 471.

12 *FTP*: 471n.

13 See "On the Basis of our Belief in a Divine Governance of the Universe," in *IWL*: 142–54, and Fichte's lecture notes on §§ 933 ff. of Platner's *Philosophishen Aphorismen*, *GA*, II/4: 288–353.

14 K.L. Reinhold, *Sendschrieben an Fichte und Lavater* (1799), *GA*, III/3: 306.

15 See Fichte's public "Announcement of a New Presentation of the *Wissenschaftslehre*," dated 4 November 1800 (in *IWL*: 186–201), in which he bemoans the fact that the *Foundations of the Entire Wissenschaftslehre* has been universally misunderstood by everyone but his own students and appears to be a text that cannot be understood properly without oral assistance. Then he adds: "But it seems to me, however, that I have been more successful in clearly expounding my thoughts concerning philosophy in general in my *Natural Right* and in my *Ethics*" (*GA*, I/7: 153).

16 *GA*, III/5: 9 (emphasis added).

17 The earlier, occasionally reprinted, translation, Fichte, *The Science of Rights*, trans. A.E. Kroeger (Philadelphia: Lippencott, 1869), though a heroic labor in its own right, was, unfortunately, wildly inaccurate and often unreadable – defects which are conspicuously absent from the new translation.

Chapter 1

Is Fichte a Social Contract Theorist?

Wayne M. Martin

After a long period of neglect, the philosophy of J.G. Fichte has returned to the attention of English-speaking scholars. No longer simply viewed as a stepping stone on the way from Kant to Hegel, his philosophical writings have been subjected to close analysis and sympathetic reconstructions, and his reputation has been at least partly salvaged from the influential distortions and caricatures that date back to his own contemporaries. Until very recently, however, this revival of anglophone attention to Fichtean philosophy has focused mainly on his controversial epistemology and metaphysics, particularly on what might nowadays be called his philosophy of mind – his account of the structures of self-conscious subjectivity.[1] Fichte's political philosophy, by contrast, has been largely neglected. Certainly there have been exceptions,[2] but for the most part Fichte's reputation as a political philosopher still finds its beginning and end with his role as a forerunner of German Nationalism. Fortunately this neglect has now begun to be rectified, and the recent appearance of the first modern English translation of Fichte's main work of political philosophy – *The Foundations of Natural Right* (1796–97) – has helped turned scholarly attention to Fichte's broadly liberal political philosophy from his Jena period. What has yet to be recognized, I shall argue, is how radically Fichte departs from traditional approaches to the central problems of political philosophy.

The discussion that follows is divided into three parts. In the first section I introduce what I take to be a standard conception of contractarian strategies in political philosophy, and undertake a preliminary survey of the conflicting evidence regarding Fichte's commitment to such strategies. In the second section I suggest an interpretative strategy for resolving the tensions that emerge in that survey. In the final section I draw on a claim from Husserl's phenomenology of intersubjectivity to suggest the shape of Fichte's alternative to the contractarian approach.

1 Conflicting Evidence

From Locke and Rousseau to Rawls and Scanlon, the mainstream of political philosophy has been broadly contractarian. I begin with a brief (and I hope boringly uncontroversial) characterization of social contract approaches in political philosophy. The most basic and central questions of political philosophy, I shall assume, are as follows:

1) What is the basis of political obligation?
2) What constitutes a just political order?

The first question in effect asks why I or anyone ought to obey civic authorities (laws, officers of the state, etc.); the second asks what forms of civic authority are legitimate and therefore deserving of my respect, allegiance, and obedience. A social contractarian approach in political philosophy, as I shall use the term, is any approach that seeks answers to these two central questions by appeal to some notion of a contract – whether among citizens or between citizens and the state. In particular, a social contract theory is one which finds the basis of civic authority in an implicit contract in virtue of which the members of a community agree to terms by which each can benefit from the fruits of social cooperation. In answer to the second basic question of political philosophy, the social contract theorist proceeds by considering whether this underlying implicit contract is fair and rational, and in that sense merits the assent of rational self-interested agents.

It is worth noticing that the contractarian approach is in a sense reductionist about political obligation. Its strategy in answering the first basic question of political philosophy in effect treats political obligation as a special (if rather puzzling) case of the moral obligation to keep one's promises. Its approach to the second question treats the evaluation of political arrangements as a special (if again rather puzzling) case of the ordinary assessment of alternatives undertaken by a rationally self-interested individual. The two cases are puzzling instances of their types because, in the first case, I find myself with an obligation to keep a promise that I never explicitly undertook, while in the latter case it is unclear *which* agent is meant to be engaged in rationally self-interested deliberation, given that every *actual* individual will have rationally self-interested motives to ride free. Many of the philosophical oddities of the social contract tradition – whether the metaphysics of Rousseau's general will or the epistemic boundaries in Rawls' original position – are motivated by the need to navigate these puzzles.

Our question, then, is whether Fichte's political philosophy, as developed in the 1796–97 *Foundations of Natural Right* (hereafter: "the *Naturrecht*"), should be considered a contractarian position in the sense just outlined.

Now there is certainly no shortage of evidence to suggest an affirmative answer to this question. In particular in Fichte's earliest political writings, we find repeated insistence that a contract provides the only legitimate basis of political authority. Most notably, his anonymously published pamphlet supporting the French Revolution (1793) is premised upon an unambiguous and characteristically rhetorical endorsement of a contractarian answer to the first of the two basic questions of political philosophy:

> [A] civil society can justly be grounded on nothing other than a contract [*Vertrag*] among its participants[.] … That much can easily be proved for even the dimmest wit. (SW, VI: 81)[3]

Moreover, there would seem to be strong evidence to suggest that this early commitment to a contractarian approach is carried over – despite a number of other prominent changes – into the more mature work. Thus in the Introduction to the *Naturrecht* we find a repetition of the insistent claim from 1793:

> [T]he association of the state can be constructed only on the basis of a contract that is original, but necessarily entered into … . (SW, III: 13)

In the body of the work, a substantial discussion is devoted to a detailed analysis of what Fichte calls the "civil contract" [*Staatsbürgervertrag*].[4]

Such concrete textual evidence is reinforced by a more abstract line of philosophical reasoning. Among all the controversies about Fichte's philosophical positions, one point beyond dispute is that freedom – in particular freedom construed as autonomy – is central to his conception of human subjectivity. Given this emphasis on individual autonomy, it is natural to turn to contractarian answers to the basic questions of political philosophy. For part of the promise of the contractarian approach is that it respects the fundamental freedom of individual citizens while at the same time underwriting state authority. Essentially this line of reasoning is expressed concisely by Beiser in connection with Fichte's early endorsement of the contractarian position:

> Autonomy means that we cannot be bound by anything but our sovereign will, that all our laws must be self-given. Hence we are obliged to obey the laws of a constitution only insofar as we have consented to them. (Beiser 1992: 81)

If we can make sense of the idea that we freely enter into a civil contract, then we can legitimately claim to be at once free individuals and at the same time obligated to the state. The contractarian approach would thus seem to answer directly to some of Fichte's deepest philosophical commitments.

Given all this evidence, the answer to our question would seem to be straightforward: Fichte *is* a contractarian, at least in his liberal period, and if there is any distinctively Fichtean contribution to liberal political philosophy it must be found in the particulars of a broadly orthodox contractarian approach. Understandably, the limited but growing scholarship on Fichte's liberal political philosophy has tended to follow this assumption.[5]

Two pieces of evidence should at least displace the sense of inevitability about the contractarian interpretation of Fichte's political philosophy. The first concerns Fichte's insistence that there is a radical division between the domains of moral and political obligation. As Fred Neuhouser has argued in detail, this is one of the major shifts in Fichte's political thought between the 1793 pamphlet on revolution and the mature liberal political doctrines of 1796.[6] In the earlier position, Fichte holds that the demands of morality – understood along orthodox Kantian lines – suffice to underwrite the basic authority of the state:

> The answer to this question [concerning the highest end of the state] is purely moral and must be grounded in the moral law, which alone … prescribes a final end to the human being.[7]

By 1796, however, Fichte's position on this point has changed. He no longer sees political right as a special application of moral right; political obligation is now held to be *sui generis*. In Fichte's preferred formulation, the science of political right is to be seen as "*eine eigene, für sich bestehende Wissenschaft*" – an individual, self-sustaining science (SW, III: 10). This shift in Fichte's position should at least give us pause in assuming that the contractarianism of the revolution pamphlet is carried over into the later work. For as we have seen, the contractarian approach in effect reduces political obligation to a species of the moral obligation to keep one's promises. It would thus not seem to satisfy Fichte's claims about the independence of political obligation and political science.

The second piece of evidence against the contractarian interpretation is mundanely textual: through the first seven sections of the *Naturrecht* there is simply no appeal to the notion of a social contract, and indeed no use of the word, *Vertrag*. Certainly the *Naturrecht* does include extensive discussion of a social contract, but this discussion begins only after the seventh section, and occurs mainly in the second main part, published separately under the title "Applied Natural Right." Fichte's original readers, working through the first published volume of the *Naturrecht*, had to read as far as the sixteenth and final section of the volume to find any substantive invocation of a social contract. And they had to wait until the following year (for the publication of the second volume) to see Fichte's substantive treatment of the workings of such a contact. This back-loading of the appeal to a contract does not of itself rule out the contractarian interpretation. But it certainly suggests that much of the distinctive work of Fichte's political philosophy is carried out independently of appeal to a contract. Here it is particularly worth noticing that by the end of the seventh section – prior to any appeal to the notion of a social contract – Fichte claims already to have established two of his main results:

> The applicability of the concept of right is now completely secured, and its limits have been precisely determined. (SW, III: 90)

In short, Fichte's deduction of natural right is carried out entirely without reliance on the notion of a social contract.

Now by itself there is nothing particularly unorthodox about invoking a conception of right prior to the introduction of an appeal to a social contract. Indeed in one sense this is the standard procedure in the contract tradition. In the *Second Treatise*, for instance, Locke simply assumes that the state of nature is "a state of liberty yet not a state of license."[8] But he is famously elusive about the warrant for this assumption.[9] What is distinctive about Fichte's procedure is, first, that he sees an independent problem here to be solved, and second, that so much of his political position is "deduced" in advance of the appeal to contract. I turn now to consider the significance of this strategy.

2 Contract Without Contractarianism

There can be no question here of mounting a full positive interpretation of Fichte's position in the *Naturrecht*. In the balance of my discussion, however, I take up two questions raised by the conflicting evidence outlined above. First, what alternative is there to a contractarian reading of Fichte's liberal political philosophy? And second, if Fichte is not best understood as a social contract theorist then why is so much of his political philosophy couched in contractarian language?

We can approach these questions in two stages. The first step is to understand Fichte's framing of the problems of political philosophy in terms of a demand for a deduction. Significantly, each of the first two main subdivisions of the *Naturrecht* (which together comprise the first seven sections of the work) are described as deductions – in the first case of the concept of right (*Recht*) and in the second case of the applicability of that concept. Within the text, little is said to explain or motivate the need for a deduction, but if we can understand this framing then we will be well on our way to seeing what is most distinctive about Fichte's political thought.

The strategy of Fichte's argument comes into relief when we consider it as closely modeled on Kant's deduction of the categories in the first critique. Recall four central features of the Kantian deduction. The deduction is required in order to meet a distinctive *skeptical challenge* – roughly the challenge of the Humean skeptic, understood as denying that we can legitimately deploy a necessitarian concept of causality. Its aim is to secure the *legitimacy* of the application of pure a priori categories such as cause and effect, while at the same time establishing the *limits* within which such concepts can be legitimately applied. Finally, the strategy of the Kantian deduction is to argue that the application of the concepts in question is a *condition on the possibility of experience* – in particular a condition on the possibility of apperceptive self-consciousness.

The case of political philosophy, as Fichte approaches it, provides analogs for each of these points. We might think of the problem of anarchism as a political variant on Hume's skepticism about causality. The Humean skeptic does not of course doubt that events of one type are regularly followed by events of another type, but he denies that such conjunction can ever warrant the claim that one event necessitates another. Analogously, we can think of the anarchist as granting that there are fruits of social cooperation and concrete benefits to be gained from the institutions of the state, but denying that appeal to such benefits itself legitimates state authority. In the face of such a skeptic, we make no progress by documenting the benefits of social cooperation or by detailing the rationality and fairness of the distribution of those benefits. What he questions is the very idea of some state authority imposing obligations on free individuals in order to secure social cooperation. As in the Kantian case, this skeptical challenge then motivates the search for a deduction of such concepts – a deduction which would establish both the legitimacy and the limits of our basic political categories. Finally, even Kant's argumentative strategy finds an analog in the political case. For Fichte's claim is that the applicability of the notion of right (*Recht*) is a condition on the possibility of self-conscious subjectivity.

Obviously much of the weight of Fichte's position will rest on this final thesis; I return below to consider how we might render it plausible. But even on the basis of this very crude sketch of Fichte's strategy, we can begin to frame answers to the two questions posed above. Consider again the analogy with the Kantian strategy. For Kant, the argument of the transcendental deduction shows us that we *must* apply the categories of cause and effect; but it does not show us *how* to apply such categories. It does not provide us with general principles for framing or assessing causal hypotheses, much less with information about the particular causes of particular effects. Kant of course has much to say about these further matters (in particular in the so-called "Analytic of Principles" and in his writings on the foundations of natural science) but this falls outside the scope of the deduction of the categories of cause and effect.

What we find in Fichte's political philosophy, I submit, is an analogous division of labor. We can capture the division as follows: when it comes to answering the *second* basic question of political philosophy – the problem of determining what political arrangements are just – Fichte's approach is indeed orthodoxly contractarian. As we have seen, he explicitly holds that a just social order must be based on the consent of the governed, and that such consent can only be expected or demanded insofar as social cooperation is ordered by a social contract. But we can now see the sense in which such contractarian claims do not by themselves provide an adequate answer to the *first* question of political philosophy. For the contractarian presupposes what Fichte holds must be established by deduction: namely that the very category of political obligation (of *Recht*) has a legitimate employment. His answer to the first question of political philosophy is accordingly not contractarian, but relies rather on his bold thesis that a self-conscious subject must *ipso facto* recognize the categories of political justice (*Recht*).

3 Objectivity and a Community of Others

This brings us to the second stage in addressing the questions set out above. For while such an account of the structure of Fichte's argument shows an important sense in which his political philosophy diverges from contractarianism, it also serves to focus attention on his most provocative (and, it must be admitted, *prima facie* implausible) thesis. How should we understand a political philosophy which claims to find the basis of political obligation in the conditions on self-conscious experience? In the space remaining I offer a few remarks about how Fichte's boldest and most original political claim might be sustained. These remarks will certainly not suffice to establish Fichte's thesis, but perhaps they will provide a clearer sense of the shape of Fichte's alternative to contractarianism.

Here I find it useful to take a step away from Fichte's own categories in order to consider a close variant of the Fichtean thesis developed over a century later in the phenomenological writings of Edmund Husserl. For in his discussion of solipsism and intersubjectivity Husserl develops an argument which closely parallels Fichte's.[10] Husserl's central claim in this context is that the notion of another subject – a distinct ego with a different perspective, or simply "an Other" – is more fundamental than the notion of an object or an objective world.[11] In making this claim, Husserl is not denying the obvious truth that we encounter other subjects ("Others") by finding them as animated portions of an objective world. (As Husserl himself puts the point: when looking out the window on a winter's day, I do not see egos but only hats and coats.) But if we set out to explicate the *sense or content* of the notion of an object, he argues, we find that we must appeal to the notion of an "Other." His reasoning rests on the claim that the very notion of an object is the notion of something which retains its identity and properties through the variation of perspective upon it. To treat a state of affairs as objective is in effect to claim that anyone who undertakes the appropriate investigation ought to acknowledge it – no matter what the peculiarities of their perspective or subjective constitution. It is in this sense that the notion of an Other – an individual with a perspective and constitution distinct from mine – is said to be a constituent in our notion of an object.

Husserl's thesis is not the same as Fichte's,[12] but it provides us with enough to articulate the core of the Fichtean alternative to orthodox contractarianism. If we are to find the grounds for political obligation we must look first for the basis of our obligation to acknowledge the viewpoints of others – in particular those whose needs and perspectives differ substantially from our own. This obligation cannot itself have its basis in a social contract, insofar as the very idea of a social contract presupposes that such acknowledgement is already sustained. Fichte's alternative is to find the basis of this most fundamental (and fundamentally liberal) political obligation not in the expectation of mutual benefit but rather in the conditions on the very possibility of self-conscious experience of an objective world. Whenever I freely make an objective claim about the state of affairs in an objective world, I find myself already implicitly committed to acknowledging the viewpoint taken by Others on that selfsame objective world. In incurring this commitment I situate myself (or as Fichte would say: I posit myself) in a primitively and distinctively political framework – that of a community of distinct individuals with overlapping but diverging interests and perspectives, each making demands on the agency of the others.[13]

Notes

1 Among the contributions to the recent revival in this area are Pippin (1987–88), Neuhouser (1990), Wood (1991), Martin (1997), Zöller (1999), and the many papers, translations and editions due to Daniel Breazeale, who has played a leading role in the recovery of Fichte's thought.

2 Beiser (1992) and Williams (1992) deal with Fichte's political thought, though in both cases only in the context of broader surveys of political philosophy in the post-Kantian period. Sluga (1993) treats Fichte's politics in connection with its influence on political thought in the period following Germany's defeat in the "Great War" of 1914–18. Neuhouser (1994) proposes an account of some of the early shifts in Fichte's political philosophy, particularly in connection with the distinction between moral and political obligation.

3 Citations to Fichte's works refer to the pagination in I.H. Fichte (ed.). *Johann Gottlieb Fichtes sämmtliche Werke* (Berlin: Veit & Comp, 1845–46; reprint: Berlin: Walter de Gruyter, 1971). Citations are given in the text in the form (SW, I: 91), indicating volume and page number. Both the modern academy edition and modern English translations provide marginal pagination indexed to this edition.

4 See in particular SW, III: 191–209.

5 Several recent papers occasioned by the new translation of the *Naturrecht* have taken this tack. In this volume see in particular the chapters by Baur, Kinlaw and Williams.

6 Neuhouser (1994). See also Verweyen (1975).

7 SW, VI: 62, as translated in Neuhouser, 1994: 161.

8 Locke, 1690: §6.

9 See for instance Locke, 1690: §12: "For though it would be beside my present purpose, to enter here into the particulars of the law of nature, or its measures of punishment; yet, it is certain that there is such a law, and that too, as intelligible and plain to a rational creature, and a studier of that law, as the positive laws of commonwealths."

10 For an interpretation of Fichte's own argument see Michael Baur's essay in this volume.

11 See in particular Husserl, 1931: 106–7.

12 Most importantly, Fichte's variant on this argument focuses on the appeal to the viewpoint of an "Other" (a distinct autonomous subject) as a condition on the possibility of *self*-consciousness. Husserl's argument, as I have sketched it here, turns on the conditions of *objective* consciousness. The divergence is important, though ultimately the difference of emphasis is complementary, particularly given the insistence of both thinkers on the interconnection of the notions of subject and object.

13 An earlier version of this paper was read at the 2002 Pacific Division meetings of the American Philosophical Association. Thanks to Ryan Hickerson and Susan Shell for their helpful comments on that draft.

References

Baur, M., "Fichte's Impossible Contract," forthcoming in the proceedings of the sixth biennial conference of the North American Fichte Society (2001).

Beiser, F., *Enlightenment, Revolution, Romanticism: The Genesis of Modern German Political Thought* (Cambridge, MA: Harvard University Press, 1992).

Fichte, J.G., *Grundlage des Naturrechts nach dem Principien der Wissenschaftslehre* (1796–97), new translation by M. Baur, ed. and with an introduction by F. Neuhouser, *The Foundations of Natural Right According to the Principles of the Wissenschaftslehre* (Cambridge: Cambridge University Press, 2000).

Husserl, E., *Méditations Cartésiennes: Introduction à la Phénoménologie* (1931). Citations refer to translation by D. Cairns, *Cartesian Meditations: An Introduction to Phenomenology* (Dordrecht: Kluwer, 1950).

Kinlaw, J., "Political Obligation, Intersubjectivity, and the Imagination in Fichte's Naturrecht," forthcoming in the proceedings of the sixth biennial conference of the North American Fichte Society (2001).

Locke, J., *Second Treatise of Government* (London: Awnsham and Churchill, 1690).

Martin, W., *Idealism and Objectivity: Understanding Fichte's Jena Project* (Palo Alto, CA: Stanford University Press, 1997).

Neuhouser, F., *Fichte's Theory of Subjectivity* (Cambridge: Cambridge University Press, 1990).

Neuhouser, F., "Fichte on the Relationship Between Right and Morality," in D. Breazeale and T. Rockmore (eds), *Fichte: Historical Contexts, Contemporary Controversies* (Atlantic Highlands, NJ: Humanities Press, 1994): 158–80.

Pippin, R., "Fichte's Contribution," *The Philosophical Forum*, 19:2–3 (1987/88): 74–96.

Sluga, H., *Heidegger's Crisis: Philosophy and Politics in Nazi Germany* (Cambridge, MA: Harvard University Press, 1993).

Verweyen, H.-J., *Recht und Sittlichkeit in J.G. Fichtes Gesellschaftslehre* (Freiburg: Alber, 1975).

Williams, R., *Recognition: Fichte and Hegel on the Other* (Albany, NY: State University of New York Press, 1992).

Williams, R., "Recognition and Social Contract," forthcoming in the proceedings of the sixth biennial conference of the North American Fichte Society.

Wood, A., "Fichte's Philosophical Revolution," *Philosophical Topics*, 19 (1991): 1–28.

Zöller, G., *Fichte's Transcendental Philosophy: The Original Duplicity of Intelligence and Will* (Cambridge: Cambridge University Press, 1999).

Chapter 2

Fichte's Impossible Contract

Michael Baur

1 The Pursuit of Normativity without an Antecedently-given "Nature" or Teleology

In the draft of a letter to Jens Baggesen from 1795, Fichte explains that there is an intrinsic, non-accidental link between pre-critical or dogmatic epistemology and metaphysics (on the one hand) and oppressive social-political thinking (on the other). Contrasting his own post-Kantian philosophy with the positions of pre-critical thinkers, Fichte writes:

> My system is the first system of freedom. Just as France has freed man from external shackles, so my system frees him from the fetters of things in themselves, which is to say, from those external influences with which all previous systems – including the Kantian – have more or less fettered man. Indeed, the first principle of my system presents man as an independent being.[1]

For Fichte, the task of a critical epistemology and metaphysics – i.e., a theory of knowledge and being that genuinely appreciates and respects human freedom and autonomy – will be to give an account of our knowledge of objects, yet without relying on the pre-critical or dogmatic assumption of an antecedently-given, causally-efficacious thing-in-itself *outside* the human knower. In a 1793 letter to F.I. Niethammer, Fichte explains the theoretical imperative in the following way:

> Kant demonstrates that the causal principle is applicable merely to appearances, and nevertheless he assumes that there is a substrate underlying all appearances – an assumption undoubtedly based upon the law of causality (at least this is the way Kant's followers argue). Whoever shows us how Kant arrived at this substrate without extending the causal law beyond its limits will have understood Kant.[2]

In other words, Fichte is claiming here that whoever gives an account of the finite or limited character of human knowing – yet without appealing to the pre-critical or dogmatic metaphysical premise of an antecedently given, independent thing-in-itself – will have truly understood Kant. This same set of issues can be transposed from their epistemological and metaphysical context into a practical and political context. Recall that Kant initiated a "Copernican revolution" in the realm of practical and political thought as well as in the realm of epistemology and metaphysics.[3] As Kant explains the matter in his *Critique of Practical Reason*, it is our own free agency and the principles of our own autonomous willing that provide the criterion for determining what is good, and not the other way around.[4] Thus it is *not* the case that the rightness of our willing is to be determined or judged on the basis of some antecedently-given, teleologically-ordained good. Just as it is our own knowing that determines what properly counts as an object (and not the other way around), so too it is our own free willing that determines what counts as good or worthy from a moral point of view (and not the other way around). So in the realm of practical and political philosophy, one can say on Fichte's behalf (and borrowing the language that Fichte himself uses in his letter to Niethammer):

> Whoever can given an account of the norms or obligations to which we are committed in the realm of practice – yet without relying on the pre-critical, dogmatic premise of an antecedently-given, teleologically-ordained order of things or notion of the good – will have truly understood Kant.

For Fichte, the task is to give an account of practical normativity, yet without appealing to any antecedently-given teleology. Stated differently, the task is to give an account of the normative constraints by which we are properly bound in our practical activity, yet without relying in any way on some notion of nature, or the good, or "ends *an sich*," which are allegedly given independent of or antecedent to our own self-legislative willing. To complete the French Revolution's project of emancipatory politics, Fichte implicitly argues, one must complete the Copernican revolution's project of overcoming the residual dogmatism of all naturalism and teleology.

As I hope to show later in this paper, Fichte's rejection of traditional social contractarian accounts of human social relations is related to his rejection of the search for a criterion, or external standard, by which we might measure our knowledge in epistemology. More specifically, Fichte's account of the impossibility of a normative social contract (as traditionally construed) is related to his account of the impossibility of our knowing things as they might be "in themselves," separate from and independent of our own activity in knowing them. Addressing the question of whether we finite human knowers can ever transcend the limits of our own consciousness, Fichte argues that Hume was not sufficiently critical:

> … the Humean system holds open the possibility that we might someday be able to go beyond the boundary of the human mind, whereas the Critical system proves that such progress is absolutely impossible, and it shows that the thought of a thing possessing existence and specific properties *in itself* and apart from any faculty of representation is a piece of whimsy, a pipe dream, a nonthought.[5]

In a very real sense, then, Fichte aims to "out-Hume" Hume on the question of whether we can ever know "things-in-themselves" or an external criterion for testing our knowledge. That is, Fichte goes beyond Hume and insists on the *necessary* – and not merely contingent – character of our ignorance of so-called things-in-themselves (i.e., things that supposedly exist antecedent to and independent of our consciousness of them). But unlike Hume, Fichte argues that radical skepticism regarding all possible knowledge of things-in-themselves does not undermine – but actually confirms and sustains – our belief in the emancipatory power of reason.

In a similar vein, Fichte can be said to "out-Rousseau" Rousseau on the issue of the social contract that allegedly grounds society and all social relations. Fichte's theory of right aims to show that it is simply wrong to think of the original "social contact" that grounds relations of "right" among human beings as any kind of representable or imaginable hypothetical "agreement" at all (even if one is willing to admit, as Rousseau does, that such an agreement may not have taken place as a real event[6]). Fichte's argument entails that the original "social contract" is itself the non-imaginable, non-representable condition of there being any conscious, genuinely human relations among human beings in the first place. Thus, it is simply *impossible* for human beings to agree – or even to imagine themselves agreeing – to terms upon which they are to treat each other as free and rational beings. The conscious and deliberate making of any such agreement (whether real, imagined, or represented in any way) must always presuppose that the parties have always already "agreed" to treat each other as free and rational beings, as beings worthy of entering into agreements in the first place (otherwise, there would be no point in seeking agreement in a social contract situation). In other words, we human beings must see ourselves as subject to an original "contract" that we freely entered into, even though we never were actually conscious of having done so, and even though it is utterly impossible for us even to imagine ourselves as consciously and freely doing so. This is because the "contract" itself is the condition of the possibility of our being conscious and free in the first place. But for Fichte, the impossibility of our ever imagining or representing to ourselves any such hypothetical social contract does not undermine our belief in the critical, liberating power of reason. Properly understood, the impossibility of an imaginable or representable social contract (the impossibility of imagining a contract which binds humans to one another on the basis of antecedently-given "natural" needs about which the parties allegedly bargain and reach agreement) confirms all the more fully our radical freedom and capacity to transcend the limits seemingly imposed on us by "nature" or an antecedently-given teleological order of things.

2 Clarification by Contrast: The Problem with Rawls's Social Contractarian Account

In order to articulate the grounds of Fichte's rejection of traditional social contractarian accounts of human social relations, it will be helpful if we refer briefly to the thought of John Rawls, one of this century's most famous and influential social contractarian thinkers. In his criticism of Kant, Rawls explicitly states that it is impossible to give a sufficiently determinate account of moral obligation or normativity if one refuses to begin with at least some minimal (or "thin") theory of the good. Thus in *A Theory of Justice*, Rawls criticizes Kant for failing to provide sufficiently determinate normative content in his moral theory:

> Kant never explains why the scoundrel does not express in a bad life his characteristic and freely chosen selfhood in the same way that a saint expresses his characteristic and freely chosen selfhood in a good one.[7]

For Rawls, in other words, it is impossible to give a sufficiently determinate account of moral obligation or normativity if one does not begin with at least some minimal account of the antecedently-given set of "primary goods" that all persons (within a properly-constituted hypothetical contract situation) would identify as worthy of having, regardless of whatever else happens to be the case.

Now in the most general terms, Fichte can be understood as arguing (against Rawls and against other, similar social contractarian thinkers) that it is not necessary to appeal to any antecedently-given, heteronomously-derived content in order to "fill out" an otherwise empty, formalistic, and self-enclosed account of Kantian autonomy. Fichte holds that one *can* complete the Kantian Copernican revolution in practical philosophy – yet without relying on any antecedently-given, allegedly normative content – if we only understand more deeply what autonomy, or self-conscious selfhood means *on its own terms*. In fact, Fichte argues that we *must* complete the Copernican revolution in this way, since any retreat in the direction of naturalism or teleology – even if it involves only a very "thin" theory of the good – is equally a reversion into dogmatic, pre-critical epistemology and metaphysics and potentially restrictive, oppressive politics (a politics that does not sufficiently appreciate the radical freedom and plasticity of finite rational selfhood).

On the face of it, Rawls might well seem to escape the charge that his social contractarian account of the principles of justice is pre-critical, or teleological, or metaphysical (in the pejorative sense of this term). In what follows, I shall try to show (however briefly) that the Rawlsian account *does*, in fact, fall prey to this charge, and does not sufficiently appreciate the radical freedom or autonomy of the finite rational human being. Furthermore, I shall try to show that – in spite of appearances – it is possible (following Fichte) to arrive at a sufficiently determinate account of practical normativity or obligation without relying – as Rawls does – on any empirically-given and heteronomously-derived set of "primary goods" or human interests. The key, for Fichte, will be to see that freedom on its own terms and in abstraction from all empirical content, is not empty and self-enclosed, but is necessarily constrained and related to what is other than it. But before considering the Fichtean account, let us first consider Rawls in a bit more detail.

In *A Theory of Justice*, Rawls argues that there is no need for an explicit epistemological, metaphysical, or teleological justification of the principles of justice, since the immediate source or ground of the principles of justice needs no ground outside of itself, but rather is *self-determining or self-grounding in the relevant respects*. This is because, for Rawls, the immediate source or ground of the principles of justice is nothing other than the very personhood or selfhood whose rights and duties are to be distributed in accordance with those principles of justice; and thus the immediate source or ground is this personhood simply insofar as it chooses *its own* principles of justice for itself. This why Rawls holds that his particular brand of liberalism is "political, not metaphysical."[8]

Now the reason why the Rawlsian project is a *political* project (and not an epistemological or metaphysical one) is also the reason why it is a *social contractarian* project. Like other social contractarians before him, Rawls begins with the intuitively appealing idea that the principles of justice are supposed to have their ultimate source in personhood or selfhood insofar as such personhood or selfhood chooses principles *for itself* (the ground or source of the principles of justice is not supposed to be any antecedently-constituted human nature). Thus for Rawlsian social contractarianism, the fundamental question concerning the principles of justice is essentially a *practical* and *political* question of acceptability or consent, and not one of metaphysics, epistemology, or theoretical standards that are given independently of or antecedently to self-determining selfhood. That is, the principles of justice are supposed to be grounded non-teleologically and non-metaphysically. This is Rawls's way of expressing what is an essentially Kantian theme, namely the theme of "the primacy of the practical."

Now for Rawls, the initial choice situation (within which free, self-determining personhood is said to choose principles of justice for itself) is called the "original position."[9] But why does Rawls need to think in terms of a hypothetical "original position" at all? For Rawls, *our own, actual personhood* (the personhood that you and I factually and concretely *are*) cannot be understood as conceptually identical to the personhood in the original position, because of *the problem of bias*. As Rawls notes, "persons are not indifferent as to how the greater benefits produced by their collaboration are distributed, for in order to pursue their ends they each prefer a larger to a lesser share."[10] Now in addition to being self-interested in this way, we as individual persons are differently situated vis-à-vis others in our social world: we have different natural endowments, we occupy different social positions, and we adhere to different conceptions of what is "good" for us. If left to ourselves to deliberate about the principles of justice, these differentiating characteristics would bias us and prevent us from reaching unanimous agreement. For Rawls, then, it is necessary to construct the fiction of an appropriate choice situation (an "original position") within which personhood is *not influenced* by the particularizing characteristics that make us different as individuals and that bias us in our thinking about justice.

Now, contrary to Rawls's own self-understanding, Fichte would argue that this very act of separating personhood into two types – our own personhood versus personhood in the hypothetical original position (or in a natural, unbiased state) – implicitly contradicts his assertion of the primacy of the practical, and ensures that the personhood that is the source of the principles of justice is *not* self-determining in the sense that Rawls requires. With the Rawlsian separation, personhood that is the source of the principles of justice (personhood in the original position) is *not* self-determining in the relevant respects, because its putative interests, tasks, goals, self-understanding, and common nature are *given* to it by a source that is different from it, and given to it in accordance with a prior order of things that antecedently sets the terms of its deliberations (from "behind its back," as it were). This is the antecedent order of things that *we ourselves* set up in advance as we construct the original position and decide what types of information should or should not be filtered out of it. In other words, by constructing the original position, we construct a hypothetical, imagined kind of personhood, with a pre-existing (antecedently-given) common nature. This common nature predetermines what personhood in the original position may or may not take into consideration when deliberating about justice. Insofar as *we* construct such an original position for *our own* political purposes, we might be said to be self-determining in the relevant respects. However, insofar as personhood in the original position must *find itself* already constituted with certain interests, tasks, goals, self-understandings, and a common nature *given* to it in accordance with an antecedent order (i.e., the order that *we* have established), then *it* cannot be said to be *self-determining in the relevant respects*.

From Fichte's point of view, the fundamental problem with any such contractarian account resides in the attempt to imagine *in advance* what *particular positive content* (i.e., what particular claims or rules) free persons would agree upon for the purpose of organizing themselves into a self-sufficient social system. The problem with this approach is twofold:

1) any personhood that can be represented or imagined by us in advance as being committed to any particular positive content is necessarily *not self-determining*; instead, it is always already constituted *by us* as being committed to some particular content that *we* have chosen for it;
2) any personhood that can be imagined by us in advance as being committed to any particular positive content is necessarily *not our own personhood*; this is because it is impossible for us to give an account of such imagined personhood while simultaneously giving an account of our own imagining and account-giving. Stated differently, anything that subjectivity represents to itself is – strictly speaking – *other than* the subjectivity that does the representing. Thus by thinking in terms of an imagined social contract situation within which allegedly free selves bargain *on our behalf* about the principles of justice, and do so on the basis of a set of interests or primary goods that they find as antecedently given and normatively binding on them, Rawls slips back into a teleological, metaphysical, and ultimately dogmatic view of human agency; and thus Rawls fails to do justice to the full meaning and scope of human freedom.[11] Or to put the matter somewhat differently: Rawls seeks to provide an account of the norms that are binding on subjectivity, but – unfortunately – he does so from a point of view that is *external* to the subjectivity that is allegedly being bound;

and thus he provides an account that ultimately regards subjectivity as an instance of objectivity.

3 Fichte's Normative Social Theory: A 'Backwards' Social Contract

Unlike Rawls, Fichte does not seek to imagine *in advance* what *particular positive content* (i.e., what particular claims or rules) free persons would agree upon for the purpose of organizing themselves into a social whole. Rather, the starting point for Fichte is the exact opposite: insofar as personhood or selfhood is genuinely free and self-determining, it simply *cannot* be imagined in advance as being committed to *any* particular positive content whatsoever. Accordingly, it is not possible to specify in advance what kinds of claims one should accept or be skeptical about; in principle, personhood that is genuinely free and self-determining can and should be skeptical about any and all positive content whatsoever. Indeed, to be fully free for Fichte means to be radically skeptical; it means to be aware that no given content whatsoever is necessarily determinative for one's thinking and/or acting.

But now the following question arises: how is it possible to derive a normative social theory without relying in any way on the antecedent givenness of any particular, determinate content whatsoever? How can one arrive at normatively valid "content" for a critical social theory on the basis of nothing other than simple freedom or skepticism, or the bare activity of being aware that no particular content whatsoever is determinative for one's thinking and/or acting? As indicated earlier, Fichte's approach is somewhat counterintuitive. And the key will be to see (with Fichte) how a radically free, self-related self (the pure I = I) can *on its own terms* never be purely self-related and self-enclosed, but must be constrained by and related to what is other than it. Fichte's full argument for this position is rather complex, but it can be presented in rough outline as follows.

As self-conscious of its radical freedom, the Fichtean self knows that no given content is necessarily determinative for itself, that no given content necessarily imposes itself on the self. However, one "thing" that (for lack of a better way of putting it) *does* "impose" itself on the self is the fact that the self must always *come-to-be* aware of itself as radically free. The self's coming-to-be as a self-consciously free self always "happens" to the self, apart from any deliberate or free choosing by the self. The self cannot deliberately and self-consciously choose its own coming-to-be-aware of itself as radically free (and thus cannot deliberately choose to come-to-be the self that it is), since – "prior" to this coming-to-be – the self is "not yet" a self-consciously free self at all. The self-consciously free self is what it is only to the extent that it seemingly emerges, or awakens, *out of* a "prior" state of *not* being a self-consciously free self. Since the self was not *always* the radically free and self-conscious self that it is, the self cannot be the totality of all that is, for coming-to-be necessarily implies some otherness. Thus there must be some "other" to the self, or a not-self (a not-I).[12]

The same point can be made in slightly more Fichtean terms. To be a self is to be for oneself, and to be for oneself is to be given to oneself and thus passive with respect to oneself. And one cannot be passive with respect to oneself (or in any respect at all), if the self were a pure, infinite, activity. Conversely, a pure, unconstrained, infinite activity – if it really were unconstrained and infinite – would never have the occasion to reflect *back* on itself or to be *for* itself (as a self always is), but would extend its activity without restriction or constraint into infinity – in which case it would be a blind, unreflected activity, and would not be an activity that is aware of itself, or for itself. Thus the very definition of the self as an activity that is purely for itself also implies some element of impurity, passivity, and otherness. In order to be a self at all, the self needs an "other" in relation to which the self is the being-for-self that it is. In other words, the self-positing self cannot be the totality of all that is, and there must be some *other* to the self, or a not-self.[13]

Now in addition to arguing for the necessity of a not-self for the self, Fichte further argues (in his *Foundations of Natural Right*) that this not-self must ultimately be understood as another free self. This, then, is Fichte's argument for the necessity of intersubjectivity, or what we might call a "backwards" or "retrospective" social contact, one that is not in any way imaginable or representable, but one that must nevertheless be understood as binding free selves to other free selves. So what is the Fichtean argument?

In the present context, the most important thing to note about Fichte's argument for intersubjectivity is that it does not involve any argument about what kinds of needs or interests free persons (allegedly) all share, or what kinds of claims free persons (allegedly) can all agree upon. The argument is not grounded on any kind of givenness or positivity at all; rather, it is based on the opposite kind of claim: no given content whatsoever is necessarily determinative for the thinking and/or acting of a free self. Thus Fichte's argument for intersubjectivity implies what we might call a "backwards social contract" – a social contract into which I must understand myself as having entered, but one into which I could not have possibly entered deliberately and self-consciously. Let us now begin to unpack the argument.

We have already seen that, for Fichte, no particular content or claim is necessarily determinative for the self's thinking and/or acting; the self is radically free. We have also seen that – precisely because a free self is aware and must have come to be aware of its own radical freedom – there must be a not-self for the self. Now Fichte argues that this not-self must necessarily be *another free self*. Significantly, the argument is not about real, empirical selves or actual relations among persons or between persons and nature. It is an argument about the non-empirical conditions of the possibility of the self's ability to relate itself freely to any empirical objects whatsoever. The point of the argument is simply this: the self could not be the self-consciously free self that it is, if there were no other free selfhood outside of itself. The argument for the necessity of free reciprocity (or mutual *Aufforderung*) among free selves can be summarized – at least preliminarily – in the following proto-Hegelian terms.

There must be a not-self for the self, but this not-self cannot consist simply of "nature." Why not? Nature is that which sets no ends for itself, but rather has ends imposed on it externally, i.e., by free and purposive selfhood such as my own. Nature is simply the realm of the not-self insofar as it is given as an object to be controlled, consumed, dominated, and transformed by me for my own purposes; that is, nature is that which is given to me from the outside, only to have its apparent independence canceled by me and integrated into my own purposive activity. Indeed, this very ability to cancel the "independent" natural object as given is a sign of my radical freedom. But such cannot yet be a sign *for me* of my own radical freedom. After all, to the extent that I merely consume nature or manipulate it to satisfy myself, I am also a slave to my passions or desires, and thus determined as something that is *not* free. Thus, to the extent that I am *only* a consumer in relation to what is other than me (i.e., in relation to the not-self), I am only a slave to my own desires and thus not genuinely free, and cannot be aware of my own freedom.

In order to be genuinely, self-consciously free, I must not be a slave to my passions. I must not merely dominate what is other than me (the not-self) in order to satisfy my desires, but I must *let the other be*; I must not simply *impose* my ends on it. But if the other that I "let be" were itself purely nature and nothing else, and if I refrained from imposing my own ends on it, then the other would cancel my very existence *as a free being*. Such cancellation does not mean that the other would destroy me physically. But it does mean that the other would destroy me *as free*. After all, if the other were a merely natural, causally-determined and causally-determining being, and if I refrained from asserting my own purposiveness in relation to it, then my only relation to the other would be a relation of *being-causally-effected* by it. Thus the other's existence in relation to me would cancel my existence *qua free being*. Therefore, if I am to be capable of refraining from merely *imposing* my own ends on the other (as I must be, in order not to be a slave to my passions), and if I am still to remain in existence *qua free being*, then the other must be capable of *preventing itself* from relating to me in a purely causal manner. That is, the other must (by virtue of its *own* agency) be capable of canceling its *own* merely natural existence.[14] The other (i.e., the not-self) must be another free self.[15]

Fichte expresses this movement of mutual summons (or *Aufforderung*) in terms of the paradoxical character of *finding* oneself as *free*. The problem is that the fundamental imperative that I have as a self is to *be* a self, or to be *for* myself, which means to *find myself as free*. But that means that my imperative is to find my own free efficacy as an *object*, and thus as finite, constrained, and determined – and that means as determined *by* something. But how can *free agency* find or see itself as *determined*? It cannot just find itself directly as determined by its *own* self, for it is precisely this *self-intuition* of the self that we are trying to explain – and to appeal to the self's seeing itself in the very act of determining itself, in order to explain how it sees itself as determined, is to argue in a circle. But furthermore, the self cannot find itself or see itself as determined by a *mere object*; for in that case, the self would not be finding itself *as free*, and thus would not be finding *itself* at all. Fichte's claim is that the self can find itself as an object (as determined), only by finding itself as being-determined (summoned, or called) to be self-determining by another self, and – more importantly – as *having already freely accepted* the call by the other self to be free and self-determining. And thus the self can find itself as free only by finding itself as having always already agreed to or accepted a call or summons from another free self, even though – in a very real sense – the self was not deliberately and consciously present to itself or aware of itself in its acceptance of this call. After all, it is the self's acceptance of the summons or call (from the other free self) that serves to explain how the self comes to be aware of itself (or find itself) as a deliberate, conscious, free self in the first place.[16]

Now without going further into the complexities and subtleties of Fichte's derivation of intersubjectivity, it is possible to make some basic points about it and its relevance to any pre-critical social contractarian project (such as the Rawlsian one). Fichte's derivation of intersubjectivity implies that "before" a self can be a self-conscious free self at all, it must always already stand in relation to another free self that allows it – and is allowed by it – to be free. Thus, even "before" any free self can overtly begin reflecting on itself at all (and thus "before" it can deliberately choose to enter into any particular contract), it must have always already "agreed" to stand in a relation of reciprocity with another free self. "Before" either self can be conscious of itself as free, both must have always already agreed to be free and to let the other be free. Thus it is possible to speak of something like a "social contract" – or a "backwards social contract" – based simply on the self's radical freedom, i.e., the fact that truly free selves cannot be determined in advance to agree about any particular content or claim at all.

For Fichte, the problem for normative political theory is not that we need to articulate grounds for reasonable agreement. The problem is that we have always already "agreed" on relating to each other as free beings, but without having been deliberately conscious of such agreement and thus without knowing the "terms" upon which such agreement was made. For how would one go about imagining the terms of such an agreement? Any attempt to imagine specific "terms" about this primordial "agreement" between free beings must already presuppose that the persons are at least *aware* of themselves as free beings. Thus any attempt to *imagine* the primordial reciprocity or agreement at the basis of all relations between free beings is futile; any such attempt must already presuppose *as having already occurred* that which one is trying to explain – namely, the persons' *awareness* of themselves as *free*.

This account also indicates why the traditional social contractarian accounts necessarily fail to explain what they seek to explain. All such accounts seek to imagine persons agreeing to the *basic terms under which they are to relate to each other as free persons per se*. But insofar as such persons are imagined to be *bargaining* or *contracting* with each other at all, the imagined construct necessarily presupposes that the persons have *always already "agreed" to something*, i.e., they have always already agreed to regard each other as free beings, capable and worthy of entering into agreements. While it is possible to imagine the terms under which persons might agree to relate to one another with regard to this or that particular matter, it is altogether impossible to imagine the terms under which persons might agree to relate to each other as *free beings per se*. For the very idea of imagined contracting or bargaining presupposes that the persons have always already agreed to treat each other as *free beings per se*.[17]

Furthermore, we can now see that the normative and critical force of Fichtean social theory is not and cannot be based on any imagined story about the terms under which persons might have agreed to regard each other as free beings. For as we have seen, Fichte's starting point is the proposition that free persons – insofar as they are conscious of their freedom at all – must have always already reached "agreement" with other free beings. Such (non-empirical, non-imaginable, and non-representable) agreement manifests itself only *indirectly* in already-existing social and legal institutions, such as property, contracts, and criminal law.[18] And it is possible to criticize these institutions, but not because they allegedly fail to live up to the "standard" of an imagined, hypothetical social contract. Rather, it is possible to criticize these institutions to the extent that the human self-understanding that they embody and foster as institutions fails to accord with the "true" account of persons as radically free and self-determining and *intrinsically* related to other free beings.[19]

Finally, the Fichtean account of free selfhood and mutual recognition can be developed to underwrite a fairly robust, critical theory regarding the concrete requirements of justice in actual social practice. Recall that, for Fichte, the equilibrium of *Aufforderung* and mutual recognition cannot be brought about by force, but must be understood as resulting from the free, uncoerced activity of the selves involved. Now since such mutual recognition cannot be forced, or based on fear or oppression, it would seem to follow that there cannot be gross material inequalities between individuals within a given society. After all, the existence of gross material inequalities makes it possible for citizens to understand the existing social equilibrium as the result of force or fear, rather than free, mutual recognition. And for Fichte's social theory (based as it is on the premise of radically free selfhood), what is crucial is not just that the social equilibrium be unforced or uncoerced, but that it *be recognized* by the parties *themselves* as unforced or uncoerced. But the existence of gross material inequalities within a particular society undermines the citizens' ability to recognize the existing institutions (such as property) as the products of their own free, intersubjectively-mediated selfhood. With the Fichtean account, then, we have the beginnings of a normative, critical, progressive, non-teleological theory of society, based not on any questionable, quasi-metaphysical claims regarding what all free and reasonable persons would agree to, but based rather on the seemingly empty and skeptical premise that it is actually *impossible* to imagine in advance what all free persons would agree to. For precisely insofar as they are free – and not determined in advance by any antecedently given set of interests or teleologically-oriented drives – it is simply impossible to represent or to imagine in advance how such beings will act or what they will do. But this acknowledged impossibility – far from casting doubt on the emancipatory power of finite human reason – actually confirms it and sanctions it all the more fully.

Notes

1 This draft is from April or May of 1795. See *EPW*: 385.

2 This letter is dated 6 December 1793. See *EPW*: 369.

3 For a useful article on this topic, see John R. Silber, "The Copernican Revolution in Ethics: The Good Re-examined," *Kant Studien*, 51 (1959/60): 85–101.

4 Kant refers to this as "the paradox of method" in practical philosophy. He writes: "This is the place to explain the paradox of method in a *Critique of Practical Reason, namely, that the concept of good and evil must not be determined before the moral law (for which, as it would seem, this concept would have to be made the basis) but only (as was done here) after it and by means of it.*" See Immanuel Kant, *Critique of Practical Reason*, in *Immanuel Kant: Practical Philosophy*, ed. and trans. Mary Gregor (Cambridge: Cambridge University Press, 1999): 190. This passage can be found in volume 5 of the critical edition (or Akademie-edition) of Kant's works, at 62–3.

5 Fichte, *EPW*: 71.

6 Thus Rousseau writes: "For it is no light undertaking to separate what is original from what is artificial in the present nature of man, and to have a proper understanding of a state [of nature] which no longer exists, which perhaps never existed, which probably never will exist, and yet about which it is necessary to have accurate notions in order to judge properly our own present state." See Jean-Jacques Rousseau, *Discourse on the Origin of Inequality*, trans. Donald A. Cress (Indianapolis: Hackett Publishing Company, 1992): 11–12. A bit later in the *Discourse* (17), Rousseau makes a related observation: "Let us therefore begin by putting aside all the facts, for they have no bearing on the question. The investigations that may be undertaken concerning this subject should not be taken for historical truths, but only for hypothetical and conditional reasonings, better suited to shedding light on the nature of things than on pointing out their true origin."

7 John Rawls, *A Theory of Justice* (Cambridge: The Belknap Press of Harvard University Press, 1971), section 40: 254–5.

8 See, for example, "Justice as Fairness: Political, Not Metaphysical," in *John Rawls: Collected Papers*, ed. Samuel Freeman (Cambridge: Harvard University Press, 1999): 388–414.

9 See Rawls, *A Theory of Justice*, section 4: 17–22.

10 Rawls, *A Theory of Justice*: 4.

11 Elsewhere and at greater length I have examined the problematic character of Rawls's social contractarian thought. See Michael Baur, "Reversing Rawls: Criteriology, Contractualism, and the Primacy of the Practical," in *Philosophy and Social Criticism*, 28:3 (2002): 251–96.

12 This proposition represents the second principle of Fichte's *Foundation of the Entire Wissenschaftslehre*, namely the principle that the I is not equal to the not-I. See J.G. Fichte, *The Science of Knowledge*, ed. and trans. by Peter Heath and John Lachs (Cambridge: Cambridge University Press, 1982): 102. See also J.G. Fichte, *FTP*: 121–33.

13 Elsewhere and at greater length I have examined the Fichtean argument for the necessity of a not-self. See Michael Baur, "Self-measure and Self-moderation in Fichte's *Wissenschaftslehre*," in *New Essays in Fichte's Foundation of the Entire Doctrine of Scientific Knowledge*, ed. Daniel Breazeale and Tom Rockmore (Amherst, NY: Humanity Books, 2001): 81–102.

14 Of course, this argument implies a necessary *reciprocity*. I cannot be a free self (i.e., I cannot overcome mere servitude to my passions) unless the other is also a free self (i.e., unless it is capable of canceling its own merely natural existence). And the converse is also the case: the other cannot be a free self (i.e., it cannot overcome its servitude to its passions and cancel its own merely natural existence), unless I, too, am a free self (i.e., unless I, too, cancel my merely natural existence and overcome mere servitude to my passions).

15 This argument roughly foreshadows Hegel's "deduction" of intersubjectivity in the *Phenomenology*. Hegel's conclusion to his own presentation is as follows: "Since the

object is in its own self negation, and in being so is at the same time independent, it is consciousness … *Self-consciousness achieves its satisfaction only in another self-consciousness.*" See *Hegel's Phenomenology of Spirit*, trans. A.V. Miller (New York: Oxford University Press, 1977): 109–10.

16 Fichte's argument appears in Section 3 (Second Theorem) of his *FNR*: 29–39.

17 Thus Hume was right to argue that traditional social contractarian approaches necessarily come on the scene too late to explain what they seek to explain. See David Hume, "Of the Original Contract," in *Essays: Moral, Political, and Literary*, ed. Eugene F. Miller (Indianapolis: The Liberty Fund, 1985): 465–87.

18 See also Hegel, who – in the *Philosophy of Right* – takes the institutions of property and contract law as his starting point, and critically examines them as forms (or failed forms) of mediated, mutual, intersubjective recognition. See *Elements of the Philosophy of Right*, ed. Allen W. Wood, trans. H.B. Nisbet (Cambridge: Cambridge University Press, 1995): 73 ff.

19 For example, property regimes can be criticized to the extent that they are based on and foster the notion that private property exists primarily for the purpose of satisfying our more-or-less animalistic "natural" desires, without also – and more importantly – mediating our mutual recognition of each other as radically free beings.

Chapter 3

Recognition, Right, and Social Contract

Robert R. Williams

This chapter is constructed in three parts. In Section 1 I shall show that Fichte seeks to ground the concept of right in what we would call a fundamental ontology of human existence and freedom. Freedom is mediated by recognition; consequently freedom is intersubjective, relational and ethical. Recognition is the deep structure or ontological foundation of right and ethics. In Section 2 I take up Fichte's attempt to ground right in reciprocal recognition, and find that Fichte does not carry out his project consistently; indeed he compromises, if not undermines his project by separating right from morality. This separation entails that the human condition is considered as not informed by reciprocal recognition, but rather constituted by mistrust and egoism. The result is that the institutions of right are not grounded in reciprocal recognition, and the primordial ontological-ethical character of intersubjectivity is omitted or abstracted. Consequently relation per se becomes external and repressive. In Section 3 I investigate whether Fichte overcomes this external relationality in his complex account of the social contract. I show that his indeterminate concept of freedom stands in tension with his concept of community as an organism, and that Hegel's criticism of Fichte in the *Differenzschrift* was on target, namely, Fichte's separation of right from morality undermines his basic principle of freedom.

1 The Ontological Foundations of Right in Recognition

Recognition is a transcendental condition and foundation of both freedom and right. Fichte works in the Kantian problematic in which the self-consciousness of freedom is a central one. How do I know I am free? The difficulty behind this question is, how can the subject have access to its freedom without turning itself into an object in the theoretical, causal-mechanical sense? Such objectification would subvert the very freedom that it seeks to know. Fichte believes that the task is to show how self-consciousness of freedom is possible. He poses the question: how can the subject find itself as an object? Fichte's thesis is that the objectification requisite to the consciousness of freedom is not a reflective self-objectification; rather, only another free being can "objectify" me and make me available to myself without undermining my freedom. According to the *Foundations of Natural Law*, the full self-consciousness of freedom is one that I cannot give to myself.[1] Rather, I discover that I am free through the other, specifically, through the summons, or the appeal (*Aufforderung*) of the other.

The appeal is a "necessary fact"[2] that provides an answer to the question, how may the subject find itself as an object and thus "know" that it is free? The appeal summons the subject, not just to action, but to self-originated, self-determined action. The appeal is distinct from an *Anstoß*; the appeal is not a check on self-activity, or a physical force. The appeal is a summons to freedom that evokes it in the one summoned, and the one who summons creates a space for the realization of freedom by restricting his own.

Freedom is not something "contained" within individuals as a property. Rather freedom is relational. To say that freedom is relational means that it has a divided ground: one aspect, viz., the abstract ontological capacity, is "in" the subject; but the subject may not yet be conscious of it. The other aspect lies in another subject, who appeals or solicits the subject, awakening the subject to her freedom. The appeal mediates freedom, not in the sense of providing the ontological capacity (*ratio essendi*), but rather the consciousness of freedom (*ratio cognoscendi*).[3] What ties the inner and external "grounds" of freedom together is relation, which is initiated in the appeal and completed in an act of reciprocal recognition. Freedom is relational; it has its basis partly within the subject, and partly in another subject that is not under the control of the first. The consciousness of freedom is a mediated autonomy, i.e., a relation of the self to itself mediated by another.

The one who summons must have a concept of reason and freedom, and thus must be a being capable of concepts; i.e., s/he must be an intelligence and must possess freedom, for only a free being can restrict and/or restrain its freedom for the sake of an end. This restraint is crucial. If the other had not restricted his freedom, there would be no appeal, but only force or coercion, and the subject would not be brought to act. The subject's action is evoked, not compelled, by the action of the being outside of him.[4] The one who appeals restricts his freedom for the sake of the subject's action and freedom.

Although he is not trying to solve the problem of other minds, Fichte sometimes suggests that the appeal constitutes a "proof" of the other. If the appeal occurs, if there is such a thing as an appeal, then there must necessarily be a rational being outside of the self as its source.[5] Only such a being can restrict its freedom through the concept of the possibility of the freedom of the other, and for the sake of enabling that freedom.

Fichte's account of the appeal implies that freedom is understood as intersubjective and ethical. The appeal is an invitation or solicitation to rational freedom; the appeal has an ethical dimension. Fichte explains that the "human being becomes human only among humans … The concept of a human being is not at all that of an isolated individual – such is unthinkable – but that of a species."[6] The appeal or summons to freedom is part of a process of education.

The fact that another has restricted his freedom for the sake of inviting me to respond, demands recognition and a similar response on my part. That is, recognizing that another has restricted his freedom to make room for me invites me to reciprocate in a similar way. The "proof" of intersubjectivity establishes a reciprocal relation between co-equal rational beings, and this relation is a condition of and flows into both ethics and the *Rechtsverhältniss*.[7] Specifically, the appeal seeks to establish a relation between subjects in which each restricts its freedom for the sake of the freedom of the other. This reciprocal restriction of freedom for the sake of the other's freedom constitutes the *Rechtsverhältniss*.

> The relation of free beings to each other is therefore a relation of interaction through intelligence and freedom. Neither can recognize the other if both do not reciprocally recognize each other, and neither can treat the other as a free being if both do not reciprocally treat each other as free. This concept is of the highest importance for our procedure, because our entire theory of right depends on it.[8]

The concept of right is thus anchored in a fundamental ontology of intersubjective recognition.

Recognition is an act that has ontological dimensions which Fichte formulates as follows:

> at the basis of all *voluntarily chosen* reciprocal interaction among free beings there lies an *original* and *necessary* reciprocal interaction among them, which is this: the free being, by his mere presence in the sensible world, compels every other free being without qualification to recognize him as a person.[9]

Right, or all *voluntarily* chosen reciprocal interaction, is grounded in an original and necessary reciprocal interaction in which the free being compels every other free being to recognize her. This original ontological self-disclosure has ethical significance; it establishes a limit to my freedom: I am forbidden from reducing the other to or regarding her as a mere object. The other "is not to be treated as a thing."[10] The other, by virtue of her presence in the world, prior to all my responses to or actions towards her, compels not only my recognition of her, but appeals to me to limit and restrain my own free activity. The appeal of the other precedes my determination of my relation to her, viz., whether as contingent or necessary, as legal or moral. The recognition of other is primordial, and consequently foundational, for the concept of right.

What evokes recognition? Fichte's answer is complex, and involves his analysis of the human body. He offers a transcendental-genetic account of the human body as radically incomplete in its articulation and expression, and this very incompleteness points to the body as an expression/embodiment of a rational being. The body's articulation as an organized product of nature is unique in that its determination is to have no determination, i.e., to be infinitely determinable. "Every animal is what it is: only the human being is originally nothing at all. He must become what he is to be: and since he is to be for himself, he must become this through himself."[11] The human body is never merely a body, but a radically incomplete being that has to complete itself through its own self-determination.

> Formability as such is the characteristic of humanity. Because it is impossible to superimpose upon a human form any concept other than the [indeterminate] human itself, every human being is inwardly compelled to regard every other human being as his equal.[12]

However, it is not only the human body that compels recognition but also the face.[13] Fichte had previously discussed the face in his earlier *Lectures on the Vocation of the Scholar*. He thematizes the face in his discussion of the social drive, a drive that "aims at interaction, reciprocal influence, mutual give and take ...."[14] The face belongs to the way human beings freely communicate and influence each other.

> Everyone can say, "Whoever you may be, because you bear a human face, you are still a member of this great community ... I have an effect upon you, and you have an effect upon me. No one whose face bears the stamp of reason, no matter how crude, exists for me in vain."[15]

When we take Fichte's concept of the face together with his concept of the appeal, we find a rather striking anticipation of Levinas: it is but a short step from Fichte's account in which the other restricts his freedom and thus appeals to me to restrict my freedom, i.e., not to treat him as a thing, to Levinas' account of the original signification of the face: "You shall not kill." In both cases the relation to the other is ethical.[16]

In *Foundations of Natural Right* Fichte raises the question, how do we come to transfer the concept of rationality to some objects but not to others?[17] Again his answer points to the face. The recognition of face is not reducible to concepts, arguments and inferences. Prior to these there is an immediate recognition of the human shape.

> However, one should not think – and only a few need to be reminded of this – that the human being must first go through the long and difficult reasoning process we have just carried out, in order to understand that a certain body outside him belongs to a being that is his equal. Such recognition either does not occur at all, or it is achieved instantaneously, without one being aware of the reasons for it. Only the philosopher is required to give an account of such reasons.[18]

There is an immediate recognition of the face of another as a human face that is independent of inferences and philosophical theories. This is a recognition, not of a being with a fixed nature, but of a being that, as free, not only has no nature, but *determines* and *expresses itself.* It is the "whole expressive face" which "compels everyone with a human countenance to recognize and respect the human shape everywhere ... the human shape is necessarily sacred to the human being."[19] That is, the self-active, expressive face compels recognition of a being that has no fixed nature and thus is radically free. The appeal makes manifest an immediate equality that is accompanied by a restriction: not to treat the self-expressive face as a mere thing. This would violate not only its radical indeterminacy; it would violate its freedom, whereby it determines itself and makes itself be what it is supposed to be.

Recognition then is a condition of freedom and relationship prior to being a condition of right. Fichte conceives individuals as already bound and obligated to each other, not through an explicit consent, but rather through their very existence.[20] This existential relation constitutes community, not as the nemesis, but as the condition of individuality, and serves as the deep structure of rational lawfulness. Community in this ontological sense reflects a union of individuals that is deeper than contracts which are conditional, contingent unions of wills. This deeper concept of community is what Fichte refers to when he says that human beings become human only among humans and that the concept of humanity is not that of an individual but that of a species. This means that the other is co-posited with the same necessity and certainty with which the self posits itself; self and other are equi-primordial.[21] All positing is co-positing, and equi-primordiality signifies the priority of relation over individual subjects in isolation. They are affected by and mutually co-constituted through reciprocal relation. Recognition is that act through which the primordial existential relation between subjects is constituted as reciprocal, i.e., the *Rechtsverhältniss*. As such it is the prior condition of the contingencies of rights as well as prior to arguments that seek to infer "other minds."

2 From Recognition to Right

The first seven paragraphs of the *Foundations of Natural Right* constitute an argument concerning mutual recognition as the foundation of the concept of right. The next several paragraphs (§§8–17) seek to apply this concept of right. However, Fichte here introduces additional considerations that are in tension with his initial analysis: specifically the separation of right from morality, and in spite of mutual recognition, a context or situation in which mutual trust and confidence have been lost. In their place is a universal, anxious egoism concerned about security. Ludwig Siep notes that:

> The concept of recognition was introduced as transcendental a priori condition and criterion for any *Rechtstaat*, namely the state must realize, support and be grounded in the reciprocal recognition of its members … However Fichte does not show that and how different relations of recognition underlie determinate institutions and are themselves made possible by these institutions.[22]

Siep believes that this step was first taken by Hegel. Siep notes that Fichte's treatment of recognition is restricted in that although it is supposed to mediate free efficacy, it does not constitute the actual intention of individuals in Fichte's state:

> for Fichte rightful recognition must be given as a fact, but not necessarily as the intention of individuals in the rational state. As the end of individual actions, recognition is dispensable in the rational state. The institutions securing right must, according to Fichte, rather derive from the contrary motivation of universal egoism. In the doctrines of coercive right and social contract, the principle of self-preservation displaces the principle of recognition … Coercive right does not reckon with free reciprocal recognition, but with the concern of each for his own security.[23]

The need for security displaces mutual recognition. Siep observes that:

> according to Fichte the end of common security can be attained through institutions that make superfluous precisely that type of recognition through which individual self-consciousness [of freedom] can first arise, namely the voluntary self-limitation that has the freedom of others as its end. In his *Staatsphilosophie* Fichte fails to develop the original concept of recognition that is the foundation of his deduction of the concept of right.[24]

One central and contentious issue in Fichte's analysis is his separation of right from morality. The separation of right from morality suggests that each is a completely distinct sphere of existence, with its own version of intersubjectivity, relation, community and principles. This separation introduces implications that contradict and undermine Fichte's ontological analysis of recognition and relation. Specifically, the separation of right from morality implies that within right, relation is treated independently of ethics. Relation is no longer necessary but contingent. Instead of being a condition of individuality, community is now regarded as optional and contingent. In right there is an interhuman relationship, but it is one which has been abstracted from the face and the ethical dimension of summons and recognition. It is not surprising that relation, conceived apart from the ethical and from the face, turns into something merely external and coercive. Consequently, Fichte fails to do justice to his own rich and suggestive account of recognition. He subordinates the ontological dimension of recognition (as ethical relation to the other as face) to right as an external contingent shape of relation.

Fichte follows Kant in distinguishing between right and morality. Right is a permission, not a moral duty. A permission is a "you may" or "no one may prevent you from so doing …." As such, right presupposes an independent, self-sufficient, self-determining individual. Moral law commands categorically without exception. If I fail to do my duty, then I violate the moral law and lose moral worth. But a law of right never commands that a right has to be exercised. If I fail to exercise my right, I still retain my right. A right that is not exercised does not cease to be a right.[25]

The basic principle of right is that I must recognize the free being outside of me in all instances as free, i.e., I must restrict my freedom through the concept of the possibility of his freedom. This means that "no one has a right to an action that makes the freedom and personality of another impossible; but everyone has a right to all other free actions."[26] This relation between rational beings in which each restricts his freedom through the concept of the possible freedom of the other, *under the condition that the other likewise restricts his freedom*, constitutes the *Rechtsverhältniss*.[27]

Note that the original relation of *immediate* recognition is different from the conditional necessity of the concepts of right and contract. The difference is that in recognition the other is equiprimordial and so relation between selves is necessary, not optional. Selves exist only in relation, and this has ethical implications. Community is not optional but a condition of free individuality. But in right, living in community with other is optional, contingent, and requires individual consent. From the perspective of right, the individual precedes the community that he enters by his voluntary consent. Thus Fichte writes:

> I must think of myself as necessarily in community with other human beings with whom nature has united me, but I cannot do this without thinking of my freedom as limited through their freedom; now I must also act in accordance with this necessary thought; otherwise my acting stands in contradiction with my thinking, and I would stand in contradiction with myself. I am bound, in conscience, by my knowledge of how things ought to be, to limit my freedom. Now in the doctrine of right there is no talk of moral obligation; each is bound only by the free arbitrary decision to live in community with others.[28]

When Fichte treats right as a relation, he characterizes relation as optional, contingent and conditional. Rights are not necessary, but become necessary only if one chooses to live in community. The necessary reciprocal relation between the divided grounds of freedom is now qualified as contingent and conditional. The *Rechtslehre* adds reciprocity as an explicit condition: I restrict my freedom *on the condition* that the other similarly restrict his freedom.

> As certainly as I recognize him, that is treat him [with respect] it is certain that he is bound and obligated by his first problematic expression, and through theoretical consequences compelled, to recognize me categorically, and to do so in a way that is valid for both of us, i.e., he is required to treat me as a free being.[29]

By actually recognizing him I obligate him to recognize me and obligate myself as a result of his recognition of me to treat him likewise. If one party fails to do this, then right, as a conditional agreement between the two, is canceled, suspended. This account, which is plausible as an account of that contingent union of wills constitutive of contract, is both troubling and problematic if read as an account of intersubjectivity and ethics.

My thesis is that Fichte slides from the primordial sense of right – namely recognition of face in which the other compels recognition by his very presence and community is a condition of individuality – to right as a conditional union of wills, founded upon explicit consent or agreement. Right in this sense is precarious because it rests on a conditional union of wills that is optional and may be reversed. However, this contingent, reversible union of wills is not the original sense of right arising out of the encounter with the other as face that compels recognition by its very presence.[30]

Whatever legitimate reasons may have led Fichte to stress the conditional reciprocity of right, it is also the case that Fichte, in thinking the *Rechtsverhältniss*, conceives individuals as isolated from and mistrustful of each other. He observes that a single transgression shatters trust and confidence in immediate right, or the immediate observance of right by others. Such a transgression reveals that the other does not really will right, or wills it merely for self-serving tactical reasons. Realization of this leads to the loss of trust and confidence.[31] Trust and confidence, once lost, cannot be restored through confessions, apologies, or expressions of regret and repentance. Once the immediate security of right is destroyed, right cannot be maintained by good will alone. Immediate right has been shattered and must be replaced by coercive right.

In morality the issue of the good will is central. But in right the good will has nothing to do; if no human being had a good will, right must nevertheless be actualized.[32] Morality may remain a pure *Sollen*, ought to be, but the social and political order cannot. Consequently Fichte spends a good deal of time discussing *Zwangsrecht*, the coercive aspect of right. Fichte even asserts that "in this domain physical force – and it alone – gives right its sanction."[33]

However, Fichte's notion of *Zwangsrecht* is not simply an appeal to physical force. Rather, coercive right is directed at the will to keep the will in conformity with legal behavior. Fichte advocates a deterrence theory of right and punishment. The *Zwangsrecht* is a quasi-mechanical arrangement whereby the person who would act contrary to right, is deterred by the realization that his action will bring about the opposite of what he intends, and thus will be led to police, i.e., restrain himself. Coercive or deterrent right must restore security after immediate trust and confidence have been lost. External coercion, i.e., deterrence, will accomplish the necessary security and thus make the good will superfluous to the realization of right.[34]

Once the realization of right is separated from the good will (i.e., once right has been separated from morality, ethics from politics) the ethical nature of intersubjective recognition is obscured, and freedom, which is supposed to be the basis of the state, is itself undermined.[35] Fichte's state is based on mistrust, on the breakdown of trust and confidence: "The state has neither the right nor the power to command citizens to trust one another, for it is itself constructed on the premise of universal mistrust. Even the state is not to be trusted …."[36]

The state is not an end in itself but merely an instrument of coercion, for only a state can fulfill the conditions of surveillance necessary to detect the bad will (so that it can be certain that its action will be detected and punished) as well as the conditions of force necessary to deter and punish. Only the state can deter the bad will by compelling it to restrain itself and remain within prescribed legal limits. Instead of a mutual recognition that mediates freedom and unites human beings in trust and confidence, Fichte's separation of right from morality threatens to reduce recognition to external surveillance, and reciprocal recognition to mere isolated existence: "Both recognize each other in their inner being, but they remain isolated as before."[37]

3 Fichte's Threefold Social Contract

It is well known that Fichte's account of the social contract is highly complex, proceeding from consideration of a property contract to a protection contract to a union contract. Since contract involves a union of wills, and such a union implies intersubjectivity, it may be that Fichte's analysis of social contract can provide a clarification of the relation between recognition, right and community.

The property contract is a union of wills whereby each agrees to renounce any claims to the other's property on the condition that the other do the same. This contract means that one's own possession becomes property mediated through the recognition of the other.[38] The other recognizes my right to exclude him from my property. However, even though the possession becomes property through recognition, and even though the property contract includes mutual recognition, the positive focal point of such recognition is not the other, but one's property. Since ownership is intersubjectively mediated, the will of the property contract undoubtedly extends beyond property; nevertheless this reference to another is merely negative.[39] Each party agrees to refrain from making any claims to the other's property, and is indifferent to the other.

So the property contract is minimalist and intersubjectively negative. It therefore requires supplementation by the protection contract. The protection contract is an agreement whereby each party agrees to come to the defense and protection of the other's property, on the condition that the other agrees to do the same. This contract is positive, in the sense that it requires not merely that people refrain from disturbing or appropriating another's property, but that they actually come to the defense of that property should it be threatened. Like every other contract, the protection contract is dissolved should one side fail to fulfill it. But a problem arises precisely at this point: since the protection contract requires that each do something – namely protect the other's property against violations by a third party – and since protection is not something needed at all times but only under certain conditions, it is clear that the protection contract is more like a promise, rather than an actual performance. Hence the question turns on the issue of the promise and its acceptance. Since Fichte explicitly rules out the good will and declares that mutual trust and confidence have been lost, how can anyone believe, much less accept that promise of protection? In short, the protection contract does not really deliver a right to be protected, because it shipwrecks on the mistrust and universal egoism that render the problem of promising insoluble.[40] "Thus we remain, as before, in a state of insecurity and dependence on the good will of others, a will upon which we are neither inclined, nor obligated, to rely."[41]

Since the conditions of the protection contract are never met, Fichte argues that a third contract is necessary, namely the union contract. The union contract is supposed to show that from the mere entrance into the state, the question whether anyone has met his obligations under the protection contract is no longer problematic. Fichte's argument concerning the union contract is far from clear; to the extent that it is clear, it appears to be quasi-Rawlsian. Invoking the concept of indeterminate oscillation in the imagination, Fichte contends that the issue of who is to be protected remains indeterminate. No one knows whose property will be attacked or transgressed. As long as we believe transgression will happen to someone else, we may not be inclined to take the protection issue seriously, nor are we willing to risk ourselves in protecting someone else. But if we do not and cannot know whose property will be transgressed, then we have to assume the worst, namely that it will be ours. The oscillation in the concept of who is to be transgressed not only functions like Rawls' veil of ignorance, it also provides a negative unifying basis of solidarity – or so Fichte asserts. We have to make the worst case assumption that it will be our own property that is going to be transgressed. In this scenario we would want the state to protect us.

> Thus each individual can believe that this whole protective arrangement has been established solely for his benefit, and so will gladly make his own small contribution to it … this oscillation in the imagination is the real bond that unites the different individuals. It is by means of this that all merge together into one.[42]

This argument is not terribly plausible, largely because the union with the state or community that it establishes seems to be not only negative, but also indeterminate and reflective merely of self interest. While this is consistent with

Fichte's view in the *Rechtslehre* that community is fundamentally negative, it is difficult to see how it overcomes the problem of promising, much less binds people together in community. However Fichte does have a reply.

> In the sphere of right there is no way to bind human beings together other than through the insight: whatever you do to the other, whether good or bad, you do not to him, but to yourself. In the case at hand, this means I would have to be able to see that, in protecting the other, I protect only myself.[43]

This is an important formulation. However, while it may appear to imply a reciprocal recognition and solidarity, it remains largely egocentric rather than affirmatively intersubjective: the other may be regarded as merely an extension of the self and is of interest only insofar as the other is identifiable with the self's own interest. Further, Fichte does not explicitly relate this insight to his concept of recognition. This is a telling omission, for it suggests that the principle is merely egocentric and reflective and has no intersubjective significance whatsoever.

Further, it remains unclear how indeterminate freedom and indeterminate potential victimhood could solve the problem of promising and effectively unite people. For not only the problem of promising but also any genuine non-repressive community would seem to require an affirmative and reciprocal self-recognition in other. But in the *Rechtslehre*, Fichte brackets affirmative mutual recognition because he separates right from morality and so refuses to rely on the good will. What connects the predominantly negative egocentric freedom and self-interest with the whole? To answer this question, Fichte invokes not mutual recognition, but the concept of organism:

> The concept we have presented can be well illustrated by the concept of an organized product of nature, e.g., a tree. If each individual part of the tree were endowed with consciousness and will, then each part, just as certainly as it wills its own self-preservation, must also will the preservation of the tree, since it can be preserved only if the tree is preserved. Now from the perspective of the individual part, what then is tree? The tree in general is nothing other than a mere concept, and a concept cannot be harmed. But the part wills that no part among all, regardless of which one it is, should ever be harmed, because the part would also suffer if any other part were harmed. Such is not the case with a pile of sand, where each part can be indifferent to whether any other part is separated, trampled upon, or strewn about.[44]

Fichte is one of the first to propose the concept of organism as an account of the civic relation. However, he fails to connect it with his account of reciprocal recognition, and he fails to appreciate the full significance of the concept of organism for the social whole. In the concept of organism, the distinction between means and ends is supposed to be suspended in favor of reciprocal interdependence between whole and parts. Fichte understands that the unity of the organism is constituted by the reciprocity between whole and parts: "without the reciprocal interaction of organic forces that keep each other in equilibrium, there would be no enduring form at all …."[45] However, in Fichte's explanation of organic union, individual freedom and its relation to the whole are still negatively conceived and determined. The whole is regarded only instrumentally as a means to egoistic self-preservation. The whole is willed and valued not as something good in itself, but only as a means to the self-preservation of the individual. On Fichte's reading, the concept of organism fails to suspend indeterminate freedom and egoism, and when he applies it to the civic relation, he fails to overcome the instrumental view of the state and the asymmetrical relation between individual and whole.

These deficiencies in Fichte's account are identified and criticized by Hegel. In Hegel's view, Fichte begins as authentic thinker of freedom, but his entanglement with *reflexionphilosophie* leads Fichte to elevate non-union into an absolute principle that returns at every crucial point, not only in his *Wissenschaftslehre* but also in his *Grundlage des Naturrechts*. Hegel asks rhetorically, "What union is possible … once absolute opposites are presupposed? Strictly speaking none at all, obviously."[46] Not only is the non-ego opposed to the ego, it is determined negatively,[47] and this negativity recurs on every level, including the practical and the political. This means not only that the other is a negation, but also that community is constituted by a necessary limitation on freedom.[48] Hegel observes that although freedom is the summit of Fichte's system, "In a community with others … freedom must be surrendered in order to make possible the freedom of all rational beings living in community."[49] But this fact "makes it clear that freedom is here something merely negative, namely, absolute indeterminateness, i.e., it is a purely ideal factor. …."[50] Hegel singles out for criticism Fichte's concepts of indeterminate freedom and abstract individuality:

> If the community of rational beings were essentially a limitation of true freedom, the community would be in and for itself the supreme tyranny. But only freedom as indeterminacy and as ideal factor is being limited at this point in Fichte, so that tyranny does not arise in the community directly from this idea itself. But it does arise in the highest degree from the way that freedom is to be limited in order to make possible the freedom of other rational beings.

> For freedom is not supposed to lose, through community, its form of being something ideal and opposite; on the contrary it is going to be fixed in this form and made dominant.[51]

This is precisely what occurs in Fichte's discussion of the union contract from the standpoint of right, namely, freedom is fixed in indeterminate form and the state is regarded as instrumental to the preservation of this individual freedom.

Hegel appropriates from Fichte the concept of recognition. He agrees that recognition provides a grounding, not merely for right in the legal sense, but also for ethics in a broad sense, including morality and ethical life.[52] For Hegel recognition means that the I becomes a We, and the We is an organic union of transformed and enlarged individualities. This means that intersubjectivity and community "with others must not be regarded as a limitation of true freedom of the individual, but essentially as its enlargement. Highest community is highest freedom ...."[53] Hegel points out that Fichte's concept of abstract indeterminate freedom must be overcome in order to realize his original insights about the organic unity of freedom, community and right. Indeterminate freedom is *aufgehoben* when one becomes an authentic member of an organic community.

> But it is precisely in this highest community that freedom as an ideal factor and reason opposed to nature disappear completely ... Through a genuinely free community of living connections [sic organism] the individual renounces his indeterminacy [which is what Fichte calls] his freedom. In a living connection there is only freedom in the sense that it includes the possibility of suspending itself and entering into other connections. *But [abstract] freedom as an ideal factor, as indeterminacy, falls away*. In a living relation, insofar as it is free, the indeterminate is nothing but the possible; it is neither something actual made dominant nor a concept that commands. In the *Grundlage des Naturrechts* however, this suspension of indeterminacy is not what is understood there as the free limitation of one's freedom. On the contrary, when limitation by the common will is raised to the status of law and fixed as a concept, true freedom, the possibility of suspending a determinate connection, is nullified.[54]

Hegel believes that Fichte's separation of right from morality is bound up with his conception of freedom as indeterminate individuality, and that such indeterminate freedom undermines his concept of community as an organic unity. Fichte's concept of indeterminate freedom goes hand in hand with the "pile of sand" metaphor for community that Fichte says he rejects. Hegel believes that Fichte's consideration of recognition and community is merely external. As such it turns right into something external and coercive and:

> offers us a picture of the complete lordship of the intellect and the complete bondage of the living being. It is an edifice in which reason has no part and which it therefore repudiates. For reason is bound to find itself most explicitly in its self-shaping as a people, which is the most perfect organization which it can give itself. But that state as conceived by the intellect is not an organism at all but a machine, and the people is not the organic body of a rich communal life, but an atomistic, life-impoverished multitude … *Fiat justitia, pereat mundus* is the law, and not even in the sense that Kant gave it: "let justice be done though all the scoundrels of the world perish." But rather in this sense: right must be done, even though for its sake all trust, all joy and love, all the potencies of a genuinely ethical identity, must be eradicated root and branch. …[55]

Fichte's *Rechtslehre* grounds right and ethics in mutual recognition, but fails to execute this idea consistently. Although recognition has an ontological depth that constitutes individuality and community as reciprocal and ethical, when he separates right from morality, Fichte treats relation as external, so that after recognition – which is supposed to unite human beings – humans remain isolated as before.[56] Hence for Fichte recognition generates no "We," no community, and is displaced by abstract universal egoism. The latter conception of abstract and indeterminate freedom is incompatible with recognition, relation and community, and these are either displaced or restricted to being vehicles of external coercion. Fichte begins the *Naturrecht* by thinking relation as a condition and requirement of freedom, but he ends it with a universal egoism from whose perspective relation appears only as external compulsion:

> In this way the external character of oneness is utterly fixed and posited as something absolute and inherently necessary; and thereby the inner life, the rebuilding of lost constancy and faith, the union of the universal and individual freedom, and ethical life itself, are made impossible.[57]

In his account of recognition which the *Philosophy of Right* presupposes, Hegel develops Fichte's original insight into the inseparability of inter-subjectivity and ethics. Thus Hegel agrees with Fichte that right is grounded in recognition. He also agrees that right can be distinguished from morality as a permission in contrast to a duty. However, this distinction between right and morality is an abstraction, and not an absolute separation. Hence abstract right is part of Hegel's mature theory, and what it abstracts from is morality. Indeed, for Hegel both abstract right and morality are abstractions that are not self-standing, and as such presuppose recognition and ethical life (*Sittlichkeit*).[58]

Notes

1 In the *System der Sittenlehre* 1798 Fichte develops the consciousness of freedom without reference to recognition but in reference to the moral law. There is a lack of clarity about transcendental grounding and its relation to ordinary consciousness. See Joachim Widmann, *Fichte Einführung in seine Philosophie* (Berlin: de Gruyter, 1982): 153.

2 *Grundlage des Naturrechts, Fichte Werke*, Band III, ed. I.H. Fichte (Berlin: Walter de Gruyter, 1971): 35, hereafter cited as GNR; ET, *The Foundations of Natural Right*, ed. Frederick Neuhouser, trans. Michael Baur (Cambridge: Cambridge University Press, 2000): 34; hereafter FNR.

3 I take these terms from Kant. In the *Second Critique* Kant had argued that the self-consciousness of freedom is mediated by the natural law, that obligation implies freedom, because only a free being can be aware of the *Sollen* as something that ought to be. Fichte is making a similar point, only claiming that the other's *Aufforderung*, rather than the moral law, is the *ratio cognoscendi* of freedom. And this is equivalent to claiming that the *Sollen* and consciousness of freedom are intersubjectively mediated. But then the consciousness of freedom is no longer a priori in the strict Kantian sense, but rather a social-psychological-historical discovery.

4 GNR: 43; FNR: 42.

5 GNR: 39; FNR: 37. Cf. C.K. Hunter, *Der Interpersonalitätsbeweis in Fichtes früher angewandter praktischer Philosophie* (Meisenheim am Glan: Verlag Anton Hain, 1973).

6 GNR: 39; FNR: 38.

7 GNR: 41; FNR: 39.

8 GNR: 44; FNR: 42.

9 GNR: 85; FNR: 79. Italics mine.

10 GNR: 86; FNR: 80.

11 GNR: 80; FNR: 74.

12 Ibid. I have modified the English translation. Here in the constitution of the other as equal (*seines Gleiche*) Fichte's transcendental account merges with his phenomenological account. The result is something like Husserl's concept of appresentation, a mediate apprehension of an equality that is neither directly sensibly present, nor simply absent and inferred, but appresented.

13 GNR: 84; FNR: 78.

14 *Lectures Concerning the Scholar's Vocation*, in *Fichte: Early Philosophical Writings*, ed. and trans. Daniel Breazeale (Ithaca: Cornell University Press, 1988): 158.

15 Ibid.: 160.

16 The difference between Fichte and Levinas is that the latter holds that the relation to the face is asymmetrical and heterological between unequals, whereas Fichte believes it is reciprocal between co-equals.

17 Fichte asks how do we know which beings are rational ends? This is one of the central political questions of the modern period. He continues: "How do I know which particular

object is a rational being? How do I know whether the protection afforded by that universal legislation [Kant's kingdom of ends] befits only the white European, or perhaps also the black Negro; only the adult human being or perhaps also the child?" (GNR: 80; FNR: 75).

18 GNR: 81; FNR: 75–6. If recognition of the other is pre-theoretical fact, how is such pre-theoretical givenness clarified, much less "explained" by the basic philosophical principle of idealism, that everything in the subject exists through the subject? Is an explanation, much less a proof, of the other even necessary? Fichte does not succeed in clarifying the relation of the transcendental standpoint to the standpoint of ordinary consciousness. On the one hand the transcendental standpoint inverts ordinary consciousness such that everything that exists *for* the I exists *through* the I. But on the other hand, Fichte also contends that the standpoint of speculative idealism is not a real standpoint; idealism can never be more than *a way of thinking* that seeks to make life and natural consciousness comprehensible (Second Introduction to the *Wissenschaftslehre*, in *Introductions to the Wissenschaftslehre*, ed. and trans. Daniel Breazeale (Indianapolis: Hackett, 1994): 38n). If the transcendental perspective is only a way of thinking, what could it add to the immediate recognition of the face? Whatever it adds, it does not add the face, because the face expresses itself. Thus it cannot be reduced to my representation. Günter Zöller fails to heed Fichte's qualification of transcendental idealism when he rejects the "realist" interpretation of the appeal: "Yet the solicitation is not really an appeal issued from outside the individual but is the individual's 'clandestine' representation to itself of its own finite being under the form of the solicitation" (Zöller, *Fichte's Transcendental Philosophy* (Cambridge: Cambridge University Press, 1998): 119). To be sure, Zöller is discussing Fichte's *Wissenschaftslehre Novo Methodo*, in which intersubjectivity is subordinate to transcendental philosophy. Zöller treats the transcendental as an independent, self-subsistent standpoint that explains ordinary consciousness. If there were such a thing as a transcendental "causal explanation" of ordinary consciousness, ordinary consciousness would not apprehend any realities beyond itself. Transcendental "explanation" of its "realities" would reveal them to be merely projections of its own self-limitations. Ordinary consciousness of the face and the appeal would be false consciousness. At the transcendental level there would be no face and no appeal, only self-limitation. This interpretation undermines the very appeal that it seeks to "explain," and it may be one reason why Fichte abandoned the *Wissenschaftslehre Novo Methodo* and the attempt to give a transcendental explanation of intersubjectivity in favor of a more nuanced existentialist position in the *Vocation of Man*. My view is that Fichte believes that neither the transcendental perspective nor ordinary consciousness can be collapsed into the other, and that both perspectives are necessary. (See *Wissenschaftslehre* 1794, *Werke* I: 282: "No ideality, no reality, and vice-versa. Accordingly we can say that the final ground of all consciousness is an interaction of the ego with itself by means of a non-ego that must be considered from different perspectives. This is the circle from which the finite spirit cannot escape … .") Thus Fichte has the problem of maintaining and reconciling the two perspectives. For starters on this problem, when Fichte says that everything in the ego exists *through* the ego, in reference to the self-expressive face the "through" (*durch*) has no metaphysical-causal but only hermeneutic phenomenological significance.

19 GNR: 84–5; FNR: 78–9.

20 GNR: 48; FNR: 45.

21 Fichte sketches such equiprimordiality in the following passage: "The rational observer is completely unable to unite the parts of the human body except in the concept of his equal … Because it is impossible to superimpose upon a human shape any concept other

than that of the [indeterminate] human itself, every human being is inwardly compelled to regard every other human being as his equal": GNR: 80; FNR: 74. This passage is one in which Fichte's descriptive phenomenology and transcendental explanation appear to merge, thereby modifying the very idea of transcendental explanation.

22 Ludwig Siep, *Anerkennung als Prinzip der praktischen Philosophie* (Freiburg: Alber Verlag, 1978): 35. Hereafter cited as APP.
23 APP: 35.
24 APP: 36.
25 GNR: 54; FNR: 50
26 GNR: 93–4; FNR: 86–7. Here is a possible intersection between right and ethics.
27 GNR: 52; FNR: 49.
28 GNR: 11; FNR: 11–12
29 GNR: 47; FNR: 44.
30 This distinction between primordial right grounded in the act of recognition, and right as conditional reciprocal consent, may help clarify some puzzles in Fichte's account of intersubjectivity and right. For example, Frederick Neuhouser notes that Fichte's account of right grounded in recognition appears to generate the implausible claim that individuals become conscious of themselves as discrete agents only by inhabiting a political order that protects individual rights (FNR: xvii). The implausibility here turns on a confusion of right in the derivative conditional sense, with a necessary condition of intersubjectivity and freedom. This gets the cart before the horse: intersubjective recognition is a condition of the self-consciousness of freedom and grounds the concept of right. In this primordial sense right is a condition of self-consciousness. However, right in the conditional legal sense is not a condition, but a modification or qualification, of intersubjective recognition.
31 GNR: 139; FNR: 125.
32 GNR: 54; FNR: 50.
33 Ibid.
34 GNR: 142; FNR: 127.
35 Widmann observes that the universal mistrust is ultimately connected not with crime and transgression, but with freedom itself. "The source of mistrust can be completely excluded only if the possibility of free decision itself is excluded. But this is utterly unthinkable for Fichte's attempt to base the state on the idea of freedom," op. cit.: 160.
36 GNR: 244 ; FNR: 213.
37 GNR: 86; FNR: 79.
38 GNR: 129–30; FNR: 116–17.
39 GNR: 194; FNR: 167.
40 GNR: 198–200; FNR: 171–3.
41 GNR: 201; FNR: 174.
42 GNR: 203; FNR: 176.
43 GNR: 199; FNR: 172.
44 GNR: 203; FNR: 176.
45 GNR: 208; FNR: 181.
46 Hegel, *Difference between Fichte's and Schelling's System of Philosophy*, trans. W. Cerf and H.S. Harris (Albany: State University of New York Press, 1977): 126.
47 Ibid.: 128.
48 Ibid.: 144.
49 Ibid.
50 Ibid.: 144–5.
51 Ibid.:145.

52 Hegel, *Philosophy of Right*, §33 Zusatz, Nisbet translation (Cambridge: Cambridge University Press, 1991).
53 Ibid.
54 Ibid.: 145. My italics. I have revised the English translation.
55 Ibid.: 148–9.
56 "Both recognize each other in their inner being but they remain isolated as before": GNR: 86; FNR: 79
57 Hegel, *Natural Law*, trans. T.M. Knox (Philadelphia: University of Pennsylvania Press, 1975): 84–5.
58 See Williams, *Hegel's Ethics of Recognition* (Berkeley: University of California Press, 1998): chs 6 and 7; Kenneth Westphal, "The Context and Structure of Hegel's *Philosophy of Right*," *Cambridge Companion to Hegel* (Cambridge: Cambridge University Press, 1993) and Paul Franco, *Hegel's Philosophy of Freedom* (New Haven: Yale University Press, 1999): ch. 6.

Chapter 4

On the Fundamental Connection between Moral Law and Natural Right in Fichte's *Contribution* (1793) and *Foundations of Natural Right* (1796/97)[1]

Violetta L. Waibel

Whereas Johann Gottlieb Fichte's work *Foundations of Natural Right*, which appeared in 1796 and 1797 in two volumes, attracts attention in research especially due to its theory of interpersonality and its theory of recognition, another work by Fichte on natural right is often not taken into consideration. Its title is *Contribution toward Correcting the Public's Judgements Concerning the French Revolution* (*Beitrag zur Berichtigung der Urtheile des Publicums über die Französische Revolution*) and appeared in 1793. The comparision of both works demonstrates that Fichte postulates a common systematic foundation of both moral law and natural right in the *Contribution*, whereas he denies explicitly the possibility of a deduction of natural right from moral law, which Fichte accuses some philosophers to have done.[2]

In the *Contribution* Fichte writes:

> One used to think, – if I may point this out in passing – that one had to trace natural right back to an original state of human nature; recently, one has objected to this method, complaining that it is the origin of many kinds of absurdities. Yet this method alone is the correct one. In order to discover the foundations of obligation in all contracts, one has to think of humanity as not yet bounded by any outer contracts, but as only subject to the law of human nature, i.e., to the moral law; and this is precisely the *natural condition of man*.[3]

In the *Foundations of Natural Right* Fichte maintains:

> This entire presentation of the concept of right has refrained from refuting in detail those who attempt to derive the doctrine of right from the moral law; this

> is because, as soon as the correct deduction is given, every unbiased mind will accept it of its own accord, even if the incorrectness of the other deductions has not been shown; but as for biased minds and those who have their own axes to grind, every word uttered for the purpose of refuting them is wasted.[4]

In reading both passages, written in the span of three years, one might suspect that there is a deep contradiction regarding the fundamental connection between moral law and natural right. Whereas the systematic difference of the two positions is beyond question, there are several interpretations to explain the nature and reason of this difference. To be sure, the *Contribution* doesn't belong to the system of the *Wissenschaftslehre* in the narrow sense, the presentation of which began with the *My Own Meditations on Elementary Philosophy* (*Eigne Meditationen über ElementarPhilosophie*) in the winter of 1793/94. We have to see that the question of the systematicity and hierarchy of philosophical principles is not only a Fichtean obsession[5] but a necessary demand where claims of validity have to be considered even if it is true that Fichte shows not to have fully mastered this problem.

Being situated earlier, the *Contribution* seems to be sketched out in contradiction to the following *Wissenschaftslehre*. But otherwise, the strict separation of moral law and natural right in the *Foundations* which at first sight may seem self-evident, in fact appears to outline new systematic problems that we have to take into consideration. The problems relate to the status of morality and right as applied sciences in the *Wissenschaftslehre* and how their principles relate to the absolute ego.

1 The Connection of Moral Law and Natural Right in the *Contribution*

In 1796, Fichte denies the possibility of deducing natural right from moral law. In the earlier work of 1793 however, Fichte does not explicitly speak of a deduction, but rather of a foundation of natural right in the natural condition of man. In a further step, he identifies this state of human nature with the moral law. Thus we should first examine what exactly the connection is between natural right and moral law as portrayed in the *Contribution*.

Fichte's aim is to show that natural right is something that cannot be grounded in experience but in reason, just as the question as to whether a people is legitimated in initiating a revolution or not is not a question of knowledge but of judgment. Knowledge only describes what occurs or has occurred. In this way the French Revolution is a "historical painting" of the events in question. But the question of its legitimation goes beyond the historical facticity and thus becomes a question of validity. As Fichte intends to show, validity can only be grounded in eternal laws, because it touches things not as they are but as they ought to be. The eternal laws of what ought to be can only be found in what Fichte calls even in 1793 the pure ego, representing human reason. The expression of the pure ego or of reason is, as Fichte stresses in 1793, the moral law.

In addition, Fichte reminds us that the real end of man is to bring about more and more individually and generally the realization of the moral law by subsuming all acts under it.

Fichte expands on three possible cases concerning the rights given by the moral law:

1) the moral law gives commands and these are called human duties;
2) the moral law forbids what is contrary to human duties;
3) the moral law is silent and therefore allows for actions done by human arbitrariness.

Fichte underlines the difference between the first two and the third case. In the first two cases, human duties and that which is contrary to them coincide with human rights (in the first case) and their opposite (in the second case), whereas the third case permits either the realization of or refrainment from a human right. We have and we must have the right to do our duties and to abstain from the contrary of our duties, legitimated by the moral law. When the moral law is silent we are completely free with respect to whether we observe a right or not, legitimated by the allowance of the moral law.

> What this law [the moral law] commands, is generally called *just, a duty*; what it forbids, *is unjust, contrary to duty*. The first is what we ought to do; the latter is what we ought not to do. – If we, as rational beings, are subject absolutely and without any exception to this law, we can not, as such, be subject to another; thus, when this law is silent, we are not subsumed under any law, we are given licence to do anything. We are permitted to do anything not forbidden by law. We have a right to do what we are permitted to do because this permission is by law.
>
> That aspect of our nature, without which the law wouldn't be at all possible, as well as what the law actually commands, belongs, together with what is simply permitted, to the concept of what is not forbidden by law; we can therefore just as well say that we have a right to be rational beings – we have a right to do our duty; as we can say that we have a right to do what the moral law allows.

> But here an important distinction immediately becomes apparent. We have a right to do what is merely allowed by the moral law; but we also have the contrary right not to do it. The moral law is silent and we are only subject to human arbitrariness.[6]

The connection between moral law and natural right proposed by Fichte in the *Contribution* can be resumed as follows:

1) the moral law is the only law to which man is subject by his rational nature;
2) the rational nature of man defines fundamental duties, such as to be moral and to be free, and defines the contrary of duties, such as to be unmoral or not to be free. The natural rights of the rational being are only determined in a negative manner, namely by not contradicting the moral law and its duties or the contrary of duties. Further, the scope of natural rights begins where the scope of the moral law ends and the latter does not include claims extending beyond that point.

Fichte thinks that there exists a natural hierarchy of obligations, which he demonstrates by overlapping spheres with the same centre, each of which becomes smaller towards the centre, symbolizing the range of each: the largest domain is that of conscience, followed by the domain of natural right, then the domain of contracts in general, and finally the domain of the civil contract.[7]

Thus we can state that the connection between moral law and natural right is only a negative one. The latter may not contradict the former. But therefore it is negatively dependent on the former. Fichte doesn't really work out the difference between a moral duty and a natural right. He only touches implicitly on this problem when he lets us know that we also ought to have the right to do what is required by moral duty.

Because, for Fichte, the purpose of man, both as an individual and as the totality of mankind, is defined by what Kant calls positive freedom, that is, the rationality and morality of mankind, natural rights are determined such that they contribute to realizing this purpose. Therefore, to put it briefly and in a manner which focuses the main reason of Fichte's work in question, a people has the right to a revolution against a civil constitution that undermines what conscience demands and suppresses positive freedom, when there are no other means of establishing and defending freedom. Fichte's arguments on the relation of morality and right depend on Kant's theory of morality but leave out of consideration the important difference between moral and mere legal motives of one's maxims and actions – a familiar distinction since the

Critique of Practical Reason of 1788. Persons can act in conformity to right without being moral in a strong sense. This is, what causes a deep shift in Fichte's claim of subjectivity in relation to morality and right.

2 On the Refutation of a Deduction of Natural Right from Moral Law in the *Foundations of Natural Right*

As we have just seen in the quotation above, in 1796 Fichte denies strictly the possibility of deducing natural right from moral law. Unfortunately, he has the opinion that the arguments against such a deduction are more or less self-evident with the presentation of the *Foundations of Natural Right* and that those who claim or believe in this deduction need not be refuted in detail. Fichte does not mention whom he supposes to have presented such a deduction.[8]

We have now to turn to the investigation of whether Fichte's rejection of the deduction in the *Foundations* of 1796 delivers a substantial clarification and conceptual development of the connection between the moral law and natural right or has to be taken as a systematical step backwards.[9]

To begin with, we should read the passage of the introduction that follows the quotation mentioned above, where Fichte gives some hints as to how one can understand the rejection in question.

> The rule of right, "limit your freedom through the concept of the freedom of all other persons with whom you come in contact," does indeed receive a new sanction for conscience through the law of absolute agreement with oneself (the moral law); and then the philosophical treatment of conscience constitutes a chapter of morality; but this is not part of the philosophical doctrine of right, which ought to be a seperate science standing on its own. One might say that several learned men who have put forth systems of natural right would have dealt with that chapter of morality without knowing it, had they not forgotten to state why compliance with the moral law (which they must always have had in mind regardless of the formula they used to express it) conditions the agreement of the rational being with itself. Similarly – I mention this in passing – the teachers of morality have generally not considered that the moral law is merely formal and therefore empty, and that a content cannot be obtained for it through sleight of hand, but must be rigorously deduced. It is possible to indicate briefly how the matter stands in our case. I must think of myself as necessarily in community with other human beings with whom nature has united me, but I cannot do this without thinking of my freedom as limited through their freedom; now I must also act in accordance with this necessary thought, otherwise my acting stands in contradiction with my thinking, – and

> thus I stand in contradiction with myself; I am bound in conscience, by my knowledge of how things ought to be, to limit my freedom. Now in the doctrine of right there is no talk of moral obligation; each is bound only by the free, arbitrary [willkürlichen] decision to live in community with others, and if someone does not at all want to limit his free choice [Willkür], then within the field of the doctrine of right, one can say nothing further against him, other than that he must then remove himself from all human community.[10]

This passage gives hints as to how to determine more precisely the connection of moral law and natural right that Fichte did not find worthy of detailed treatment in the *Foundations of Natural Right*. Fichte states that a close connection between both is possible and that natural right establishes a chapter of morality, but as Fichte mentions, it is not acceptable that morality is a chapter of natural right. To be sure, morality and natural right each have to constitute a science of their own. Thus we have to ask what the fundamental difference is between the two philosophical sciences that makes Fichte reject the possibility of deducing the one from the other.

In the following passage, Fichte insists on the thesis that the natural right has to be treated totally independently of morality and that examining how morality and natural right possibly coincide does not belong to the domain of the doctrine of right.

> The deduced concept has nothing to do with the moral law; it is deduced without it, and this fact is enough to prove that it cannot be deduced form the moral law, for there cannot be more than one deduction of the same concept. Furthermore, all attempts at such a deduction have failed completely. The concept of *duty*, which arises from the moral law, is directly opposed to the concept of right in most of its characteristics. The moral law commands duty categorically: the law of right only permits, but never commands, that one exercise[s] one's right. Indeed, the moral law often forbids a person to exercise his right, and yet – as all the world acknowledges – that right does not thereby cease to be a right.[11]

These statements by Fichte are directly opposed to what he believed in 1793. There, he thought that conscience might even reign in the domain of right and that right ought not contradict the commands of morality. Now he confirms that it is possible to have a right that may be morally forbidden. The idea of the *Contribution* that the relation of morality and right can be understood as a complete disjunction between the coincidence of both principles on the one hand and the allowance of arbitrariness in using rights licenced by the moral law on the other hand is here no longer valid. Does this insight show progress in Fichte's consideration of the concept of natural right and its relation to morality, or is this a step backwards?[12]

The disjunction that is now valid for the relation of both principles is threefold: 1) a possible coincidence, or 2) a possible reciprocal indifference of the claims towards each other, or 3) the possibility that the claims are contradictory. One argument that Fichte puts forward is that the "moral law commands duty categorically: the law of right only permits, but never commands." But indeed, the difference made apparent in this phrase is in fact already stated in 1793, where Fichte told us that we may or may not make use of a right whereas morality obliges absolutely.

This remark finally brings some light to Fichte's notion of deduction, especially if we take into consideration a further remark in the *Foundations* on the difference of both principles in question:

> The concept of right is the concept of a relation between rational beings ... Rational beings enter into reciprocal interaction with one another only through actions, expressions of their freedom, in the sensible world: thus the concept of right concerns only what is expressed in the sensible world: whatever has no causality in the sensible world – but remains inside the mind instead – belongs before another tribunal, the tribunal of morality. Thus it is nonsense to speak of a right to the freedom of thought, freedom of conscience, and so forth. There is a faculty that performs these inner actions, and there are duties, but no rights, with respect to them.[13]

Fichte's idea of a deduction is that the concept in question must be developed and continually elaborated in full recognition of the fundamental division of the inner pure intellectual relation of morality and the outer relation in the sensible world of right. This coincides with the Kantian difference between an action that is founded in a pure moral motivation of one's mind (rein moralische Gesinnung) and a mere legally motivated action that takes into consideration the outer coincidence with the demands of morality or right. Fichte's notion of deduction does not seem to allow for an overlapping of these domains, but rather demands a rectilinear development of concepts and separateness of each domain.

The difference between the commands of duties in an inner relation of the self and the permission to employ natural rights in an outer relation of rational beings in reciprocal interaction appears to Fichte not only sufficient for claiming different deductions of moral law and natural right, but also sufficient for not treating the possible coincidence of both principles within the philosophical doctrine of right. He rather sees reason to attach this to morality, as he mentioned in the introduction.

But we have to ask whether any serious systematic problems arise, if it is still true that both principles ought to be grounded in the pure ego of the *Grundlage* or however else the foundation of the applied sciences in the *Wissenschaftslehre* may be called. As Fichte resumes at the end of the "First main division":

> Therefore, in consequence of the deduction just carried out, it can be claimed that the concept of right is contained within the essence of reason, and that no finite rational being is possible if this concept is not present within it – and present not through experience, instruction, arbitrary human conventions, etc., but rather in consequence of the being's rational nature.[14]

To assert that right is justified in the rational nature of man is an argument that we know from the *Contribution* of 1793. But there Fichte confirmed that the rational nature of man is identical with his morality. Therefore we have to examine what in 1796 is meant by the essence of rationality and whether there is a rupture with regard to the absolute ego of the *Grundlage*.

3 The Rule of Right and the Demand of Agreement with Oneself

The deduction of the reciprocal recognition of rational beings in interaction and the condition of limiting one's freedom in order to give way to the freedom of others is due to the law of cognition only and not to the law of morality, as Fichte urgently stresses in the following passage:

> As has been demonstrated, the concept of individuality is a *reciprocal concept*, i.e. a concept that can be thought only in relation to another thought, and one that (with respect to its form) is conditioned by another – indeed be an *identical* – thought. This concept can exist in a rational being only if it is posited as *completed* by another rational being. Thus this concept is never *mine*; rather it is – in accordance with my own admission and the admission of the other – *mine and his, his and mine*; it is a shared concept within which two consciousnesses are unified into one.[15]

A few passages later Fichte says explicitly:

> Hence the *positive element* in the concept of right, whereby we believe that we impose on the other an obligation not to resist our way of treating him, but even to approve of it. The source of this obligation is certainly not the moral law: rather, it is the law of thought; and what emerges here is the syllogism's practical validity.[16]

If we accept the strict prohibition of a deduction of right from morality, and if we hence accept that the right results from the law of thought we have in the end to pay a high price. First, Fichte's submission consists in a concept of right whose power varies according to its realizability. A concept of right, loaded with high moral demands that, for many reasons, can not become effective manifests itself in its total impotence. This right appears to be untrustworthy.

But, even though we should be convinced that treating the case of coincidence of morality and natural right should be excluded from the doctrine of right, we must not forget that this question influences profoundly the quality of a community in which individuals limit their freedom partially by their own will and partially by coercion. We must suppose that the rejection of treating the possible coincidence in question is responsible for the character of a community's being essentially based on the right of coercion, as it is traced out in the *Foundations*. Coercion is justified by protecting people from those who are not willing to sufficiently limit their own freedom in favour of the freedom of others. Finally we ought to expect that not only morality but even natural right need to be grounded in the complete concept of the pure ego which includes a theoretical and practical aspect of rationality. But what Fichte deduces in his work of 1796 is the very contrary of what he sketched out in 1794 in the published part of *Some Lectures on the Destination of the Scholar*, where he presents the thesis that:

> society in general should not be confounded with the empirically conditioned society that one calls the state. Life in a state doesn't belong to the absolute purposes of mankind, whatever great men may say to the contrary; rather it is a means, realized only under certain conditions, serving the foundation of a perfect society. The state, like all human institutions which are no more than means, works for its own destruction: it is the purpose of every government, to make government superfluous. This moment in time has surely not yet come ... but it is certain that in the course designated a priori to man, there is a point when every state binding will be superfluous. It is at this point that instead of force and cleverness pure reason will be acknowledged in general as the supreme arbiter. [17]

It is true that the claims of right cannot place moral demands on a person. Moral obligation is only possible in the first person perspective whereas in the third person perspective it can only be desirable. In case people fail to attain reasonable insight, coercion might really be the only means to protect the legal order of a community. In the *Foundations of Natural Right* Fichte makes the difference between the original rights of man and the right of coercion that are necessary in case of conflicting legal claims. "*The possibility of a relation of right between persons in the sphere of natural right is conditioned by mutual honesty and trust.*"[18]

The loss of honesty and trust is the reason for the necessary appearance of the principle of coercion. "As soon as honesty and trust between persons who live together have been lost, mutual security and any relation of right between them become impossible, as we have seen."[19]

But Fichte clearly claims in the *Foundations of Natural Right* that the mutual interaction of persons based on honesty and trust are not a question of right in the strict sense.

Fichte has a larger range of possibilities to arrange communities in the sensible world in the *Lectures on the Destination of a Scholar* than in the *Foundations*. In the former, the possibilities range from a utopian state (that according to Fichte is not a state in the literal sense) to a state of coercion, whereas in the latter they range from self-limitation of one's freedom by the law of cognition to the limitation of one's freedom by the law of coercion.

Unfortunately, Fichte only mentions in the quoted passage of the introduction an important addition to the rule of right that demands "limit[ing] your freedom through the concept of the freedom of all other persons with whom you come in contact." The addition is that the rule of right "receive[s] a new sanction for conscience through the law of absolute agreement with oneself (the moral law)."[20]

There is a revision of the theses of 1793 concerning a fundamental difference between moral law and natural right. Whereas in 1793 right is subordinated under the moral law, in 1796 both are thought to be coordinated. The three possibilities of connecting both principles – 1) coincidence, 2) indifference, 3) contradiction – confirms this revision. Furthermore it seems that Fichte holds fast to the idea that the moral law is the highest law to which a human being as a rational being is bound. But as we have worked out it is no longer the unique one. However, the moral law is the unique law that pronounces whether one is capable of establishing what Fichte calls agreement with oneself.

The idea of the agreement of the ego with itself is an idea that Fichte has established in the *Grundlage der gesamten Wissenschaftslehre* of 1794/95, especially in paragraph 5. Generally said, the absolute ego requires that the empirical ego has to think and to act in accordance with it. Therefore, its fundamental idea is that the intelligible and practical acts of the ego, namely every thought, intention and act, need to be appropriated by its freedom and spontaneity. The ego as a rational being should not be forced to do something that it finally cannot accept and posit by its own will. Thus we can even read in the *Foundations of Natural Right*, too: "Willing is the genuine and essential character of reason."[21] Therefore the question arises as to whether a rational being really can have a right justified by the law of cognition that contradicts the moral law and also the demand to agree with itself. Isn't there finally a contradiction between the absolute ego that represents the idealistic concept of freedom and the philosophical doctrine of right that develops the concept of freedom realizable in the sensible world?As it stands, we have to distinguish the concept of the absolute ego's freedom from empirical freedom. It can be assumed that the concept of freedom ascribed to the absolute ego embraces the full range of what freedom may be, but only as an ideal possibility and capacity of pure reason as a mere formula and rule. This possibility includes pure spontaneity as a reasonable cause of thoughts or actions as well as the practical aspect of morality in a broad sense. Finally, freedom is also the freedom of choice, namely arbitrariness, to do what one ought to do or not. Each of the three aspects has also its source in reason and are therefore in any case ideal. But can arbitrariness really be an aspect of the absolute ego, or do we have to search for its source elsewhere? It is important to keep this in mind because with the absolute ego and its idealistic capacity of freedom and humanity on the one hand, and the aspects of realizing freedom under conditions of right in the sensible world on the other hand Fichte points out the polarity between idealistic and realistic ends of the theory of freedom, not completely developed in the *Foundations of Natural Right.* Instead of treating bifurcations of following or refuting the rule of right, the latter leading to the right of coercion, we could have expected a sort of trifurcation, taking into consideration the possible coincidence, indifference and contradiction of both principles in question as opposed to the breach of law that demands the law of coercion.

The first aspect of the projected state, based not only on right but also on morality in a broad sense, would create the case in which the rule of right of limiting one's freedom in respect of the freedom of others is accompanied by a moral intention, receiving this moral component clearly from the absolute ego as something additional. The second and the third aspects would be the cases of either reciprocal indifference beween both principles or their contradiction. A willing that doesn't take notice of morality or is against it, might still be in conformity with right and coercion isn't necessary. This conformity can be guaranteed by another kind of intention, for example by rules of prudence, by fear, by adaptation to given conditions and so forth. These are cases in which, in Fichte's terms, the ego doesn't acquire agreement with itself, because it in the end is determined by some extrinsic force instead of having appropriated a thought or action intrinsically by its spontaneity and freedom. Therefore we have to assume that arbitrariness is not founded in the absolute ego or only in its part that is due to an intelligible relation to the sensible world. But, if this is true, the doctrine of right is only partially founded on the first principle of the *Wissenschaftslehre*, the absolute ego, namely on its theoretical law of cognition.

Furthermore, as Fichte teaches, freedom of the individual is awakened by other individuals. Freedom is innate to reason but in reality we have to be educated to freedom. Certainly this idea of education to freedom has a correspondence in reality, but consistently thought out, it either leads to an infinite regress or the first individual has been awakened to freedom by God. Otherwise, it may really be a majority of individuals that have to be educated to be free. But in the summer lectures of 1794 in Jena on the topic "I intend to examine, how letter and spirit differ in philosophy in general," Fichte has spoken of geniuses of all kinds, who are not conscious of their spontaneity at all, but whose minds act absolutely and without any outer impulse: "there is an aesthetic genius. There is a genius of truth. There is a genius of virtue."[22] If the philosophy of right is the science of the community of individuals and their realization of freedom, this latter aspect also has to be taken into consideration. Thus, Fichte has a one-sided generalization of the idea of human education to freedom, and has passed over the possibility of its realization by the spontaneity and self-education of the absolute ego along with the many modifications between self-education and education by others.

4 Summary

We can state that the connection between moral law and natural right in the *Contribution* is only a negative one. The latter may not contradict the former. But therefore it is negatively dependent on the former. Fichte doesn't really work out the difference between a moral duty and a natural right. He only touches implicitly on this problem when he stresses the difference of commands of duties and mere permission to have natural rights.

The idea of the *Contribution* that the relation of morality and right can be understood as a complete disjunction between the coincidence of both principles on the one hand and the allowance of arbitrariness in using rights licenced by the moral law on the other hand is in the *Foundations* no longer valid. This insight seems on the first hand to show progress in Fichte's consideration of the concept of natural right and its relation to morality. The disjunction that is valid in the *Foundations* for the relation of both principles is threefold: 1) a possible coincidence, or 2) a possible reciprocal indifference of the claims towards each other, or 3) the possibility that the claims are contradictory. There is a revision in comparision with the theses of 1793 concerning a fundamental difference of moral law and natural right. Whereas in 1793 the natural right is subordinated to the moral law, in 1796 both are thought to be coordinated.

Fichte's idea that morality is an inner and ideal relation of the self (first person perspective) whereas natural right is an outer relation of the rational beings in the sensible world (third person perspective), forces him to present a deduction that permits no overlapping of the concepts of morality and natural right. But there arises the problem that natural right is in the end only partially grounded in the absolute ego which consists of the theoretical and practical basic capacities of cognition and self-agreement.

In the *Foundations of Natural Right* Fichte has thereby departed from the thought that the legal order of a community should serve to realize the purpose of man. Fichte does not further take into consideration that a state more or less founded on morality cannot abolish itself, but rather must appropriate a legal order.

Notes

1 I owe my appreciation to Ken Caskie for his careful and patient revision of this chapter.

2 See Wolfgang Kersting, *Die Unabhängigkeit des Rechts von der Moral (Einleitung)*, in: *Johann Gottlieb Fichte. Grundlage des Naturrechts. Klassiker Auslegen, 24*, ed. Jean-Christoph Merle (Berlin: Akademie Verlag, 2001): 21–37, especially 27–29. Kersting maintains that Fichte's first position of natural right belongs to those of the Kantians who founded the natural right in the Kantian principle of morality in a way other than Kant himself would do when his doctrine of right appeared in 1797.

3 Johann Gottlieb Fichte, *Sämmtliche Werke*, 8 vols, ed. Immanuel Hermann Fichte (Berlin: Veit & Comp, 1845/46), reprint, Berlin: de Gruyter, SW, VI: 82 (trans. Violetta L. Waibel and Ken Caskie).

4 Johann Gottlieb Fichte, *Foundations of Natural Right*, Cambridge Texts in the History of Philosophy, ed. Frederick Neuhouser, trans. Michael Baur (Cambridge: Cambridge University Press, 2000): 10; SW, III: 10.

5 See Frederick Neuhouser, "Fichte and the Relationship between Right and Morality," in Daniel Breazeale and Tom Rockmore (eds), *Fichte. Historical Contexts/Contemporary Controversies* (New Jersey: Humanities Press International, 1994): 158–80, who wonders whether Fichte on the one hand shows an obsession with the topic of philosophical systematicity and on the other hand has not developed a criterion to articulate the relationship of morality and right in his work *On the Notion of the Wissenschaftslehre* (see Neuhouser: 175 and 34n.). Against Neuhouser we have to remember that in spring 1794 Fichte actually did not dispose of the whole system in detail and the intrinsic relationship in question.

6 Fichte, SW, VI: 60 (trans. Waibel and Caskie).

7 See Fichte, SW, VI: 133.

8 See Kersting 2001 and Wolfgang Kersting, "Sittengesetz und Rechtsgesetz. Die Begründung des Rechts bei Kant und den frühen Kantianern," in Reinhardt Brandt (ed.), *Rechtsphilosophie der Aufklärung* (Berlin, 1982) – Kersting holds that Fichte ascribes this position to the early Kantians.

9 The opinions in the research are obviously divided on this question. Luc Ferry accepts Fichte's separation between moral law and natural right and supposes that Johann Benjamin Erhard gave the impact to the Fichtean revision between the *Contribution* and the *Foundations of Natural Right* in his work, "Apology of the Devil" ("Apologie des Teufels"), *Philosophisches Journal einer Gesellschaft Teutscher Gelehrten*, 1:2 (1795): 73–103). See Ferry, "Sur la distinction du droit et de l'éthique dans la première philosophie de Fichte," *Archives du philosophie du droit*, 26: 286–301. Wolfgang Bartuschat compares the Kantian and Fichtean foundation of the right preferring the position of the first ("Zur Deduktion des Rechts aus der Vernunft bei Kant and Fichte," in Michael Kahlo, Ernst A. Wolff and Rainer Zaczyk (eds), *Fichtes Lehre vom Rechtsverhältnis. Die Deduktion der §§1–4 der "Grundlage des Naturrechts" und ihre Stellung in der Rechtsphilosophie* (Frankfurt am Main: Klostermann, 1992): 71–92 and 173–93).

Paul Anselm Feuerbach decisively claims in his "Essay on the Concept of Right" ("Versuch über den Begriff des Rechts"), *Philosophisches Journal einer Gesellschaft Teutscher Gelehrten*, 2:2 (1795): 138–62) a separate deduction of moral law and natural right, too (see Feuerbach: 157).

10 Fichte: 10–12; SW, III: 10/11.

11 Fichte: 50; SW, III: 54.

12 According to Wolfgang Kersting it is a step backwards. He decisevely prefers the Kantian conception of an imperative of right that places us under obligation in the same way as the categorical imperative of morality does. Kersting defends the Kantian categorical validity of right although it is true that the application and execution of right under historical conditions in fact shows it to be a mere permissive law. The validity of right must be founded independently of what the executive organs are contingently able to realize as a right. See Kersting, 2001.

13 Fichte: 51; SW, III: 55.

14 Fichte: 49; SW, III: 53. The fact that Fichte makes a distinction between morality as an inner relation of the self and right as an outer relation of individuals in the sensible world does not permit the conclusion that Fichte's natural right is based on a mere empiricism. The Fichtean doctrine of right is rather a manifestation of the pure reason that demands validity in the actions of individuals in the sensible world.

15 Fichte: 45; SW, III: 47/8.

16 Fichte: 47; SW, III: 50.

17 Fichte, SW, VI: 306; (trans. Waibel and Caskie).

18 Fichte: 124; SW, III: 139.

19 Fichte: 125; SW, III: 139.

20 Fichte: 10/11; SW, III: 10.

21 Fichte: 21; SW, III: 20/21.

22 Fichte, GA, II 3: 303 (trans. Waibel and Caskie).

Chapter 5

Fichte's Hypothetical Imperative: Morality, Right, and Philosophy in the Jena *Wissenschaftslehre*

Yolanda Estes

This chapter addresses the deduction of the concept of right in J.G. Fichte's *Grundlage des Naturrechts* (1796–97), or the *Foundations of Natural Right*, with the aim of clarifying the relation between morality, right, and philosophy in the Jena *Wissenschaftslehre* (1794–1800).[1] Section 1 reviews Fichte's account of individuality, intersubjectivity, and summoning in the *Wissenschaftslehre nova methodo* (1796/99), or the *Foundations of Transcendental Philosophy (Wissenschaftslehre) nova methodo*, and the *Foundations of Natural Right*. Section 2 considers Fichte's description of the relation between morality, right, and philosophy in the "Deduction of the Subdivisions of the *Wissenschaftslehre*" and the *Foundations of Natural Right*. Section 3 explains how the rule of right functions as a hypothetical imperative in the *Foundations of Natural Right*.

1 Individuality, Intersubjectivity, and Summoning

In the *Wissenschaftslehre Nova Methodo*, the central task is answering the question: "How do I discover myself? Or – since thinking is an ideal act, which presupposes that its object is given – how am I given to myself? … This act of thinking refers to an intellectual intuition {of myself as a willing subject[.]}"[2] Since willing presupposes the concept of a goal, which requires an objective cognition, and since an objective cognition cannot occur apart from willing, the argument of the *Nova Methodo* appears viciously circular.[3] Fichte extricates the argument from this circle by introducing the concept of a pure will, which contains a goal-concept within itself.[4]

Pure willing is just a hypothesis in the *Nova Methodo*, so Fichte warns: "Pure willing, at this point, is not supposed to be anything more than the explanatory ground of consciousness; it is still a hypothesis, *not yet* an object of consciousness."[5] The *Nova Methodo* presupposes the pure will as the supersensible ground necessary for the possibility of consciousness, but transcendental philosophy describes nothing real unless the pure will appears within empirical consciousness.

In empirical consciousness, the pure will appears as an act of willing, which Fichte describes as "*ein Sollen, ein Fordern.*"[6] As a necessary feature of consciousness, the pure will is felt – specifically – as a feeling of obligation to remain within the sphere of the "ought," or "*das Gefühl des Nichtdürfens.*"[7] Within this sphere, the subject "appears to itself as determined to determine itself" through an *Aufforderung*, or summons, to act freely issuing from another rational, free being.[8] By means of the law of reflective opposition, the (determinate) subject is related to a (determinable) realm of rational being and consequently, reciprocal interaction between individuals (i.e., intersubjectivity) is shown to be a necessary condition for any consciousness.[9]

In the *Foundations of Natural Right*, the initial project is deducing the concept of right, or the necessary relation of free beings to one another.[10] This project requires answering the question: "How can the subject find itself as an object?"[11] "The rational being *is*, only insofar as it *posits* itself *as being*, i.e., insofar as it is conscious of itself."[12] A rational being cannot posit itself without attributing a free efficacy to itself, which requires it to posit an object that opposes its efficacy, but it cannot posit an object if it is not really efficacious.[13] Like the argument in the *Nova Methodo*, the argument in the *Foundations of Natural Right* appears circular. Fichte explains that "The reason the possibility of self-consciousness cannot be explained without always presupposing it as already actual lies in the fact that, in order to be able to posit its own efficacy, the subject of self-consciousness, must have already posited an object, simply as an object."[14] This fact compels Fichte to introduce the hypothesis that the rational being's efficacy must be precisely this "already posited" object.[15]

The presupposed synthetic unity of the subject and object seems to generate a contradiction. The rational being feels the object as a determinate limitation on its activity, but the object and the subject are supposed to be united, so the subject must find itself as constrained and free simultaneously?[16] The rational being finds itself in this manner only if "we think of the subject's being-determined as *its being-determined to be self-determining*, i.e., as a summons [*eine Aufforderung*] to the subject, calling upon it to resolve to exercise its efficacy."[17]

In order for the subject to find itself as determined in any manner, it must feel some external influence on itself, or in other words, it must encounter a sensible limitation.[18] However, if this check [*Anstoß*] were to cancel the subject's freedom, or if it were to compel the subject's action, it would not serve as a determining impulse that initiates the rational being's self-awareness. For just this reason, the rational being must receive a concept of itself as a merely possible freedom – "something that *ought* to exist" – through an external summons to act.[19] The summons initiates the rational being's self-awareness without undermining its freedom because, in grasping the summons, the subject chooses freely to act or not to act.[20]

The rational being must think of the summons as issuing from another rational, free being.[21] Consequently, the subject's self-concept is necessarily connected to the thought of reciprocal interaction between individuals – a relation of mutual determination – and thus, "a particular sphere is allotted to the subject as the sphere of its possible activity."[22] This concept of individuality is determined through the law of reflective opposition.[23] This reciprocal concept "is never *mine*; rather it is ... *mine and his, his and mine*."[24] Consequently: "I must in all cases recognize the free being outside me as a free being, i.e. I must limit my freedom through the concept of the possibility of his freedom."[25]

2 Morality, Right, and Philosophy

In the "Deduction of the Subdivisions of the *Wissenschaftslehre*," Fichte claims that "simply by means of analysis, one must be able to proceed from the Foundations [of the *Wissenschaftslehre*] to every particular science."[26] Theoretical and practical philosophy together explain the world as it is necessarily, potentially, and ideally.[27] Practical philosophy considers the world, as reason *ought* to transfigure it.

The "ought" appears within experience through a summons to act, which each individual must interpret before its own conscience, but moral theory concerns this summons insofar as it is directed categorically to rational beings in general.[28] Empirical individuals sometimes heed this moral summons, but they often disagree in their interpretations of it or choose to disregard it entirely.[29] This fact generates the need for a separate "mixed" science – specifically, the philosophy of right – which mediates theoretical and practical philosophy.[30] The theory of right is theoretical insofar as it addresses an ideal world, yet it is practical insofar as it considers the means whereby human activity might produce such a world.[31] "The task of the theory of right can be described as follows: the free wills [of many different individuals] are to be reconciled with one another in accordance with a certain mechanical connection and interaction."[32]

In the *Foundations of Natural Right*, Fichte describes how the "joint efficacy of nature and reason" could unite many free individuals and bring them under a legal constitution. The *Foundations of Natural Right* deduces the concept of right to provide an account of a possible juridical world wherein the law of right prevails and thus, to reveal a means for securing individuals' formal freedom. "The concept [of right] acquires necessity" because an individual's formal freedom presumes the existence of other rational beings, which the subject cannot posit without "positing itself as standing with those beings in a particular relation of right [*Rechtsverhältniß*]."[33]

An individual's decision not to enter into community with others – not to limit its freedom through their freedom – contradicts its rational, free nature. A fully developed rational being knows that we are "*bound* and *obligated* to each other by our very existence," but many individuals are not fully developed.[34] It follows that "in the doctrine of right there is no talk of moral obligation; each is bound only by the free, arbitrary [*willkürlichen*] decision to live in community with others."[35] Thus, the concept of right "has nothing to do with the moral law."[36]

Fichte claims that deducing the concept of right from the moral law is impossible, because the *Foundations of Natural Right* deduces right from the philosophical concept of the I and "there cannot be more than one deduction of the same concept."[37] Moreover, he asserts that "[i]t is absolutely *impossible* to see how a permissive law should be derivable from the moral law, which commands unconditionally and thereby extends its reach to everything."[38] The concept of right implies a limited, conditioned law, which delineates what an individual is permitted to do with its formal freedom.[39] A rule of right secures individuals' rights in the sensible world but does not require individuals to exercise their rights.[40]

Morality provides no basis for right because the moral law never generates rules that motivate sensible beings; but the rule of right appeals to the sensible being.[41] "The concept of right concerns only what is expressed in the sensible world: whatever has no causality in the sensible world – but remains inside the mind instead – belongs before another tribunal, the tribunal of morality."[42] Intelligible willing has no causality in the sensible world and thus, "no role to play" within the province of right.[43] Nonetheless, moral subjects, as empirical beings, certainly act within the sensible world. If their moral education were complete, a rule of right would be needless.[44] Likewise, rational subjects, as empirical beings, certainly think within the sensible world. If their rationality were fully cultivated, a coercive power would not be necessary to enforce their compliance with the law of right.[45]

The moral law commands the moral subject to strive for the complete development of all rational free beings, but the moral law has no causality in the sensible world.[46] Consequently, a juridical world provides for a "joint efficacy of nature and reason" that reconciles flawed individuals without annihilating the freedom that allows them to change.[47] In other words, within the domain of sensibility, the only sanction of right is a "physical force" that enforces the "law[s] of thought" regardless of human beings' levels of moral development.[48] The moral law provides no sanction for relations of right, because all empirical subjects have not been elevated to the level of moral consciousness.

As far as Fichte is concerned in the *Foundations of Natural Right*: "The question of whether the moral law might provide a new sanction for the concept of right is not part of the doctrine of natural right, but belongs instead to an account of real morality ...."[49] Indeed, the "Deduction of the Subdivisions of the *Wissenschaftslehre*" admonishes "If the goal of reason is to be achieved in a moral world, then a juridical world, thanks to which the struggle between efficaciously acting forces is restrained and limited, must already exist."[50]

3 Fichte's Hypothetical Imperative

In the *Wissenschaftslehre Nova Methodo* and the *Foundations of Natural Right*, Fichte relieves the circularity of the account of self-consciousness by introducing a philosophical hypothesis – a synthetic unity of subject and object – that generates the notion of a summons. In both cases, the summons represents a call for the subject to freely determine itself. However, the summons urges a possible action rather than compelling it directly, for otherwise it would nullify the freedom of the summoned subject. Moreover, this call to freedom is presented as something that actually appears in consciousness as an influence on the rational being. Finally, the content of the summons relates the subject's internal self-consistency to reciprocal interaction within a human community:

> I must think of myself as necessarily in community with other human beings with whom nature has united me, but I cannot do this without thinking of my freedom as limited through their freedom; now I must also act in accordance with this necessary thought, otherwise my acting stands in contradiction with my thinking; I am bound in conscience, by my knowledge of how things ought to be, to limit my freedom.[51]

In the *Nova Methodo*, Fichte often relates the summons to the categorical imperative – usually with a warning that one must not view it as the moral law in the Foundations of the *Wissenschaftslehre* but rather as a hypothesis, which functions as the categorical imperative in the *System of Ethical Theory*. Thus, he reminds us, "The pure will is the categorical imperative. Here, however, it will not be employed as such, but will be employed only for the purpose of explaining consciousness in general."[52] In the *Foundations of Natural Right*, Fichte stresses the extra-moral character of the summons – advising repeatedly that the rule of right is not the moral law. The rule of right does not command the intelligible subject categorically but rather appeals to the sensible subject hypothetically.

All imperatives contain an "ought" and thus urge some possible action rather than determining the will directly.[53] This, of course, is precisely how the summons operates on the rational being in the *Foundations of Natural Right* (and in the *Nova Methodo* as well). Otherwise, the subject would not find the ground of its activity as resting partly within and partly outside of itself, which it must do in order to discover itself as efficacious. Nonetheless, the "ought" expressed by the rule of right does not appeal categorically to the intelligible will of a moral being. It does not represent the urged action as "good *in itself* and therefore as necessary, in virtue of its principle, for a will which of itself accords with reason."[54] The rule of right represents the requested action "as a means to something else."[55] Thus, it is a hypothetical imperative.

Hypothetical imperatives are conditional insofar as they state that if one wishes to accomplish a particular goal, then one ought to perform some action, which is conducive to that desired end.[56] Some hypothetical imperatives, such as "rules of skill," are problematic insofar as they refer to arbitrary and thus merely possible ends.[57]

> There is, however, *one* end that can be presupposed as actual in all rational beings (so far as they are dependent beings to whom imperatives apply); and thus there is one purpose which they not only can have, but which we can assume with certainty that all *do* have by a natural necessity – the purpose, namely, of *happiness*.[58]

"Counsels of prudence," or hypothetical imperatives that command actions as conducive to the universal end of happiness, are assertoric insofar as they apply to everyone. Counsels of prudence recommend actions as means to human well-being and thus, they remain hypothetical imperatives.[59] Moreover, "imperatives of prudence, strictly speaking, do not command at all – that is, cannot exhibit actions objectively as practically *necessary*; that they are rather to be taken as recommendations (*consilia*), than as commands (*praecepta*), of reason."[60]

The rule of right is a hypothetical imperative, because it urges mutual limitation of freedom in order to preserve the individual's formal freedom, or capacity to act toward its own freely chosen ends.[61] These ends are freely chosen and thus vary according to individual interest. Nonetheless, the ultimate end for each individual is the preservation of its freedom and its very life, which it may use in the pursuit of pleasure, intellectual or moral self-development, or any other conceivable purpose.[62] Although the desire for formal freedom is not precisely a matter of "natural" necessity, Fichte obviously believes that every individual desires to live and to act efficaciously toward its own ends and thus, that the rule of right appeals universally. The rule of right, like counsels of prudence, "does indeed involve necessity, but necessity valid only under a subjective and contingent condition."[63] The desire to preserve one's formal freedom presumes a willingness to enter into community, but the decision to enter any particular community is arbitrary.

4 Conclusion

Fichte's hypothetical imperative provides a strong extra-moral incentive for establishing a juridical world and thereby securing a place in the sensible realm wherein sensible subjects may find themselves as intelligible subjects. Indeed, it is difficult to imagine how to raise an empirical subject above mere sensibility without it. The categorical imperative exerts no influence on the sensible subject, but the hypothetical imperative motivates the empirical will without annulling self-determining activity. However, could the hypothetical imperative be the categorical imperative; or to state the matter differently, could the moral law provide an external sanction for the science of right?

If, as Kant says, apparent categorical imperatives can be "covertly hypothetical," then perhaps an apparent hypothetical imperative can be "covertly categorical."[64] For the empirical subject, as a member of the sensible world, the summons expresses a hypothetical imperative, which the science of right takes as its starting point. For the empirical subject, as a member of the intelligible world, the summons expresses a categorical imperative, which a system of ethical theory takes as its starting point. For the transcendental philosopher, "the 'ought,' or categorical imperative, is also a theoretical principle."[65] Consequently:

> The world of the senses and belief in the reality of that world is produced in no other way than through the conception of the moral world, even for the person who may never have thought about his own moral vocation (if there could be such a person), or, if he should have thought about it, has not the least intention of fulfilling it at any time in the indefinite future. Even if he does not apprehend the world through the thought of his *duties*, he will yet surely do so through the demand of his *rights*.[66]

The rule of right has a philosophical sanction in the theoretical *Wissenschaftslehre* as well as a moral sanction in the categorical imperative. This does not imply that right depends on morality, for if it did, neither would be possible. Right must carry an incentive that renders the good will superfluous in the sensible realm. Morality, likewise, renders juridical duty superfluous in its domain. The theory of ethics articulates the goal of reason in general; and the theory of right describes the means for accomplishing it. This interpretation has the advantage of reconciling different aspects of the Jena *Wissenschaftslehre*. Moreover, Fichte seems to approve of it in the Introduction to the *Foundations of Natural Right*.

The rule of right, "limit your freedom through the concept of the freedom of all other persons with whom you come in contact," does indeed receive a new sanction from conscience through the law of absolute agreement with oneself (the moral law); and then the philosophical treatment of conscience constitutes a chapter of morality; but this is not part of the philosophical doctrine of right, which ought to be a separate science standing on its own.[67]

Notes

1 Frederick Neuhouser addressed this relation in "Fichte and the Relationship between Right and Morality," in Daniel Breazeale and Tom Rockmore (eds), *Fichte: Historical Contexts/ Contemporary Controversies* (Atlantic Highlands, NJ: Humanities Press, 1994): 158–80. It was also treated albeit less directly by Alain Perrinjaquet, "Duties Concerning Natural Beings in Fichte's Practical Philosophy," in Daniel Breazeale and Tom Rockmore (eds), *New Perspectives on Fichte* (Atlantic Highlands, NJ: Humanities Press, 1996): 153–78.

2 FTP: 290.

3 "The difficulty that faced us was actually this: to explain an act of willing without {presupposing} any cognition of the object {of this act – a pure act of willing – one that is present in itself – therefore something original and a condition for the possibility of all consciousness. Such an act must be possible, because this act of willing, even if it is considered only as an empirical one, already contains within itself cognition of an object.} The reason for the above-mentioned difficulty lay in the fact that we considered empirical willing (i.e. the movement of transition from what is determinable to what is determinate) to be the only kind of willing" (FTP: 292–3).

4 FTP: 292–3.

5 FTP: 293–4. Note also: "Individuality is given to me precisely through this summons: individuality = the summons to act freely. Is this true? What does 'a summons to freedom' mean? This is a concept that would produce an action on the part of a free being – if, that is, such a concept were endowed with causal power … Such an action, however, is [only] possible, and therefore, we have postulated it only hypothetically … This concept [of a summons] is not supposed to be able to exercise any causality, for if it did, then it would determine us in a purely mechanical manner; instead, it is thought of hypothetically" (FTP: 355–6).

6 "It appears there as an act of willing; according to what was said above, however, willing can be characterized as an 'ought' or as a demand. Therefore, this determinacy of the I would have to appear as a determinate, absolute ought, as a categorical demand" (FTP: 291).

7 "Since this act of thinking is a necessary one, {and since everything that is necessary is grounded in a feeling,} the mediating link between it and willing must be supplied by a feeling of some sort. {Consequently, some feeling must lie between this categorical demand and this act of thinking.} What kind of feeling can this be? A feeling is a limitation of striving; accordingly, striving must extend beyond the sphere of striving that was originally determined by pure willing, and the limitation of striving by an act of pure willing would produce a feeling of prohibition, of not being permitted to go beyond this sphere, a feeling of being obliged {to remain} within this sphere of the 'ought'" (FTP: 292).

8 This passage reads in full: "The Idea that we ourselves first originate within time is contained in this. The I here appears to itself as determined to determine itself in just the way it does determine itself, and the movement of transition is here thought of not as free, but rather as necessary. It is something discovered. This determinacy, which constitutes my basic character, consists in the fact that I am determined to determine myself in a certain way; it assigns me an 'ought.' Man's determinate nature or 'vocation' is not something he gives to himself; instead, it is that through which a human being is a human being" (FTP: 300).

9 "The I is reason – determinate reason. What is determinable in this case is reason as a whole (my generic essence). I myself am what is determinate {(through a feeling), as what is *posited in opposition* to this sphere} namely, I as an individual (for I posit a sphere of rational beings in opposition to myself)" (FTP: 302). See also FTP: 125. See also Fichte, *The Science of Knowledge*: 258–9 and Solomon Maimon, *Versuch einer neuen Logik oder Theorie des Denkens* (Berlin: Ernst Felisch, 1794): 310–4.

10 FNR: 9.

11 FNR: 32.

12 FNR: 4.

13 FNR: 30.

14 FNR: 30–31.

15 FNR: 31.

16 Ibid.

17 Ibid.

18 FNR: 32–3.

19 FNR: 32. "The subject cannot find itself necessitated to do anything, not even to act in general; for then it would not be free, nor an I. Even less can it, if it is to resolve to act, find itself to act in this or that particular way; for then, once again, it would not be free nor an I. How and in what sense, then, must the subject be determined to exercise its efficacy, if it is to find itself as an object? Only insofar as it finds itself as something that *could*

exercise its efficacy, as something that is summoned to exercise its efficacy but that can just as well refrain from doing so" (FNR: 32–3). Compare FTP: 355. See also FNR: 32n3. For a more detailed discussion of Fichte's "Doctrine of the *Anstoß*," see Daniel Breazeale, "Check or Checkmate? On the Finitude of the Fichtean Self," in Karl Ameriks and Dieter Sturma (eds), *The Modern Subject: Conceptions of Self in Classical German Philosophy* (Albany: State University of New York Press, 1996): 87–114.

20 "The rational being is to realize its free efficacy; this demand [*Aufforderung*] upon it belongs to the very concept of a rational being, and just as certainly as the rational being grasps this concept, so to does it realize its free efficacy, and in one of two ways: *either* by *actually acting* … *or* by *not acting*" (FNR: 33).

21 FNR: 39–40. Note: "Therefore, the cause of the summons must itself necessarily possess the concept of reason and freedom; thus it must itself be a being capable of having concepts; it must be an intelligence, and – since this is not possible without freedom, as has just been shown – it must also be a free, and thus a rational, being, and must be posited as such" (FNR: 35). See also FNR: 35–7 for Fichte's detailed account of why the rational being must attribute the summons to another rational being.

22 FNR: 37–8. "The summons to engage in free self-activity is what we call up-bringing [*Erziehung*]. All individuals must be brought up to be human beings, otherwise they would not be human beings" (FNR: 38). I think this passage implies that the summons is best construed as a communal process rather than a particular message from one individual to another. In other words, while education involves reciprocal activity between individuals, no particular encounter constitutes an education.

23 FNR: 40. See note 10 above. See also FNR: 43–4. The individual is defined by having a particular sphere of potential activity wherein it alone may choose to act, but its having this sphere depends in turn on another rational being, which it treats as such, refraining from acting in that sphere.

24 FNR: 45.

25 FNR: 49.

26 FTP: 46–8.

27 FTP: 468–9. Note also: "Remark: Both theoretical and practical philosophy are [included within] the *Wissenschaftslehre*. Both are based upon the transcendental point of view: Theoretical philosophy is based upon the transcendental point of view precisely because it deals with the act of cognizing, and thus with something within us, and it is not concerned with any sort of {mere} being. *Practical philosophy* is based upon the transcendental point of view because it does not deal with the I as an individual at all, but instead deals with reason as such, in its individuality. {The theory of ethics maintains that individuality is contained within and follows from reason. That I am precisely this specific individual, however, is not something that follows from reason.} The former theory is {in a certain respect} concrete; the latter is the highest abstraction {present within thinking and involves an ascent} from the level of what is sensible to the pure concept as a motive [for action]" (FTP: 470).

28 "Everyone bears his own conscience within himself, and each person's conscience is entirely his own. {Everyone has his own ethical law, his own duties.} Yet the manner in which the law of reason commands everyone can certainly be established *in abstracto*. Such an inquiry is conducted from a higher standpoint, {where the individual beings coincide,} where individuality vanishes from view and one attends only to what is universal or general. I must act; my conscience is *my* conscience, and to this extent the theory of ethics is an individual matter. This, however, is not the way it is dealt with in the general theory of ethics. {If one attends only to what is universal, there arises} the practical

Wissenschaftslehre, which becomes the particular [science of] ethics, {of 'ethics' in the proper sense of the term}" (FTP: 469).

29 FTP: 470.

30 Ibid.

31 FTP: 470–71.

32 FTP: 471. Note also: "Closely related to the theory of right and sharing the same domain is the philosophy of religion. Together, these two constitute a third {part of} philosophy: 'the philosophy of the postulates.' {There is a postulate that theory addresses to the practical realm: that many free individuals ought to maintain a certain order and enter into peaceful relations with one another. This is a postulate that theory addresses to freedom as well as to reason, and this is how we obtain the theory of right" (FTP: 471).

33 FNR: 9 and 39.

34 FNR: 45.

35 FNR: 11–12.

36 FNR: 50.

37 FNR: 50.

38 FNR: 14 (my emphasis).

39 "The union of prohibition and desire produces {not an 'ought,' but merely} a [feeling of] being permitted to satisfy the desire {in a certain respect, without any immediate expression of the categorical drive within the power of feeling}. Whatever is included within the sphere of what I am allowed to do is permitted" (FTP: 292).

40 FNR: 50.

41 FNR: 51. "{The 'ought' first arises from the unification of pure willing, insofar as this exercises an influence upon our power of feeling, and thus upon some desire, which is thereby restricted to a narrow sphere, from which everything that is prohibited is excluded. Consequently, an 'ought' arises when what is permitted accords with pure willing. Consider, for example, [the difference between] natural law and morality:}" (FTP: 292).

42 FNR: 51. Compare: "The theory of natural law or natural right is concerned with what we are permitted to do, rather than with what we ought to do. It refers only to empirical willing. Morality tells us that we ought to do something, which, from the standpoint of natural right we are merely permitted to do. {The latter deals with empirical human beings and permits justice toward others; morality, on the other hand, makes justice a duty for the intelligible person.}" (FTP: 295).

43 FNR: 51.

44 FNR: 132.

45 FNR: 127.

46 FNR: 81.

47 FTP: 471.

48 "The source of this obligation is certainly not the moral law: rather, it is the 'law of thought[.]'" (FNR: 47): "[T]he concept of the individual was previously proved to be a condition of self-consciousness; thus the concept of right is itself a condition of self-consciousness. therefore, the concept of right has been properly deduced *a priori*, i.e., from the pure form of reason, from the I" (FNR: 49); "In this domain, physical force – and it alone – gives right its sanction." "Right must be enforceable, *even if* there is not a single human being with a good will; the very aim of the science of right is to sketch out just such an order of things" (FNR: 51).

49 FNR: 50–51. Compare: "The rule of right, … does indeed receive a new sanction for conscience through the law of absolute agreement with oneself (the moral law); and then the philosophical treatment of conscience constitutes a chapter of morality; but this is not

part of the philosophical doctrine of right, which ought to be a separate science standing on its own" (FNR: 10–11).

50 FTP: 470.

51 FNR: 11. See *Some Lectures Concerning the Scholar's Vocation* in EPW: 149.

52 FTP: 293.

53 "All imperatives are expressed by an 'ought' (*Sollen*). By this they mark the relation of an objective law of reason to a will which is not necessarily determined by this law in virtue of its subjective constitution (the relation of necessitation)." Immanuel Kant, *Groundwork of the Metaphysics of Morals*, trans. H.J. Paton (New York: Harper and Row, 1964) [henceforth *Groundwork*]: 81.

54 "If the action would be good solely as a means *to something else*, the imperative is *hypothetical*; if the action is represented as good *in itself* and therefore as necessary, in virtue of its principle, for a will which of itself accords with reason, then the imperative is *categorical*" (*Groundwork*: 81).

55 Ibid.

56 *Groundwork*: 82.

57 *Goundwork*: 82–3.

58 *Groundwork*: 83

59 *Groundwork*: 83.

60 *Groundwork*: 86.

61 "Juridical duties are thus hypothetical imperatives, whereas ethical duties are exactly as in Kant, categorical imperatives" (Alain Perrinjaquet, "Duties Concerning Natural Beings in Fichte's Practical Philosophy" in Daniel Breazeale and Tom Rockmore (eds), *New Perspectives on Fichte* (Atlantic Highlands, NJ: Humanities Press, 1996): 153–78, 154. See also GA, I, 3: 387–8 [SW, III: 89–90].

62 FNR: 107.

63 *Groundwork*: 84.

64 *Groundwork*: 87.

65 FTP: 437.

66 *Vocation of Man*, trans. Peter Preuss (Indianapolis: Hackett, 1987: 78. The passage continues: "What perhaps he never expects of himself he will, however, surely expect of others in relation to himself: that they treat him with consideration, thoughtfully, and purposefully, not as a nonrational thing but as a free and independent being. And so, if they are even to be able to meet this requirement, he will be obliged to think of them too as considerate, free, self-sufficient, and independent of the mere power of nature."

67 FNR: 11.

Chapter 6

The Role of the Human Body in Fichte's *Grundlage des Naturrechts* (1796–97)

Angelica Nuzzo

> In the present century, black people are believed to be totally different from whites in race and origin, yet totally equal to them with regard to human rights. In the sixteenth century, when blacks were thought to come from the same roots and to be of the same family as whites, it was held, most of all by Spanish theologians, that with regard to rights blacks were by nature and divine will greatly inferior to whites. In both centuries, blacks have been bought and sold and made to work in chains under the whip. Such is ethics; and such is the extent to which moral beliefs have anything to do with action.

This reflection by Giacomo Leopardi speaks to us indeed from a very different tradition than the one in which Fichte develops his *Naturrecht*. It aptly serves, however, to illuminate the complex constellation of problems that situate the topic of the human body in German philosophical thinking at the end of the eighteenth century in the aftermath of Kant's critical philosophy. For Fichte, the issue of the human body directly concerns the first condition for the constitution of a human community ruled by juridical relations in the sensible world. The body is the first and foremost agent (not just the medium) of human concrete interpersonal activity and freedom. The body is the material principle of individuality but is also, at the same time, that which makes visible the intrinsically public and intersubjective dimension of human individuality.

To philosophical reflection, the human body represents something like a *Grenzbegriff* – a notion placed at the intersection between anthropology, ethics, the theory of right, and even aesthetics. The fluidity of the separation among these thematic spheres, however, is precisely what is at stake in the definition of the human body and its social and juridical status. Accordingly, the issue of where to place, systematically, the philosophical significance of the body carries with itself the most relevant consequences.

The questions that Fichte raises in this regard, namely questions such as: how can we identify the free and accountable subject of moral action in the world of the senses? How can we recognize who is the subject of rights and who or what is excluded from right's protection? – are no longer Kantian questions. They are Fichte's own translation of Kantian problems at the level of a concrete, "real" doctrine of right placed from the very outset in the interpersonal, human context of the sensible world. These questions bear directly upon the understanding of the issue of embodiment. The human body belongs to nature and is subject to the mechanical laws of matter and motion. On the other hand, however, it participates in freedom and reason, whereby its "motion" as well as its "figure" and organization must be explained according to a different order of lawfulness. To be sure, the body almost displays a causality of its own as well as a type of "purposiveness" of its own – a specific purposive constitution or articulation. It is a causality that takes place immediately in the sensible world (as opposed to freedom's formal, intelligible causality). The body is the primary source of "effective action" (*Wirksamkeit*), is able to modify matter, to work, to form and preserve its own environment, but even more originally it is that which exercises an influence (*Einwirkung*) over the bodies of other human beings. The human body is also fundamentally vulnerable and hence is the first source of human insecurity. I will argue for the claim that in Fichte's *Naturrecht* the human *Leib* appears as the concrete embodiment of the reflective faculty of judgment explored by Kant in both parts of the *Critique of Judgment*. The body is the first original art-product or art-work that arises from human free activity. And yet, at the same time, it is also natural possession of the individuum just as, for Kant, the faculty of the "'genius' is the natural talent presupposed to all artistic creation."

According to a long-standing tradition, the body plays a crucial role in defining notions such as "subjectivity," "individuality," and "personality," and is thereby an important component of the idea of human agency. Two main models dominate the historical tradition. The body is seen, according to the first model, as the merely material principle that marks out the agent as a finite individuum; in this role, the body is the "instrument" or medium of the subject's action, that through which the will, rationality, and freedom become actual in the world. The body is something that "the person *has*, owns or possesses." According to the second model, on the contrary, the body *is* the person itself in its worldly existence, is the external "expression" of rationality and is constituted in organic unity with it. The body is, as Fichte puts it, the "representative" of the self in the sensible world, and is thereby identical with it – the body is the whole self made sensibly visible. According to these two positions, the body is defined either through nature as a naturally given, as something that the subject "finds" as immediately (and deterministically) assigned to it, or through culture or art as a construction, something that still needs to be cultivated and formed, something that the subject must deliberately ascribe to itself with a voluntary act. Clearly enough, from these two views of the body very different implications for moral theory and the theory of right follow. The present considerations frame Fichte's own conception of the human body in relation to these two models.

The question that I want to address is the following one: How does Fichte position the human body with regard to moral, anthropological, and juridical issues in the *Grundlage des Naturrechts*? I will concentrate my considerations on Fichte's argument in the second main division of the 1796 work (and I will also follow its implications in the sections dedicated to the *Urrecht*, the original and absolute right that grounds the possibility of all society based upon the application of right). I start out by formulating the main question that guides my interrogation of Fichte's text; then I lay out the argument with which Fichte progressively develops the characters of the human body as the condition for the "applicability" of the concept of right, and hence also, successively, for the definition of the person's original right to property and self-preservation. Finally, I discuss some implications of Fichte's argument by showing how they follow from his major transformation of Kant's theory of sensibility (or "aesthetic").

1 The Problem: How to Recognize a Human Body

It is essential to Fichte's aim in the *Grundlage des Naturrechts* to establish the sphere of natural right as an independent domain. On the one hand, the sphere of *Naturrecht* must be radically separated from the doctrine of morals (*Sittenlehre*), i.e., from the moral law of Kantian origin as well as from the moral significance of "person" and "personality." The science of right and the science of morality are, for Fichte, "originally" separated and even "opposed to one another." On the other hand, the question must be addressed of who can be the subject of rights and in relation to what or whom can rights be claimed.

Fichte's account of the human body – first *Körper* and then *Leib* – is framed by three different but interconnected issues: (i) the issue of the self's or the person's act of embodiment; (ii) the issue of the person's relation to another individual as a similarly embodied rational being; (iii) and the assumption (or the possibility for me of assuming) that the other's body is same in kind as my own. This latter assumption proves itself crucial as it grounds the very possibility for me to know and foresee the effects of my influence on the other and hence to establish the juridical relation.

The problem that frames my present considerations is raised by Fichte, for the first time, at the end of the first main division of the *Naturrecht* – the division that leads from the deduction of the concept of right to the deduction of its applicability. An analogous question is repeated, a second time, at the end the deduction of the applicability of right, so as to reassure us that we can indeed proceed to the actual application of the concept of right. For, we are now sufficiently equipped with the theoretical means necessary to distinguish a human figure or body from what does not have human figure at all. Fichte has learned from Kant that in order to concretely *apply* a concept to real cases we must first solve a problem of judgment, namely we must be able to distinguish what falls under that concept and what is excluded from its extension. The notion of "body" provides Fichte with the key for the solution to the problem of right's applicability.

The argument by which Fichte establishes the basic conditions of his theory of right already in the "deduction of the concept of right," assumes the presence of the body and embodied individuals. In the first division of the *Naturrecht*, Fichte shows the way in which as free beings we come in contact with other rational free beings and are summoned to engage in communal and reciprocal action through *Anerkennung*. In the sphere of right (as opposed to morality), recognition must necessarily express itself in the external world and take on a reality of its own (*Entäußerung* is here a necessary condition). The condition, Fichte argues, "is *not* that I merely grasp the concept" of a certain individual "as a rational being." It is not just an act of internal understanding and conviction that is required from me. What is needed is "*rather* that I act in the sensible world. A concept in the innermost regions of my consciousness remains accessible only to me, and to no one outside me." For "the other cannot know what I think" (45, I, 3, 352). Hence we are summoned to find a concrete – physical – point of contact (*Berührungspunkt* – 48, I, 3, 355) with the other by way of action. Yet, the very possibility for me to distinguish between my intellectual *internal* concept of a rational being and the *external* figure of a rational being that summons me to action in the sensible world is rooted in my own embodiment. For the only condition that allows me to distinguish the concept that lies *internally* within myself from another person *outside* of myself towards whom my action is directed is the physical and sensible condition of my body. Action is possible in the sphere of right only as it proceeds out of that dividing line between the internal me and the external other that is my own body. On the other hand, if what is required from me is not just intellectual internal recognition through a concept but practical external recognition through an action that seeks a point of contact with the other, then I must somehow be able to recognize the other's rationality by means of an "external sense" to which an external physical shape must correspond. In other words, I must be able to *see* and *perceive* the figure and the body towards which I direct my own activity. And I must be able to classify this figure specifically as the body of a rational being, i.e., as that which represents the way in which a rational being must look like. Thus, the human body poses to Fichte a specific problem of *physical* recognition that is essentially connected with the general conceptual figure of *Anerkennung*. The solution to this more specific problem grounds the idea of membership in the juridical community.

Fichte's notion of right is a *communal* notion. "The concept of right is the concept of a relation between rational beings. Thus, it arises only under the condition that rational beings are thought in relation to one another." Accordingly, there cannot be any right to nature, to land, to animals, and to things in general. In these relations, we are told, the "question of right does not arise at all" (55, I, 3 360). The issue of the "right" that I might have "to a certain thing" properly regards what should be called my "right in relation to another person" who claims the use or the property of the same thing as I do. How does the specific question of right arise as opposed to a mere question of prudence or to a purely moral question? On Fichte's account, how are we to distinguish what applies to the sphere of nature, of animals, and things from what belongs, instead, to the sphere of those peculiar finite rational beings that we encounter and recognize under the shape of a synthetic unity of sensibility and reason? In the framework provided by Fichte's intersubjective notions of *Aufforderung* and *Anerkennung* we must ask: how are we supposed to recognize the other human being as a member of the *Rechtsverhältnis*, and to treat her accordingly in a way that is juridically different than the way in which we engage with nature, with animals, and things?

In concluding the deduction of the concept of right, Fichte contends that "the question of right between rational beings is possible only if the rational beings are *actually* (*wirklich*) in relation to one another," and can thus act in such a way that the action of the one has *real consequences* for the other, consequences that can be immediately felt and measured by the other (not just speculatively inferred). This is the result of the deduction of the concept of right which, Fichte repeats, "always presupposes a *real* (*reell*) reciprocal interaction." Fichte's emphasis on the "real" and "actual" character of the confrontation among rational beings as condition for the *Rechtsverhältnis* must be taken quite seriously. It is this condition that leads Fichte to introduce a further limitation to the validity of the juridical relation. In his view, it holds not only that human/rational beings alone as opposed to nature, land, animals, and things can be subjects of the *Rechtsverhältnis*. These rational beings must also be engaging in a very special relation with one another, since "there is no relation of right between those *who do not know each other* (*sich nicht kennen*) or those whose spheres of efficacy are completely separate from one another." Accordingly, Fichte suggests that it neither makes sense to talk about the rights of the dead (or, we could add, the rights of future generations) nor can we have an obligation toward someone that we merely *assume* to be a "*possible* rational being"[1] without knowing it for sure. What is then, for Fichte, the minimal condition required for *really* "knowing" someone (what or who someone is)? What is the kind of acquaintance that qualifies rational beings as condition for entering the juridical relation? The crucial restriction that Fichte puts on the validity of the notion of right already hints at his answer. Right and the juridical relation presuppose some kind of explicit *bodily contact* (and action) between beings that thereby first recognize each other as human rational beings (Fichte talks, as we have seen, of "*Berührungspunkte*" – material, physical points of contact: 48, I, 3, 355). These beings recognize each other – in the very first place and with the immediacy of that first bodily contact – as *beings that have the same kind of physical body or external figure*. Thus, the human body is what provides "reality" or real content to our knowledge and recognition of the other person as a free rational being.[2] The original act of physical recognition is explicitly opposed by Fichte to mere philosophical speculation. It is an immediate action that takes place in the *Augenblick*, leaving no time for reflection. It is, Fichte contends, an "amazing, instantaneously grasped connection" (84, I, 3, 383) that is given to our physical senses and no philosophical abstraction can hope to dissect or split.

At the end of the deduction of the applicability of the concept of right, when the notion of human body has been fully developed, defined, and deduced, Fichte raises a problem that parallels the one discussed at the beginning of that same development. "How do we come to transfer the concept of rationality on to some objects in the sensible world but not on to others; what is the characteristic difference between these two classes of objects?"[3] Fichte suggests that Kant's solution of the problem was provided by the universal moral law: I am required to treat certain beings so that I can will that they, in turn, treat me in accordance with the same maxim. Or, in a somehow different formulation, which does not necessarily endorse a Fichtean intersubjective perspective: any being for which the moral law is valid is a rational being. It is immediately apparent that this is hardly an answer to the proposed question. To be sure, the problem that Fichte is thereby addressing is not at all a question to which Kant's moral theory means to be responding. It is instead a specific issue internal to Fichte's own theory of right. For, Kant's principle of morality does not discriminate among the beings towards which I have to act morally (or I do act morally). Its sole function is rather to define what a "good will" is, i.e., what is the *Bestimmungsgrund* of the will to moral action. With regard to this question, the nature of the subject or object towards which I direct my action is utterly immaterial. Fichte rejects as still insufficient what he claims would be Kant's "moral" answer to his own problem, and looks instead for a solution that would play itself out in the different realm of right. Hence, with regard to Kant's alleged solution, Fichte argues that the question can still be raised of "who is to be included in the kingdom" governed by the moral legislation? This is, however, from the very outset, a purely juridical question. Evidently, what is at stake is not the application of the moral law but the applicability of the concept of right. Thus, Fichte reformulates the problem by lending to it a more concrete form: how do I know which particular and determinate object in the sensible world is a rational being; how do I know whether the protection afforded by the legislation (moral or better juridical legislation) "benefits only the white European, or perhaps also the black Negro; only the adult human being, or perhaps also the child. And how do I know whether it might not even befit the loyal house-pet?"[4] (80–81, I, 3, 380). The problem is indeed crucial. For as long as this question remains unanswered, Fichte warns, the principle has no applicability and hence no reality at all. This is, however, Fichte's own question of right. It is certainly not Kant's question of morality. It regards the principle of right not the moral law. Thereby, Fichte expresses the main issue concerning the juridical organization of the human community under the form of the *Rechtsverhältniß*.

What is then Fichte's solution to such a problem? In the passage that I have been discussing, Fichte's answer is highly problematic. It can be read as alluding to further developments provided by the science of "anthropology" on the one hand (77, I, 3, 378), and as hinting at some kind of teleological explanation involving the notion of nature's purpose with regard to the natural production of the human being, on the other hand. To answer the question of how to recognize a rational being in the sensible world, Fichte simply intimates that "nature has decided this question long ago." Relying on anthropological and psychological observation, he claims that "surely there is no human being who, upon first seeing another human being, would immediately take flight (as one would do in the presence of a rapacious animal) or prepare to kill and eat him (as one would do to a beast)." What we expect instead, at the simple sight of a human being even without further reflection, is reciprocal communication (81, I, 3, 378). Even though this might be indeed nature's answer, it is evidently not the final philosophical solution of the problem. What still needs to be explained is the set of assumptions that allows us to qualify a certain being, which we encounter in our action in the sensible world, as another human being similar to us, and furthermore allows us to explain why we don't take flight at the simple sight of this being, expecting, on the contrary, reciprocal communication. What is it that counts for us as "human being" given that, as Fichte suggests, we are not dealing with formal concepts to be grasped in the interior of our conscience but with an encounter whose *external* reality prompts us to immediate action (the range of possibilities that Fichte enumerates is: run away, kill and eat, or communicate)? In other words, since it is not a generic universal notion of "humanity" that determines my action, for humanity is rather disclosed to me in its first immediate determination by the other's body, what is the shape of what I ought to call a human body; how does a human being look like *externally*? It is at this point that is most appropriate to ask Fichte's own question: would only the white European or also the black Negro qualify as "human being" (evidently, Fichte is recurring here to a physical mark of differentiation)? Would only the adult human being, or perhaps also the child be appropriate? (Moreover, we also don't take flight from the "loyal house-pet" as we do indeed from rapacious animals.) As Fichte asks in his letter to Reinhold dated August 29, 1795: how can it be decided whether my riding a horse is committing an injustice towards the poor animal similar to the injustice which the Russian nobleman commits in giving away and selling his slaves? In both cases, common sense perceives no injustice. Is there "injustice" here at all? How are questions of racism and slavery to be posed in the first place and what are these questions really concerned with? Do they regard the moral person or the juridical person, do they include animals or are they limited to the human being? And, in the latter case, where is the dividing line between animals and human beings to be drawn? What is the *quid juris* of this distinction anyway?

The crucial issue entailed in these questions is the fundamental problem that I want to address. We must look back at the development of Fichte's argument in §§5–6 of the *Naturrecht* in order to see how he constructs the juridical or pre-juridical figure of the "human body" as the key to the solution of the problem of right's "applicability."

2 What Is the Human Body?

In a doctrine of right that claims from the very outset the character of a "real" science against all types of formalism (or *Formular-Philosophie*), the human body is attributed a crucial function in the "deduction of the applicability" of the concept of right from which the "reality" of the theory depends. The body, first of all merely and generally *Körper*, is what identifies finite and discrete individuals in the world. The progressive determination or deduction of the *Körper* toward the fully-fledged figure of *Leib* will reveal, at the same time, the determination of the individual agent and the determination of the world, sphere, or environment of its action. It is to this complex of relations mediated by the figure of the body – but first generated through it – that the concept of right will be applied. Fichte's aim is to prove that the figure of the human body shows the rationality and freedom proper to the human being as "person." Moreover, Fichte's argument in these sections completes the "deduction" of intersubjectivity from its material side. For Fichte, the human body is the expression of the person's intersubjective determination and destination (*Bestimmung*). The "deduction" of the body proceeds from lesser to greater "determinateness." At the end of the deduction, the body's *determination* is proved identical with the person's act of self-determination, whereas the body's physical *limitation* amounts to the person's act of self-limitation by which the sphere of right is first established.

In the very opening of the proof of the fourth theorem, the essentially juridical (not moral) figure of the "person" comes to the fore as embodied individual: "The rational being cannot posit itself as an individual that has efficacy without *ascribing* a material body (*materieller Leib*) to itself, and thereby determining this same material body" (56, I, 3, 361). Fichte's demonstration moves from the human body as material *Körper* to the human body as the articulated totality of the *Leib*. In a traditional way, Fichte connects the issue of the body to the issue of the subject's material individuation. By means of the body, the abstract and formal self becomes a material and determinate person. The fact that the body is the condition for the person's "efficacy (*Wirksamkeit*)" in the world brings Fichte's important Leibnizian heritage to light. The body is the site of human activity and efficacy in the world, not a principle of passivity or receptivity. As I will argue in the concluding part of these reflections, this assumption is the fundamental key to Fichte's transformation of Kant's theory of sensibility ("transcendental aesthetic"). Moreover, the body is the principal source of human *vulnerability* and fundamental *insecurity*, an issue that will prove crucial to the further developments of Fichte's theory of right at the level of the state. While the body is essential to our freedom in the world, it also permits us to encroach on one another's sphere of action and to do violence to that freedom. In this sense, human embodiment is the condition of the juridical community.

The body is first determined in relation to the self or the I as a "part of the world." It is, however, a special – somehow the most "original" – part of the world. The subject constructs it and appropriates it in the immediacy of an intuition (space and time), which is, more precisely, the formative act of the "productive imagination" (57–8, I, 3, 362). The body is, from the very outset, an active construction of the individual not a naturally given. To this extent, the body resembles an art-product. Thus, the person "ascribes" (§§5, 6 theorem formulation) to herself a body and as a consequence of this act it properly becomes a person. Fichte argues that in the perspective of the synthesis the body is "produced;" while in the perspective of the analysis it is merely "found."[5] Placed at the intersection between giveness and active production, the status of the body can be further explained by recalling Fichte's characterization of the "aesthetic standpoint" in the 1798 *Sittenlehre*: "from the transcendental standpoint the world is produced (*gemacht*), from the common standpoint it is given: from the *aesthetic* standpoint it is given but only according to the perspective in which it is produced" (SW IV, 353 f.).[6]

The person is defined in immediate identity with her body: the person exists and ceases to exist with her body. The body is the person's existence in space and time. Yet the body (*Körper*) receives at the same time a characterization according to freedom: it is not just space-time existence, but is the free existence of an original activity. The body is "posited as the sphere (*Umfang*) of all possible free actions of the person" (59, I, 3, 363). The person's sphere of freedom extends as far as the body extends and is capable of action and motion. In Fichte's dynamic view, the body is chiefly a source of movement and activity, not of receptivity and passivity. Physical movement is the material translation of – and specular counterpart to – both the dynamism of freedom and the "agility" of thinking. It follows that no material determination alone exhausts the description of the human body, for matter is unchangeable and incapable of (self-)movement. For the human body, however, this would be the state of death. Hence, a distinction of form and matter must be introduced. This allows Fichte to understand the body's dynamism in terms of the differential movement of its "members" and in terms of its organic constitution (60–61, I, 3, 364). There arises the crucial notion of "articulation" that makes of the body a totality whose independent members are able to move each one in its own way. Articulation accounts for the body as the site of the person's freedom and as the source of her free efficacy. The body is "*Äusserung*" of freedom (62, I, 3, 366) – in the sense of being both exteriorization and expression of freedom. As articulated whole, the generic *Körper* has clearly become human *Leib*. The *Leib* accounts for the person's identity and uninterrupted duration. In its articulated constitution, the *Leib* is what we ascribe to ourselves by calling it "*our* own body" (61, I, 3, 365).

Once the body has been deduced or completely determined as *our* personal, individual human body, Fichte's task is to demonstrate its intersubjective validity. The body defines, at the same time, personality and the possibility of interpersonality. The fifth theorem establishes that "the person cannot ascribe a body to himself without positing it as standing under the influence of a person outside him, and without thereby further determining it" (61, I, 3, 365). Thereby Fichte brings the determination of the body to bear on the previously achieved deduction of intersubjectivity. The condition of self-consciousness is to posit an influence or affection (not just *Wirksamkeit* but *Einwirkung*) upon another person as a similarly embodied individuum. All activity exercised upon an individuum is an activity exercised upon its body. The consequence is that certain activities and movements of the articulated body – and hence certain exteriorizations of freedom – are restricted or impeded by this external affection (Fichte's notion of *Hemmung*). Articulation provides the body with a differential sensibility and capacity of affection (which obviously increase the possibilities of escaping a *total* limitation of movement). Fichte distinguishes a "higher organ" or inner sense from a "lower organ" or outer sense. To this distinction corresponds a difference in the material composition of the body, and hence a difference in its mobility and capacity of free activity. In its external projection, the articulate body is essentially "sense (*Sinn*)" (65, I, 3, 368). The body as sense positions the person in relation to what lays outside of her – in the first place, in relation to the other person, whose activity it perceives and towards which, in turn, it acts; and then in relation to the "sensible world," the material world of the senses (*Sinnenwelt*). "Sense" is possible only in relation to an external activity that the body can reproduce as its own. There is something like a "physical recognition" at work in this bodily intelligence that is "sense." "Sense" is the body's own form – a physical form – of *Anerkennung*. My body can feel only that which it can itself produce, namely another human body's action. Hence, originally and constitutionally my sense is directed towards other human bodies and their action, not towards rigid unmovable matter. In the former case, the body exercises free causality, in the latter it merely opposes "physical force" to the opposition of resistant matter (68, I, 3, 370). The former sense (a "sense" for embodied persons) is original and is the condition to the second (a "sense" for impersonal matter).

On this account, Fichte institutes the relation of reciprocal *Anerkennung* between embodied persons. The other person recognizes (i.e., senses or feels) that my body is not mere solid unmovable dead matter, that its action is not mere compulsion and exertion of physical force but is free action and free causality. Free action, according to Fichte, is realized and made visible by the human body's specific way of movement and articulation (more precisely by its "higher organ"). This is, quite remarkably, an "aesthetic" consideration of the human figure that, transposed from the realm of aesthetic appreciation and contemplation (we could think of Schiller's notion of *Anmut* or grace) to the sphere of action becomes a relevant practical and juridical "criterion of reciprocal action." On the ground of this moment of reciprocal bodily recognition we act on each other under the assumption "that the object of my *Einwirkung* has a sense," i.e., is a sensible and also *vulnerable* being – a being that will feel my action upon it and possibly get hurt by it (69, I, 3, 371). Thereby it also starts to be palpable what it means, in Fichte's theory, "to know" the other person as person. At this point, the answer to the question that I initially raised: how do we recognize a human body? would sound: we recognize another human body from its action, from its way of moving, which is the material and physical complement of freedom; from its differential articulation, which betrays a sense; and from its way of acting (and reacting) differently upon ourselves than upon resistant matter.

In the act of bodily recognition we become aware of the possibilities entailed in our own free causality on other persons as well as on the external world. The body is not only "sense." It is also the "instrument (*Werkzeug*) of freedom" (71, I, 3, 373). Fichte employs a (Leibnizian) notion of "expression" to indicate the body's relation to freedom and purposive rationality. The human body is not a naturally given "behind" which the causality of the will or freedom is at work so as to determine the bodily movement. In Fichte's "monistic" view, the bodily movement is identical with the will as its immediate sensible expression.[7] The body is shaped and formed in its articulated members in order to *express* freedom by carrying its purposes through in the external world. Accordingly, the further determination of the human body – and correspondingly the determination of the sensible world – is inferred from the necessity of a community of free beings. The sensible world is thereby determined as the intersubjective "world of free beings" (73, I, 3, 374). At this level, I do not only attribute to the other person a "sense" analogous to mine. I also recognize that we all share "the same type of intuition" (73, I, 3, 375).

On this ground, Fichte constructs the physical, bodily encounter between two persons, i.e., the necessary reciprocal (self-)limitation of their respective spheres of freedom. This is the condition for the possibility of the *Rechtsverhältnis* and its application. Fichte contends that the reciprocal relation of *Einwirkung* takes place in the body and yet is not simply violence, coercion, or raw impediment (*Hemmung*) as when action is exerted upon matter. In Fichte's phrasing, to simply act upon the other person's "lower organ" would not be a fair treatment for the body of another free human being. Instead, the bodily contact must take place in the "higher organ" – which means through the voice and the act of making oneself visible. Not solid matter but air and light are the elements in which and through which the first human interpersonal contact takes place. "My body must be visible to the person outside me, it must appear to him through the medium of light, and it must have appeared to him as sure as he exercises an efficacy on me" (75, I, 3, 376; 76, I, 3, 377). The "aesthetic" importance of the human figure in Fichte's theory is thereby further underscored. But the requisite of visibility and exchange of signs through the voice are also basic cautionary ways of protecting our bodily vulnerability and fundamental insecurity. Therein Fichte's preoccupation regarding our need to guarantee a certain amount of security in the relation with other persons comes for the first time to the fore. The issue of security, which will become so important in the further development of the *Naturrecht*, in particular at the level of the state, in Fichte's compilation of complex police regulations, has here its remotest origin and justification. On this ground, we can understand how acts otherwise juridically indifferent such as being on the street at night without a light, can become unlawful for Fichte so as to prompt the police regulation that forbids to anyone to be out at night without a light. We can also understand the origin of Fichte's suggestion that the police must be able at any time to "identify citizens as this or that determined person" (SW X, 295), knowing identity and whereabouts at all time of every citizen.

Fichte observes that by relating to the other person's body in an exchange of visible appearances and voice our body "acts" or exerts an influence even though it is physically still. Our body brings about "modifications" in the other person even without exercising violence or immediate coercion on her body. Such is freedom's specific way of producing motion and modification. It is Fichte's translation of Kant's notion of "causality through freedom" at the level of the body (and at the level of psychology). The issue of what it means, for Fichte, "to know" the person who can enter in a juridical relation with us receives here a further specification. We come to know that someone is a human being as soon as we can *see* her body and we can *speak* to her. It also becomes clear why, for Fichte, no *Rechtsverhältnis* can bind us to the dead or to the not yet born, and more generally to "those whose sphere of efficacy lay too far apart from each other," in a word, to "those who we do not know" by bodily sensory contact.

Fichte's conclusive determination of the human body raises an issue that will lead me to briefly address the relation between his theory of the body as the site of human sensibility and Kant's *Critique of Judgment*. It is the issue of the human body as both artistic construction or artifact, and as source of an artist-like activity (a technique of the body, we could say in a variation on Kant's "technique of nature"). In general, Fichte's deductions can be considered concluded when the notion to be deduced has been completely determined. In the present case, a sufficient explanation must be reached for the human body, which neither its mere articulation nor its organization and movement alone could yet provide. Fichte's final contention is that I cannot "understand" the specificity of the human body unless I have the ground to claim that it is the "*Leib* of a rational being." Hence, in order to sufficiently explain or grasp this specificity, thereby bringing the deduction to an end, Fichte draws the distinction between "*Naturprodukt*" and "*Kunstprodukt*."

It is immediately evident that in his construction of the human body Fichte is no longer working within the dualistic opposition between mechanism and organism or natural necessity and freedom. He is rather operating within the more advanced conceptual frame provided by Kant's notion of "purposiveness" in the third *Critique*, which allows for the analogical relation between nature and art. Both organized products of nature and products of art are wholes or totalities whose parts cannot be separated. Yet, only apparently does the question concern the alternative of subsuming the human body either under the category of natural product or under that of art product. Fichte's argument tries, as it were, to avoid taking sides for one solution with exclusion of the other. The human body must certainly be explained as a natural product insofar as it must necessarily be thought of as an organized totality. Its peculiar articulation, organization, and movement all point in this direction. Fichte claims, however, that the specificity of the human body cannot be exhausted by the organic explanation of its natural articulation, organization, and movement. For, in this respect, the human body would not differ from that of any other animal (the rapacious animals at whose sight we take flight included). What really makes the difference is the "aesthetic" element that intervenes in our "reflection" on the human figure. Thus, the notion of "*Kunstprodukt*" suggests an additional feature in order to determine the specificity of the human body. In the natural product, the whole exists for the sake of the parts. There is no further "purpose" than the production of those parts. In the product of art, on the contrary, the whole refers to an aim that is not immanent in the parts but is *external* to them. The whole is "an instrument (*Werkzeug*) to something else." The totality exists for a purpose to which it is essentially related. It is precisely this possibility of referring to something external to it and other than it in a purposive way that characterizes, for Fichte, both the art-product and the human body. Interestingly, the internal purposiveness of natural organisms that for Kant defined the higher form of purposiveness proper to these beings, yields in Fichte's intersubjective perspective to a higher ranking of external teleology. In addition, the "aesthetic" purposiveness that for Kant was merely formal and without purpose yields, in Fichte's view, to the "aesthetic" character on the basis of which the human figure is set in relation to the external purpose of communication.

Moreover, Fichte argues that the close determination of the natural product fixes the animal body into a particular way of existence and into a particular form of movement and activity. The range of what is physically possible to the animal body as the sphere of its voluntary movement is closed and determined once and for all. Fichte contends, on the contrary, that no fixed determination can be imposed on the human body whose character is rather an infinite and open determinability. The human body is not formed in any particular way but is rather "formable" in all possible ways.[8] "In short, Fichte concludes, all animals are complete and finished; the human being is only outlined and sketched (*angedeutet und entworfen*)"[9] – in the same way in which the mere outline and initial sketch of an art-work is left to the artist's freedom and imagination to complete (78–9, I, 3, 378–9). Animals are already from the outset what they should be; the human being, on the contrary, is a work in progress: it must become what it is. Nature's hand has not finished its work. Education and cultivation are rooted, for Fichte, in the very art-work nature of the human body. Repeating and varying a Kantian thesis that plays itself out in Kant's philosophy of history, Fichte intimates that while nature completely determines the animal in its body, in the case of the human being nature leaves the physical body indeterminate. Thus, the body is a sphere of freedom left to the person's own choice. With this claim, Fichte initiates a rather problematic metamorphosis of the human body, whereby each one of its physical organs is transformed into an "instrument" of freedom and spirit – the "eye" is eventually transformed into that "spiritual eye" which is the "soul."

As the artist completes with the freedom of her imagination the outline of merely sketched figures, so the intimation of reciprocal bodily recognition requires that we recognize a human figure even there where it is only outlined and must still be completed and fully cultivated. To the act of recognition belongs a moment of creative imagination whose purpose is the *external* purpose of reaching out for the other, external to me. "The human figure" – so Fichte's conclusion – "is sacred to the human being" (83–5, I, 3, 382–3) everywhere and in all its even just outlined and undeveloped forms.

The question posed at the very beginning – how do we recognize the human body as the body of a rational being – receives now a final answer. What is required is an act of imagination which is, in turn, inscribed in the "aesthetic" quality of the human figure. The human body is not a fixed entity but a work-in-progress. An outline is given to us in the process of recognition, which we must complete with an intuition of the potentialities proper to the rational being. This is the "aesthetic" concept of "humanity" that Fichte is proposing in the *Naturrecht*. In the paradigmatic occurrence of the body, "humanity is neither determined, nor self-determining, as Kant would have it, but somehow determined to determine itself. In the contour of that paradox, freedom and security, for Fichte, find their common ground."[10]

3 The Human Body and Fichte's Theory of Sensibility

This conclusion allows me to further elaborate on the following thesis. My claim is that the construction and deduction of the human body in the fourth and fifth theorems of the *Naturrecht* becomes the site of Fichte's radical revision of Kant's "transcendental aesthetic" as theory of human sensibility. This revision, however, works with the conceptual apparatus that Fichte finds not in the transcendental aesthetic of the *Critique of Pure Reason* but rather in the "aesthetic" of the aesthetic faculty of judgment of the *Critique of Judgment*.[11] *Anschauung*, for Fichte, does not refer to the pure a priori forms of space and time in the first place. Fichte's faculty of intuition is rather originally – and unproblematically for him – the productive imagination. Fichte's transformation has a twofold consequence. On the one hand, the body as the mode of human existence in space and time and as the site of human sensibility is no longer something given but something produced. It is not something produced by sensible intuition or mechanical nature but is an artifact of freedom, is the art-work of the productive imagination. On the other hand, for Fichte what I call *my* body still functions as the dividing line that separates an inside from an outside. This becomes the separation between the concrete determinate self that I am and the other person outside of me. The body, however, does no longer relate to the "outside" world as a passive and receptive "sense" to be affected by something given that only successively, with the intervention of the understanding's categories, is known. The body is an active instrument of freedom that originally affects the outside world. The outside world, in turn, is not given but co-original with my body's first interaction with other human beings. My body discloses to me the outside world as a world of interpersonal relations among free beings, not as the world of nature in general, i.e., the world of matter in space and time. My bodily *Einwirken* is identical with the way in which I come to know the other. External human bodies, or other persons, are known by the very act of physically (and perhaps also emotionally) affecting them – by establishing a "point of contact" – be it through sight and voice or through violent action. In Fichte's theory, the body's activity eliminates all distinction between possibility and actuality, theoretical and practical access to the world. Knowledge of a *possible* human being is not knowledge that grounds a juridical relation. All our bodily actions, on the other hand, directly translate freedom into existence and are identical with freedom's actuality. Hence my conclusion: in Fichte's theory, the human body is, at the same time, Kant's "genius" and Kant's "intuitive understanding" incarnated.

Two examples will support my claim. If we look back at Fichte's very first step in the deduction of the human body, we can see how the body as a "part of the world" is posited, and thereby made real, by an "intuition" that first creates what is there as human body in space and time. "Through intuiting and exclusively through this act what is intuited arises." Yet, what is intuited is not posited as a given but precisely as that which itself intuits, i.e., is the active organ of intuition as such. To intuit a part of the world as one's own body is the original act through which reason in "intuition is by no means passive but rather absolutely active; in intuition reason is *productive imagination*." The analogy employed by Fichte is therein significant. The act of positing one's own body is like the action of the sense – is like the act of seeing, which, in turn, is analogous to the creative activity of the painter. In the act of seeing, intuition projects something outward "somewhat like … the way in which a painter projects the completed shape out of his eye onto the surface of the canvas and "looks towards," so to speak, before the hand (which is slower) can copy the outline of the shape" (58, I, 3, 362). Through intuition as act of the productive imagination a person's sphere of freedom is established. The person becomes *this determinate* person by projecting out the physical body that she calls her own. The "original schema" of this activity is the act of "drawing a line" – the line which marks out the limits of my body as well as the limits of my external sphere of freedom. The body's limitation is the person's self-limitation.

For a finite and determinate human being, however, the body is still the site of "sense." Fichte transforms all receptivity and passivity inherent in sensibility as one's feeling of being affected into the activity of affecting another person's body. Reciprocally, Fichte explains that to be affected means that a possible or actual activity, which takes place in the body, is canceled by another external influence. Fichte attempts – albeit in a somehow convoluted way – to transform a suffered affection on the body into an activity of the body itself. He manages to do so by recurring to the notions of reproduction (*Nachbildung*) and imitation (*Nachahmung*). To be affected in the body only means that an expression of freedom is canceled. This, however, does not mean that an activity is made impossible. It means only that what I could produce myself has already been produced, and yet not by myself but by someone else outside of myself. In other words, in order to be affected I must recognize in my own body the product of an efficacy that I could have exerted but I have not myself exerted. Hence, I ascribe this efficacy to someone else's body outside of myself but similar to myself. This is Fichte's explanation for "perception" as the counterpart of "production." Perception is properly a production that takes place inwardly. To feel the outside world affecting me is to create it in myself. In order to perceive an outer affection in my body I have first to freely re-produce it and imitate it (*nachahmen*) in myself (in my higher organ) as my own activity. All limitation by way of affection is self-limitation. To be limited by another person's efficacy on my body is really a self-limitation of my own activity. "In general, nothing is found in the perception of a rational being that it does not believe itself capable of producing, or the production of which it cannot ascribe to itself." The sensual activity of seeing or hearing is once again paradigmatic: "a person cannot see if he does not first accept an influence upon himself and then internally reproduce (*nachbilden*) the form of the object, that is, actively construct the object's outline" (65–6, I, 3, 368). This process holds true of all the senses. While the senses exercise an activity towards the external world, they presuppose an "internal causality" (66, I, 3, 368) that imitates all external activity and recreates it in the internal sense. The person, in order to be externally affected, must internally "imitate" the affection, and this, Fichte claims, is an original act of freedom: I choose to be affectable, I choose to perceive. An internal free activity provides the "schema" for what can take place externally. Hence, in Fichte's description, the human body as the site of human sensibility functions in analogy to Kant's genius. Sensibility is the free and creative activity of a productive imagination, which projects outwardly the outline of an art-work for the purpose of human intersubjective communication.

Notes

1 Accordingly, in 122, I, 3: 412 Fichte claims: "The actual ... self-limitation of a free being is conditioned by his knowledge (*Erkenntnis*) of a particular free being outside him. Whoever does not have such knowledge cannot limit himself, and a possible being that I do not know does not obligate me to limit myself."

2 In this way, Fichte's "deduction" still maintains a Kantian meaning.

3 At the beginning of the second lecture on the *Bestimmung des Gelehrten*, Fichte raises a similar point: "How is it that the human being comes to admit and to recognize rational beings of the same species outside of itself?" (SW VI, 302). Accordingly, Fichte presents the necessity of finding characteristic *Merkmale* that distinguish the human being from the animal as condition for establishing a human community.

4 See in very similar terms, Fichte's letter to Reinhold August 29, 1795 (GA, I, 3: 301).

5 See *Das System der Sittenlehre*, §1, where Fichte explains the meaning of my *finding* myself as myself (GA, I, 5: 37 f.).

6 *Das System der Sittenlehre*, §31, see also *WL Nova Methodo* 244 (473).

7 See L. Siep, "Leiblichkeit bei Fichte," in K. Held and J. Hennigfeld (eds), *Kategorien der Existenz*, Festschrift f. W. Janke (Würzburg: Königshausen and Neumann, 1993): 107–20, who concentrates, however, on the deduction of the body in Fichte *WL Nova Methodo*.

8 *Bildsamkeit* is opposed to *Bildung*.

9 Translation modified: "intimated and projected."

10 Susan M. Shell, "'A Determined Stand': Freedom and Security in Fichte's *Science of Right*," *Policy*, 25:1 (1992): 95–121, 121.

11 The importance of Kant's *Critique of Judgment* for Fichte's *Naturrecht* has been often underscored by the interpreters. Yet, what they generally point to is the relevance of Kant's critique of teleological judgment (see for example A. Renaut, *Le Système du droit. Philosophie et droit dans la pensée de Fichte*, Paris: PUF, 1986). What I want to underline, instead, is the crucial significance of Kant's critique of *aesthetic* judgment. For Fichte's confrontation with Kant's "transcendental aesthetics" in the first *Critique*, see A. Nuzzo, "Fichte's Early Theory of Space," in J. Stolzenberg (ed.), *Kant und der Frühidealismus* (Hamburg: Meiner, forthcoming).

Chapter 7

Fichte's *Foundations of Natural Right* and the Mind–Body Problem

Günter Zöller

> The animal exists for the sake of bearing the free spirit in the world of sense and of binding it with the world of sense. (82)[1]

In Fichte's *Grundlage des Naturrechts*,[2] originally published in two parts in 1796 and 1797, the philosophical theory of right or law (*Rechtslehre*), specifically that concerning the state (*Staatsrechtslehre*) and the latter's extensions into family law (*Familienrecht*), international law (*Völkerrecht*) and cosmopolitan law (*Weltbürgerrecht*), developed in the tradition of modern natural law, is preceded by a "general doctrine of law" (*allgemeine Rechtslehre*: 12n) that links legal philosophy to its ultimate foundation in Fichtean first philosophy or *Wissenschaftslehre*. Accordingly, the reception of Fichte's main work in legal philosophy from his Jena years has proceeded in two main ways – either by discussing Fichte's place in the history of modern legal and political philosophy from Hobbes to Hegel or by addressing the foundational or transcendental dimension of the work. While the former approach has characterized much of earlier scholarship on Fichte's *Naturrecht*,[3] the latter perspective has been cultivated especially in recent years.[4] To be sure, there are also studies of Fichte's *Naturrecht*, of his legal philosphy as a whole and of his social philosophy in its entirety in which both doctrinal aspects of the *Naturrecht* are taken into consideration.[5]

The present essay seeks to supplement the foundational, transcendental line of the reception of Fichte's *Naturrecht* by focusing on the later sections of the general, transcendental part of the work, which have not received as much attention as the earlier sections of Fichte's legal proto-philosophy. In particular, the essay considers Fichte's transcendental theory of the body (*Leib*) in §§5 and 6 of the *Naturrecht* as a core component of an applied or "real philosophy" (*reelle Philosophie*: 6) that seeks to supplement the general, formal necessary conditions of possible experience with specific claims about the contents and objects of possible experience.

Fichte's treatment of the body has received some attention in recent years. Those earlier studies typically have discussed the pertinent material from the *Naturrecht* in the context of Fichte's further work on the *Wissenschaftslehre* in Jena – specifically the *Wissenschaftslehre nova methodo* (1796–99), as preserved in lecture transcripts – and of his second main work in applied practical philosophy from the Jena period, *The System of Ethics* (1798).[6] By contrast, the present account will focus on the transcendental somatology in the *Naturrecht* itself, reconstruct its argumentive structure and chief doctrinal content and relate it at a systematic and textual level to central parts and aspects of Fichte's lectures on logic and metaphysics (*Vorlesungen über Logik und Metaphysik*), based on Ernst Platner's *Philosophical Aphorisms.* Fichte held this lecture course as a general introduction into the *Wissenschaftslehre* in each of the eight semesters that he actually taught at the University of Jena (1794–99).

In the argumentative architectonic of the *Naturrecht* the theory of the body is closely linked to the theory of the Other (the other rational being). In fact, the *Naturrecht* is the work in which both the body and the Other first receive systematic philosophical attention – not only in Fichte but in philosophy in general. Expressed in the concepts and terms of transcendental philosophy, the body and the Other are syntheses of I and not-I, with the Other being a not-I-ly I and the body an I-ly Not-I. In his theory of the body Fichte transforms the modern philosophical problem of the relation between mental and physical reality by asking how the I comes to assume or "posit" its own body in the first place and what a body has to be like in order to be, and to be recognized as, the body of an I. For Fichte the problem is not the relation between distinct entities but the generation of the relata.

1 The I and the World of Sense

Fichte's theory of the body in the *Naturrecht* forms an essential part of his overall project of deducing the concept of right (*Begriff des Rechts*: 8) as a necessary condition of self-consciousness in the foundational chapters of that work. More precisely, Fichte introduces the body into the *Naturrecht* – and thereby into transcendental philosophy in general – in the systematic context of showing the necessity of the "possible application" (*Anwendbarkeit*: 56) of the concept of right. Given Fichte's general anti-formalist project of a real, contentually specific philosophy and his overall procedure of a philosophical reconstruction of the necessary conditions of ordinary consciousness and its world, this cannot mean that a previously established set of concepts and principles is subsequently brought to bear on an additional subject matter, as though something given extraneously had to be subsumed under already established rules and concepts. Rather, in discussing the possibility of applying the concept of right, Fichte undertakes a necessary further extension of the investigation into a direction which has remained unexplored so far in the argument and without which neither the deduction of the concept of right nor that of the conditions of the possibility of self-consciousness could be completed.

To be sure, the particular result of the first stage of the deduction of the concept of right (§§1–3) might seem to call into question the very project of deducing right from I, considering that the relationship implied by the concept of right (*Rechtsverhältniss*: 52), viz., that relationship among finite rational beings in which each of them with inner freedom limits the use of its external freedom through the concept of the possible external freedom of the other rational beings. For this concept of an "absolute community" (*absolute Gemeinschaft*: 86) is doubly contingent in its reality and possible or actual application. First, the original necessity of conceiving oneself as engaged in an externally free reciprocal relationship with another finite rational being like oneself, marked by the the founding cognitions-cum-actions of "solicitation" (*Aufforderung*: 33) and "recognition" (*Anerkennung*: 49), does not by itself alone imply the continuation of freely rational interaction on either side of the free rational beings involved. Only the theoretical, cognitive or logical criterion of consistencey in thinking and in action based on thinking (*fortgesetzte Consequenz*: 48) and the practical, vital interest in the security of one's right (*rechtliche … Sicherheit*: 142) from possible infringement is able to vouch for future reciprocally free interaction among finite rational beings. Second, the deduction of the concept of right as a necessary condition for the actualization of finite rationality presupposes the "real interaction" (*reelle Wechselwirkung*: 56) between free beings, i.e., the actual temporal-spatial contiguity between the potential partners of right. Temporally or spatially distant rational beings are not be to be considered as possible relata in the relatonship of right.

There remains an important sense, though, in which the concept of right and the relationship that it implies necessarily determine, if not the actual acting of the rational being than at least the basic thinking of the rational being about itself – in Fichtean terms, the way in which the rational being necessarily posits itself. The rational being as such has to think of itself as practical intelligence distinct from a world in which it is yet able to exercise efficacy by shaping or reshaping a given "stuff" (*Stoff*: 29) and as one of several such beings with which it possibly or actually shares that world. There is thus a twofold necessary further determination of the self-reverting activity – or "I-hood, subjectivity" (*Ichheit, Subjectivität*: 17) – that *is* the finite rational being: first into a being possibly *acting* on *non-rational* beings in the world and, second, into a being possibly *interacting* with *rational* beings in that world. Fichte's technical term for the I that possesses this further degree of determinacy is "individual" (*Individuum*: 8, 42), more precisely "rational individual" (*vernünftiges Individuum*: 56).[7]

The remaining step in the deduction of the individual I and its proto-legal constitution, to be carried out in the subsequent sections (§§5–6) of the *Naturrecht*, concerns the further determinations that have to be ascribed by the individual I (1) to itself, (2) to non-rational beings in the world and (3) to other rational beings in the world, in order for it to be possible that the I *qua* individual has, on the one hand, free efficacy in and on something that it is not, the world and the beings in it, and, on the other hand, is able to distinguish rational from non-rational beings in that world.

The basic problem to be solved in this concluding part of the argument is that the I as such is sheer *acting* (*Handeln*: 1, 28) – acting on itself at that, and nothing but pure self-reverting activity – while the world and the beings in it on which the individual I is to be able to act are objects or instances of "being" (*Seyn*: 28) in the "world of sense" (*Sinnenwelt*: 23). This problem is not limited to the individual I's relation to *non-rational* beings. It also holds with respect to the individual I's relation to another *rational* being whose being may well not be exhausted by their existence in the world of sense but who *first and originally* appear to the individual I as beings in the world of sense. Under the methodological restriction of the *Naturrecht* to the conditions, limits and laws of *external* freedom, other rational beings are encountered not as fellow noumena but as sensible beings with intimations of rationality. Accordingly, Fichte's theory of the individual I's necessary *embodiment* in the world of sense in the second chapter of the *Naturrecht* is designed to show that and how an individual I can be cognizant of and effective in the world of sense and can stand in relation to the non-rational and well as rational beings in it. The gist of Fichte's account is that the individual I as such necessarily *finds* itself as falling, or as having always already fallen, into the world of sense and as equipped with a sensory apparatus for acting and interacting in that world.

To be sure, these further detemination of the I and its world, without which there would not be an I nor a world for the latter, have to be taken with the same methodological *caveat* that has characterized the entire argument of the *Naturrecht* up to this point. Philosophical reflection can only elucidate how the rational being acts necessarily and how a rational being has to think of itself as a result of that necessary acting. The necessity involved is one imposed by the laws of thinking or by reason. There are no claims made or even possible about how things are "in themselves" or independent of the reference point constitued by the rational being. Moreover, such an absolute being of the I, or of any and all of its activities and their products, is not just unknowable to us but altogether inconceivable, representing nothing but an absurd notion that cannot even be entertained consistently. Fichte's argument is "transcendental" (*transcendental*: 72) in the specifically critical, limitative sense that it states how we as rational beings must *think* of ourselves and the world:

> To say that something *is* a certain way means that we must posit it that way; and because we must posit it this way, it is so. (72)[8]

This characteristic combination of ontological modesty and epistemological audacity also holds for Fichte's deduction of the Other. As posited originator of an undergone solicitation, which is in essence nothing but a *soft* "check," one that manages to maintains its recipient's external freedom, the rational being outside me has the same status as the non-rational being posited by the I in response to the hard "check," introduced in the *Foundation of the Entire Wissenschaftslehre*. The same pertains to the bodily reality of the I – a necessary appearance, more than an illusion, less than some thing in itself, and all we will ever get. To be sure, the radical limitation of being to being "for us" only comes in on the philosophical or speculative viewpoint. On the ordinary, practical viewpoint there are things, bodies, others, even a personal God as the unsolicited solicitor of the first being or beings capable of rationality (39f.). But strictly speaking, we do not have *knowledge* (*Wissen*) of any of these beings outside and independent of us; they are objects of feeling (*Gefühl*) and belief (*Glaube*).

Still the transcendental reduction of reality to how things are "for us" should not be confused with a deflation of Fichte's applied or real philosophy to an inventory of empirical data about the specifics of "us" human beings. Such an anthropological reduction would not do justice to the method and the content of Fichte's applied philosophy in general and the somatolgy of the *Naturrecht* in particular. In terms of method and procedure, Fichte is not collecting *facts* (*Thatsachen*) about human beings but reconstructing the originary acts of the self-constitution (*Thathandlungen*: 25) of a practical intelligence. In terms of content, he is not deducing such specifics as the five senses and their respective objects and media, but delineating basic functional requirements for rational agency in the world of sense, which are then, parenthetically, identified with their contingent empirical instantiations.

2 The I's Body

The "deduction of the applicability of the concept of right" in the *Naturrecht* consists of two further theorems with proofs, which complete the argument of the preceding three theorems in the "deduction of the concept of right." The two final theorems concern the rational individual's self-ascription of a material body and the latter's further determination in view of the rational individual's twofold function of acting on objects and interacting with other rational beings in the world of sense. Accordingly, the proofs proceed teleologically, detailing in a series of ever more specific determinations the structural requirements for an active-interactive rational individual to be possible.

The Fourth Theorem states:

> The rational being cannot posit itself as an individual that has efficacy without ascribing to itself, and thereby determining, a material body. (56)[9]

The free efficacy in the world of sense which the finite rational being has to posit or ascribe to itself as a necessary condition of its self-consciousness is not unlimited or absolute freedom but limited or determinate freedom. Provided that its potential for rationality has been realized in the course of a successful solication to free activity, the individual has at its disposal a "sphere" (*Sphäre*: 41) or range of actions that have been left undetermined by the solicitor and among which it is able to choose freely and "exclusively" (*ausschliessend*: 56). Any choice in that sphere is that of the rational individual in question and of no other rational individual. By ascribing such an exclusive sphere of activity to itself, the rational individual undertakes a further determination of itself and of the world on which and in which it is supposed to act.

The exclusive sphere of actvity is not only *posited* by the rational being *qua* I but also opposited or counterposited (*setzt sich entgegen*: 57) to the I by the I. The self-ascribed sphere is posited not as part of the I but as "a part of the world" (*ein Theil der Welt*: 57). Due to the clandestine workings of the "productive power of the imagination" (*productive Einbildungskraft*: 58), the sphere is further posited by the I – and accordingly appears to the I – as a spatio-temporally extended, fixed and enduring whole or "material body" (*materieller Körper*: 59), the essence of which consists in it being the "extent of all possible free actions of the person" (*Umfang aller möglichen freien Handlungen der Person*: 59), with "person" being a synomym for "rational individual" (56).

Now the material body is not only posited and opposited by the I but also self-ascribed by the I as the sphere of *its own* free actions. More precisely, it is the sphere of those possible free actions of the rational individual that are actualized solely through the latter's willing. Immediately by willing one of the actions contained in the self-ascribed sphere called "material body," that action takes place. Alternatively put, the "concept of a purpose" (*Begriff vom Zweck*: 59) is *immediately* the "cause" (*Ursache*: 59) of the object willed. But also inversely, none of the possible free actions that together constitute the self-ascribed material body can occur without this having been willed by the rational individual whose self-ascribed material body it is. The exclusivity of willing (or choosing) in relation to the sphere of free actions is an exclusivity of *immediate access* to the material body on the part of the particular rational individual whose self-ascribed material body it is. Moreover, it is a mode of access that can be described as *internal* or exercised from *within*, as opposed to any external influence that something or someone else might exercise over a given rational individual's sphere of immediate free activity.

The required possibility of immediate efficacy of the will in the correlated material body implies a further determination of the material body itself. The latter has to be thought as susceptible to the infinitely varied possible determinations which the rational individual must be able to will and at once realize by choosing from among the totality of its immediately free possible actions. For that purpose the material body has to be – has to be posited as being – composed of unchangeable but infinitely divisible matter and of infinitely changeable form, with the latter constituted of parts that move in immediate response to the determinations of the will. Given the infinitely many possible determinations of the will, the required partition of the body is not fixed but open; it depends on the actual determination of the will which parts of it are moved and which not. In sum, the material body is composed of arbitrarily partioned wholes that can be parts and parts that can be wholes or of "members" (*Glieder*: 61) due to which the material body in its entirety possesses "articulation" (*Articulation*: 61).

In the exclusive correlation between the I that self-ascribes a particular material body and the particular self-ascribed material body the latter functions as the principle of individuation of the I. The I is a "determinate material I" (*bestimmtes materiales Ich*: 57), and not just an "absolute formal I" (*absolut formales [Ich]*: 57), only by having posited or self-ascribed this particular material body. The material body first provides the basis for ascertaining the "continuation and identity of our personality" (*Fortdauer und Identität unserer Persönlichkeit*: 61). The material body as individuating the rational being and as the sphere of immediately effective willing is called our "living body" (*Leib*: 61).[10]

3 The Body as Organ, Sense, and Tool

The Fifth Theorem, the final one in the argumentative architectonic of the *Naturrecht*, further determines the body of a given rational individual as the object of the free efficacy of one or more other embodied rational beings:

> The person cannot ascribe a body to himself without positing it as standing under the influence of a person outside him, and without thereby further determining it. (61)[11]

In the proof Fichte deduces the possibility of a free rational being influencing another one in the wider context of the possibility and the principal forms of influence (*Einfluss*: 61) that bodies as such (*Körper*) as well as embodied rational beings can exercise on a given embodied rational individual. In a first step Fichte argues for the double structure of the living body's articulation. Any influence on an embodied rational being, no matter from where and by what or by whom, amounts to an infringement of that being's freedom; part of that being's free activity is "removed" (*aufgehoben*: 62); in terms of the being's embodiment, its living body is subject to a determination from without; the being's ability to will immediately in its body is "restrained" (*gehemmt*: 62). But the rational individual *qua* I is constitutively always active and nothing but active. Strictly speaking, one cannot even conceive of an influence on the I from without but only of restrained activity in the I and for the I, which is taken by the I as indicating the presence and efficacy of other beings.

In order to be able preserve its essential freedom and re-establish the exclusive voluntative determination of its body under conditions of (supposed) influence from without, the rational individual has to be posited (and to posit itself) as endowed with a body that can be at once foreign-determined and self-determined, or determined from without and determined from within. Such a body possesses a "dual articulation" (*doppelte Articulation*: 64) or a "dual organ" (*doppeltes Organ*: 64). The designation of the articulated body as an "organ" addresses the function of bodily articulation as the individual's medium of efficacy in the world of sense. The living body is posited as consisting of a "higher organ" (*höheres Organ*: 64) that is exclusively under the control of the rational individual's will, and a "lower organ" (*niederes Organ*: 64) that is subject to external influence but also capable of internal determination though the will of the rational individual. Hence there is always a part or dimension of the living body that is exlusively under the control of the will, regardless of the kind and degree of external influence.

The basic relations between the higher and the lower organs of articulation depend on the two principal functions of the body as instrument of *cognition*, specifically of sensory cognition or "perception" (*Wahrnehmung*: 64), and as instrument of *action* or as a "tool" (*Werkzeug*: 71). In perception the lower organ undergoes an external influence, which modification is at once "imitated" (*nachgeahmt*: 65) in the higher organ. The internal imitation of the external influence vindicates the essentially and exclusively active nature of the rational individual *qua* I. In perceiving, the rational individual simulates *internally*, in the higher organ, the same activity that the external influence exercises on the lower organ. Fichte illustrates this transcendental account of perception by detailing how hearing involves the internal imitation (in the *inner ear*) of what is heard through the lower, outward-directed sensory organ. The same holds for seeing, which is never only a passive imaging but always involves an activity of the *inner eye* (65).

In its capacity of internally and freely appropriating external, unfree influences, the articulated body functions as "sense" (*Sinn*: 65). This perceptive function of the articulated body is to be contrasted with the latter's function as a "tool." In the latter case the efficacy that the body undergoes does not originate from without – or is so posited – as in the case of sense perception, but originates from within, in the rational individual itself: the concept of a purpose or of an object willed modifies the higher organ, which in turn affects the lower organ manifesting itself in the correlated bodily action (71).

4 Free Influence

But the interaction between free rational beings in the world of sense is more than mutual sensory perception of each other and more than mutual influencing of each other through the articulated body functioning as a tool. Rational individuals, or individuals capable of rationality, must be able to interact with others in the world of sense *as free beings*. To be sure, their influence upon each other must be exercised in the world of sense and by means of their articulated bodies, but the organ and the sense and in general the material reality involved have to be such that it is possible for each rational individual engaged in mutual influencing to retain its external freedom for the exercise of its will and the employment of its body. Otherwise a rational individual would be influencing another one not any differently than it would act on a non-rational being; and the recipient of such unfree treatment would have no reason to attribute rationality, or the potential for it, to the perpetrator of such treatment. In short, the mutual influencing of free rational beings as such must lack the element of external *constraint* characteristic of ordinary physical influence.

The required possibility of *free influence* among rational beings leads to, or leads to posit, further determinations of the articulated body and the world of sense of which it is part. Most importantly, the matter by means of which the articulated body of one rational being acts on that of another one in free influence has to be different form the "tough lasting matter" (*zähe haltbare Materie*: 68) by means of which a given articulated body is constrained and its lower organ forcibly modified. The only freedom left to the rational individual under an influence of the latter kind of matter is the "absolute freedom of reflection" (*absolute Freiheit der Reflexion*: 66), whether or not to pay attention to the modification undergone. By contrast, free influence would have to operate by means of a matter that is "finer and more subtle" (*feinere und subtilere [Materie]*: 69). The latter's modifications of the articulated body and its organ are comparatively fragile and can be undone by an act of willing on the part of the influenced rational individual. Hence the modification is not just *formally* suspendable, as in non-reflection on the tough influence, but *materially* destructible.

To be sure, having its subtle influence on another rational being *actually* disregarded and destroyed is not the purpose of a rational individual employing finer rather than rough matter to exercise influence on another one. What is important here is the *possibility* of such a destructive reception and the freedom which this possibilty leaves to the recipient to respond in kind to the free influence excercised upon him. In free influence the purpose is not to modify the lower organ as such but to affect through the latter's modification the higher organ – provided the recipient lets this happen – and to convey through this very mode of influence that not mere efficacy but interaction is happening or is sought. In free influence the medium is the message. The function of the articulated body in free interaction is one of sense, more precisely of "higher sense" (*höherer Sinn*: 71), as opposed to the "lower sense" (*niederer Sinn*: 72) involved in the perception of influence by constraint.

A final functional requirement for the possibility of free influence between embodied rational individuals is the differentiation of subtle matter into two kinds. The first kind of subtle matter, introduced as "matter A" (*Materie A*: 76) and *en passant* identified as "air" (*Luft*: 76), is immediately modifiable through the lower organ that sets it into motion. The "constant movement" (*beständige Bewegung*: 76) of this flexible subtle matter reaches first the lower, then the higher organ of another rational individual. Matter of such a kind not only serves the puposes of formal communication or communication as such, viz., of conveying to the recipient that the originator is a rational being addressing himself to the recipient as another rational being by choosing the mode of *free* influence. It also serves as vehicle for material communication, which Fichte identifies parenthetically as "speaking with each other" (*mit einander sprechen*: 76). Flexible subtle matter makes possible the communication of cognitions.

The second kind of subtle matter, "matter = B" ([*Materie*] = *B*: 76), *en passant* identified as "light" (*Licht*: 76), is posited for the specific pupose of enabling the identification of one finite rational being by another one on the basis of the "mere shape" (*blosse Gestalt*: 76) of its living body. While the first kind of subtle matter is in constant movement and immediately influenced by the will by means of the lower organ, as rational individuals are freely influencing each other (speaking to each other by setting the air into vibration), the second kind of subtle matter is relatively stable in the shape it takes and is also not immediately subject to the influence of the will on some correlated lower organ for that kind of matter. In fact, there is no specific organ corresponding to the specific sense (sense of sight) for the modification of this second kind of subtle matter (no organ of sight). The changes in the latter have to be brought about by another organ (e.g., touch) before they can be sensed (seen).

The relative stability of the second kind of subtle matter permits the initial as well as continued identification of beings in the world of sense. In particular, the presence of such matter and the existence of a sense for it and its modifications in rational individuals is a necessary condition for a given rational individual being able to identify the potential for rationality in a being that has not yet actualized its rationality and freedom but is in need of a soft check or solicitation to free activity. But for that necessary purpose – necessary if there is to be free influence among rational individuals – the shape of the (potentially) rational individual has to be sufficiently characteristic to distinguish it and its bearer from non-rational beings. That outward, bodily mark of possible freedom and rationality is the lack of fixed determination in the articulated body in question, more precisely its "infinite determinability" (*Bestimmbarkeit ins Unendliche*: 79), its openness to an infinity of possible free determinations or its "plasticity" (*Bildsamkeit*: 79), which contrasts with the closedness of determination in all other beings to be encountered in the world of sense. To the rational observer this "open" shape of the second kind of subtle matter indicates the presence of someone like him (*seines Gleichen*: 79). At this point of the reconstruction of the I's positing, free influence among finite rational beings is possible.

5 Mind, Body, and Soul

The specific intent of Fichte's transcendental theory of the living body in the *Naturrecht*, to account for the possibility of free influence among rational individuals, belongs in the wider context of the relation between the sensible and the intelligible in finite rational beings. The comprehensive problem is not only that of accounting for the unity of the subject and its constitutive duplicity as "a being of sense and a being of reason at the same time" (*Sinnenwesen und Vernunftwesen zugleich*: 48). Rather, the very status of "our" sensory reality is at issue. If nature is nothing but objectified restrained activity of reason, then how could it be that rational individuals exist in the world of sense? The specific aspect of this basic problem dealt with in the *Naturrecht* is the transition from the merely natural to the rational in the consitution of a rational individual as such. Attributing the potential or "faculty" (*Vermögen*) for rationality to a being will not suffice for explaining its actual rationality. On Fichte's view, only reason can tease out reason; rationality in an individual can only develop through "education" (*Erziehung*: 39) by another, actually rational individual. Neither the specter of an infinite regress of educators' educators nor the latter's termination in some miraculous uneducated educator makes Fichte agree with those, like Ernst Platner, who considered a naturalistic explanation of logogenesis at the individual as well as the species level:

> The human being necessarily has to be developed by beings like him.[12]

Fichte's sustained critical commentaries on Platner *Aphorisms*,[13] as recorded in Fichte's own extensive notes for the lectures on logic and metaphysics after Platner[14] and in several student transcripts of individual sets of lectures or parts thereof,[15] accord a prominent place to the theory of the living body. This material is presented by Fichte under the heading "On the connection between the body and the soul" (*Ueber den Zusammenhang des Leibes und der Seele*).[16] There is no such heading or section in Platner's *Aphorisms*. In his lectures on Platner Fichte places the material after his discussion of Platner's account of the capacity for language (*Von der Sprachfähigkeit*).[17] The two sets of material are closely related. Both concern the origin of a specifically human trait, language and cognition, repectively. Moreover, Fichte defends a critically mitigated non-natural occurrence or "miracle"[18] at the origin of language as well as reason in finite beings. Finally, a good part of the discussion of the origin of language in the Platner lectures does not deal with the specifics of language and its acquisition and development but with the function of "language in the most general sense," of "signs" or of "language in general"[19] in the emergence of rationality. Much of the material on reciprocal interaction (*Wechselwirkung*) between rational beings to be found in §§5 and 6 of the *Naturrecht* is covered in that more general part on the origin of language in the Platner lectures. Specifically, the proto-legal act of solicitation is cast in the Platner lectures as "reciprocal interaction through signs" and declared to be a "condition of humanity."[20]

The other key concept of the theory of free influence in the *Naturrecht*, "recognition" (*Anerkennung*), plays no comparable role in the acount of communicative action in the Platner lectures. However, Platner's own text, the *Aphorisms*, contains an entire section entitled "Of the act of recognition" (*Von dem Anerkennen*).[21] For Platner, recognition is "the faculty for comprehending under concepts what is apprehended [by the receptivity for impressions]."[22] Platner may here be here taking up Kant's doctrine of the "synthesis of recognition in the concept" (*Synthesis der Rekognition im Begriffe*) in the transcendental deduction of the pure concepts of the understanding.[23] The term *Anerkennung* is the Germanic equivalent of the Latin-based word *Rekognition* used by Kant.

On Platner's understanding, in recognition an *image* (*Bild*) is held against a *concept* (*Begriff*) and "recognized as [contained] under its kind."[24] This corresponds exactly to Fichte's use of the term "recognition" in the *Naturrecht* to designate the act of recognizing another being as contained under the concept of "being like me" (*meinesgleichen*). The practical dimension accrues to Fichte's subsumptive concept of recognition due to the fact that only acting of a certain sort, viz., under conditions of free influence, can count as "commonly valid recognition" (*gemeingültiges Anerkennen*: 47).

While the section on the origin of language in the Platner lectures contains the material corresponding to the theory of solicitation in the *Naturrecht*, the section on the connection between body and soul from the Platner lectures corresponds to the account of the body's articulation, its function as organ and sense, in the *Naturrecht*. The most remarkable thing about the vast overlap between the two sets of material is the total absence of the term "soul" in the *Naturrecht*. This is not to say that the subject matter of the soul is simply missing in the *Naturrecht*. On the contrary, what Fichte says about the "higher organ," the "higher sense" and the "finer, subtle matter" in the *Naturrecht* fits exactly the concept of the *soul as inner sense* to be found in Platner's *Aphorisms* as a heritage of Wolffian school of philosophy and its traditional concern with the origin and location of the soul and the nature of its relation to the body. The very phrase "organ of the soul" (*Seelenorgan* or *Organ der Seele*), to be found in Platner,[25] indicates the bodily manifestation of the soul discussed in the "empirical psychology" (*psychologia empirica*) of Wolffian metaphysics.[26] Platner defines:

> The inner organ of the soul, or the seat of the soul, is that part of the body in which all sensory impressions terminate, all movements of the body originate and all effects of the soul in general first manifest themselves.[27]

In the Platner lectures Fichte takes up the traditional concept of the "organ of the soul" and hints at a complete reduction of the soul to its organ:

> We thereby obtain a *dual* organ An outer and an inner one: organ of the soul and organ of the body … The former might in the end turn out to be the entire soul itself.[28]

In systematic, architectonic terms, this amounts to the elimination of the metaphysical discipline of rational psychology, assigned to cover the soul alone, without its bodily organ, and independent of the body in general, with the chief purpose of establishing the immortality of the soul.

This is not say that the Fichte of the Platner lectures defends a materialism according to which there are only bodies. For one, the soul is not an object of outer sense, hence no body in the physical sense of the term. Moreover, on Fichte's account neither the body nor the soul have ultimate reality but have only being *for us* – and *through us*, due to the I's positing and counterpositing activity. In terms of their *being* (for us), body and soul are the *correlated* modes of appearance of the I *qua* subjectivity or activity in the world of sense. In terms of their *being known* (by us), the body is *subordinated* to the soul, in that every object of outer sense can be in turn an object of inner sense but not vice versa.[29] Finally, the soul and the body are not really distinct from each other but are the complementary sides or aspects of the One I, with the soul respresenting the inner activity and the body the outer product of that activity, both in the acts of cognizing and willing:

> Body and soul, inner and outer organ are One.[30]

And:

> The I is simple, self-positing. This I becomes and must become cognizing and acting in a world of sense and to that extent the I is regarded twofold, as part of the world of sense and as inwardly active, i.e., body and soul; the two are the same only viewed differently.[31]

In Fichte's understanding, the problem of the connection between the soul and the body is a pseudo problem. It is like asking how the two sides of a coin are connected: they are one and the same coin; it is not as though a second side were added to an already existing first one. One cannot be without the other, and the coin is more than the two sides put back to back. In the Platner lectures Fichte likens this identity of the body and the soul as aspects of the One I to the identity of thinking and extension in Spinoza's infinite substance:

> The same determinations of my mind, viewed from a certain side, are my acting and, viewed from another side, the object of my acting ... Just as earlier we said that soul and [body] are my I viewed from different sides.[32]

For Fichte the problematic relation is not the one between the body and the soul (what in German is called the *Leib-Seele-Problem*), but that between predisjunctive "mind" or "spirit," the I as such, the purely "mental" or "spiritual" (*Geistiges*: 57), on the one hand, and the latter's falling into the world of sense, as soul-cum-body, on the other hand. In that sense, and in that sense only, Fichte still knows a mind–body problem. And he is not about to pretend to be able to solve it in any other form than by explaining its inexplicability. Finite rational beings are not their own creatures only; before freely making themselves into what they are, they *find* themselves; their freedom is *given*, as is the medium of their free activity in the world of sense, the body:

> The I cannot produce its body as such and cannot posit itself as producing the latter.[33]

Notes

1 See note 2 for the full reference. ("Das Thier ist da, um den freien Geist in der Sinnenwelt zu tragen und mit ihr zu verbinden" (82)).

2 References to the *Grundlage des Naturrechts* are inserted parenthetically into the text using the pagination of the work's edition in *Johann Gottlieb Fichtes sämmtliche Werke*, ed. Immanuel Hermann Fichte, 8 vols (Berlin 1845–46), vol. 3, reprinted as *Fichtes Werke*, 11 vols (Berlin and New York, 1971), vol. 3. This pagination is also indicated in the new English translation: J.G. Fichte, *Foundations of Natural Right*, ed. Frederick Neuhouser and trans. Michael Baur (Cambridge: Cambridge University Press, 2000). Quotations from the *Naturrecht* are taken from this edition, occasionally with modifications; all other translations are my own. Other works by Fichte are cited and quoted according to *J.G. Fichte-Gesamtausgabe*, ed. Bavarian Academy of Sciences (Stuttgart-Bad Cannstatt: Frommann-Holzboog, 1962ff.), abbreviated as: "GA," followed by a combination of a Roman and an Arabic numeral indicating the series and the volume, respectively.

3 For a more recent example of this kind of interest in the *Naturrecht*, see Richard Schottky, *Untersuchungen zur Geschichte der staatsphilosophischen Vertragstheorie im 17. und 18. Jahrhundert (Hobbes – Locke – Fichte). Mit einem Beitrag zum Problem der Gewaltenteilung bei Rousseau und Fichte* (Amsterdam/Atlanta: Rodopi, 1995). Earlier studies in that vein (through the 1960s) are listed in the bibliography by Manfred Zahn in Johann Gottlieb Fichte, *Grundlage des Naturrechts nach Prinzipien der Wissenschaftslehre* (Hamburg: Felix Meiner, 1979): 391–6.

4 See, e.g., Michael Kahlo, Ernst A. Wolff and Rainer Zaczyk (eds), *Fichtes Lehre vom Rechtsverhältnis. Die Deduktion der §§1–4 der "Grundlage des Naturrechts" und ihre Stellung in der Rechtsphilosophie* (Frankfurt/Main: Klostermann, 1992). The programmatic basis for much of this work has been an essay by Reinhard Lauth on Fichte's philosophical discovery of interpersonality: "Le problème de l'interpersonalité chez J.G. Fichte," *Archives de philosophie*, 35 (1962): 325–44.

5 See, e.g., Hansjürgen Verweyen, *Recht und Sittlichkeit in J.G. Fichtes Gesellschaftslehre* (Freiburg/Munich: Karl Alber, 1975); Alain Renaut, *Le système du droit. Philosophie et droit dans la pensée de Fichte* (Paris: Presses Universitaires de France, 1986) and Christian Maria Stadler, *Freiheit in Gemeinschaft. Zum transzendentalphilosophischen Rechtsbegriff Johann Gottlieb Fichtes* (Cuxhaven and Dartford: Traude Junghans, 2000).

6 See especially Ludwig Siep, "Leiblichkeit bei Fichte," in *Kategorien der Existenz. Festschrift für Wolfgang Janke* (Würzburg: Königshausen and Neumann, 1993): 107–20; Virginia López-Domíngues, "Die Idee des Leibes im Jenaer System," *Fichte-Studien*, 16 (1999): 273–93; and Günter Zöller, "Leib, Materie und gemeinsames Wollen als Anwendungsbedingungen des Rechts," in Jean-Christophe Merle (ed.), *Fichtes Grundlage des Naturrechts*, Reihe Klassiker auslegen (Berlin: Akademie Verlag, 2001): 97–111. For a discussion of Fichte's theory of the human body in the context of Kant's philosophy of biology, see Alain Renaut, *Le système du droit*: 201–21. For a reconstruction of Fichte's philosophical human biology, see Reinhard Lauth, *Die transzendentale Naturlehre Fichtes nach den Prinzipien der Wissenschaftslehre* (Hamburg: Felix Meiner, 1984): 140–47.

7 On Fichte's deduction of the individual I from the pure I, see Günter Zöller, "Die Individualität des Ich in Fichtes zweiter Jenaer Wissenschaftslehre (1796–99)," *Revue Internationale de Philosophie*, 206 (1998): 641–63.

8 "Es *ist* so, heisst, wir müssen es so setzen: und weil wir es so setzen müssen, darum ist es so" (72).

9 "Das vernünftige Wesen kann sich nicht, als wirksames Individuum, setzen, ohne sich einen materiellen Leib zuzuschreiben, und denselben dadurch zu bestimmen" (56).

10 *Leib* is here rendered as "living body" in the sense of "animated body" to distinguish it from the generic sense of term "body" (*Körper*) and in line with the etymological origin of *Leib* in the middle-high German word for "life" (*lîp*), as still preserved in the *hendiadys* "Leib und Leben."

11 "Die Person kann sich keinen Leib zuschreiben, ohne ihn zu seztzen, als stehend unter dem Einflusse einer Person ausser ihr, und ohne ihn dadurch weiter zu bestimmen" (61).

12 GA, II, 4: 37 (on §1 of Platner's *Aphorisms*; cf. GA, II, 4 S: 9): "Der Mensch muß nothwendig entwikelt werden durch seines gleichen."

13 The text by Platner on which the lectures are based (*Ernst Platner's Philosophische Aphorismen nebst einigen Anleitungen zur philosophischen Geschichte*, Ersther Theil [Leipzig: im Schwickertschen Verlage, 1793]) is reprinted in GA, I: 4 S[upplement].

14 GA, II: 4.

15 GA, IV, 1: 169–450 (Nachschrift Krause, 1787/98); GA, IV, 3: 77–141 (Nachschrift Eschen, 1796/97); GA, IV, 3: 197–305 (Nachschrift Höijer, 1798).

16 GA, IV, 1: 328; GA, IV, 3: 122.

17 GA, II, 1: 292–327 and GA, II, 3: 115–22 (*Ueber den Ursprung der Sprache*); see GA, II, 4 S: 113–29 (Platner, *Aphorisms*, §§473–543).

18 GA, IV, 1: 302 and GA, II, 4: 163f.: "Wunder." See also GA, IV, 3: 117.

19 GA, IV, 1: 296: "Sprache im allgemeinsten Sinne," "Zeichen," "Sprache überhaupt."

20 GA, IV, 1: 295: "Mittheilung"; "Wechselwirkung durch Zeichen ist also Bedingung der Menschheit."

21 GA, II, 4 S: 38–42 (§§110–21).

22 GA, II, 4 S: 23 (§34): "die Fähigkeit das Aufgefaßte unter Begriffe zu bringen."

23 See *Critique of Pure Reason*, A 103ff.

24 GA, II, 4 S: 39 (§111): "anerkennt … als unter seinem [sc. des Begriffes] Geschlecht."

25 GA, II, 4 S: 303ff.

26 See, e.g., Gottlieb Alexander Baumgarten, *Metaphysica*, reprinted in *Kant's gesammelte Schriften*, ed. Royal Prussian Academy of Sciences and its successors (Berlin, later Berlin/New York: Reimer, later de Gruyter, 1900), vols 17 and 18. See also Kant's contribution to the debate in his *Beilage* to a letter to Samuel Thomas Sömmerring of 10 August 1795, included as an appendix in the latter's *Über das Organ der Seele* (Königsberg 1796), in *Kant's gesammelte Schriften*, 12: 31–5; sketches in *Kant's gesammelte Schriften*, 13: 398–413.

27 GA, II, 4 S: 31 (§67): "Das innere Seelenorgan, oder der Sitz der Seele, ist derjenige Theil des Körpers, in welchem alle Sinneneindrücke sich endigen, alle Bewegungen des Körpers sich anfangen, und alle Seelenwirkungen überhaupt zunächst sich äußern."

28 GA, II, 4: 7 : "Wir erhalten dadurch ein *doppeltes* Organ. Ein äusseres u. ein inneres: *Seelen-* u. *LeibesOrgan*. Das erstere … dürfte denn wohl zulezt die ganze Seele selbst werden …."

29 See GA, IV, 1: 334.

30 GA, IV, 1: 345: "Leib u. Seele, inneres u. äußeres Organ sind eins."

31 GA, IV, 1: 334: "Das Ich ist ein einfaches, sich selbst setzendes. Dieses Ich wird u. muß werden erkennend u. handelnd in einer Sinnenwelt, u. in so ferne wird as Ich doppelt angesehen, als Theil der Sinnenwelt u. als etwas innerlich thätiges, das ist Leib u. Seele; beydes ist dasselbe, nur verschieden angesehen."

32 GA, IV, 1: 367, in place of the word "body" the student transcript has *Geist* ("mind" or "spirit"), a slip of the pen: "Dieselben Bestimmungen meines Geistes sind von einer gewissen Seite mein Handeln u. von einer anderen Seite angesehen Obiect meines Handelns … So wie wir oben sagten: Seele u. Geist (sic) sind mein Ich von verschiedenen Seiten angesehen."

33 GA, IV, 1: 342 (erroneous page number 242): "Das Ich bringt seinen Leib als solchen nicht selbst hervor, u. kann sich nicht setzen als denselben hervorbringend …."

Chapter 8

Fichte's Materialism

Bruce Merrill

Fichte's *Foundations of Natural Right* opens with an emphatic idealism, in two senses. Taking off from the entrenchment of idealism already established by the prior *Wissenschaftslehre*, he arrives at a highly idealistic – i.e., lofty, elevated – conception of our species in its social context. As an explicit extension of the *Wissenschaftslehre*, Fichte's theory of right begins in unimpeachable subjectivity, "the I in self-consciousness" (21),[1] then observes a similar method of regressive explanation, which gives rise to a dialectical triad, the first three theorems. Thus Fichte now locates the necessary preconditions for the I's awareness of itself in our social setting. He reproduces his prior dialectical triad (I, not-I, then I and not-I in reciprocal limitation) as an analogous triad pertaining to the I in its social context: I, others, then I and others in reciprocal self-limitation. That is, beginning with the self-conscious efficacious I, Fichte contends that this awareness is possible only through a moral awareness of the efficacy of other rational persons, which, in turn, is only possible by positing the I and others as conjoined in "a relation of right" (41). With the third theorem, the reciprocal limitation of Fichte's original triad appears in a social context, as the requirement to limit one's own freedom on behalf of the freedom of another: "I must in all cases recognize the free being outside me as a free being, i.e., I must limit my freedom through the concept of the possibility of his freedom" (52). Such reciprocal self-limitation is the essence of right, and the key to a universal realization of freedom in the social setting. Freedom, which is the essence of our subjectivity, is externalized, realized in the larger setting wherein the I locates itself.

During his initial "deduction of the concept of right," we find this core conception of right expounded in an idealistic context, an elevated notion of "the distinctive character of humanity." "Only free, reciprocal interaction by means of concepts and in accordance with concepts, only the giving and receiving of knowledge, is the distinctive character of humanity, by virtue of which alone each person undeniably confirms himself as a human being"

(40). Right pertains to the direct and mutual interpersonalism between free and rational beings.

> Thus the relation of free beings to one another is a relation of reciprocal interaction through intelligence and freedom. One cannot recognize the other if both do not mutually recognize each other, and one cannot treat the other as free being, if both do not mutually treat each other as free.
>
> The concept here is extremely important for our project, for our entire theory of right … (44)

Here right supplies the framework for a horizontal community of equals, conjoined by moral awareness (of the "summons"), respect (i.e., recognition) and intelligence.

As Fichte proceeds from his initial deduction to the "applicability of the concept," and asserts our necessary embodiment, he does not abandon his sanguine horizontal interpersonalism. Because the domain of right lies within the "sensible world," we access this domain as material beings, bodies capable of sensing and being sensed. The body is the necessary medium for our externalized freedom. "The material body … is posited as the sphere of the person's possible free actions, and nothing more. Its essence consists in this alone" (59). Yet Fichte's insistence upon our embodiment, as active and public beings, remains consistent with his preceding idealistic notion of "the distinctive character of humanity." As corporeal persons, our freedom, reason and moral awareness are inescapably bound up with our embodiment. We are dual, and each aspect implies the other. "The presence of the body was inferred from the concepts of independence and freedom" (73). "I cannot understand the appearance of a human body except by assuming it to be a body of a rational being" (77). With respect to the "applicability of right," Fichte's vision of the human community remains horizontal, interpersonal, moral.

1 Fichte's Materialism

The thrust of Fichte's insistence upon our embodiment becomes clear when he turns from the "applicability" to the "systematic application of right," wherein he infers that "Original right is … the absolute right of the person to be only a cause in the sensible world and purely and simply never something caused" (113). His concern with our essentially active, efficacious nature no longer pertains to our moral aspect, and the free efficacy of practical reason, but with our physical dynamism, our causal efficacy as a body in relation to objects. With his exposition of "original right," Fichte resolves to a defining continuity between the materiality inherent to our status as embodied persons and the materiality of the inanimate targets of our rightful efficacy.

> The body, regarded as a person, must be the absolute and final cause of its determination to exercise efficacy … [A]nything that is physically possible in the body must be permitted actually to be produced in it, if and only if the person wills it. The body must be neither set in motion nor restricted in its motion by any external cause; there must be absolutely nothing that immediately exercises an effect upon it. (114)

The context for right no longer pertains to our reciprocal efficacy in a horizontal relation between other equivalent persons, but to our asymmetric causal relation to things. The brunt of our externalized freedom now pertains to our capacity to manipulate (or not) those objects which are given to us. "[T]he person is free only in the sphere in which objects are given … [I]t is within the sphere of the given and under the condition that something is given that one is free to leave the given as it is or make it into something else …" (115). Rather than a parity between morally equivalent persons, Fichte is especially focused upon our right to maintain a disparity in our relation to objects, a unilateral physical dynamism: "the absolute right of the person to be only a cause in the sensible world and purely and simply never something caused." Externalized freedom in the sensible world is now focused upon our potency as a body in motion, while right serves to enforce our claim to be an active first cause in relation to external objects, that is, "to be only a cause," never an effect. Thus Fichte has replaced his initial conception of right as providing a framework for the horizontal community of moral and intelligent persons for an alternate community based upon our individualist, unilateral, causal dynamism, in relation to things. As our direct relation to things is revealed as primary for the realization of our efficacy, our relation to other persons is found to be secondary and indirect.

Our original right to be unilaterally dynamic, "to be only a cause," grounds our right to physical property. That is, our absolute right to causal efficacy grounds our right to a stable "orientation," a rightful demand upon the stability of the physical realm in order that it remain available to our causal action. The demand for stability engenders a legitimate property claim – as determined by the horizon of our knowledge of given objects.

> The person has the right to demand that in the entire region of the world known to him everything should remain as he has known it, because in exercising his efficacy he orients himself in accordance with his knowledge of the world, and

> as soon as change occurs in the world he immediately become disoriented and impeded by the course of the world's causality, or he sees results completely different from the ones intended.
>
> Here is the ground of all property rights. The part of the sensible world that is known to me and subjected to my ends – even if only in thought – is originally my property ... No one can affect that part of the sensible world without restricting the freedom of my efficacy. (116)

The most notable aspect of this unusual case for property rights is an extremely expansive conception of legitimate private property, since the extended horizon of cognition determines the practical horizon of agency and possession. By means of knowing, we transform the given into the owned.

In sum, the human agent whose free efficacy is justified by Fichte's philosophy of right is an essentially economic being, inherently possessive, focused upon his private property as a sphere for his causal activities. Moreover, he is aggressively possessive, primed to appropriate "the entire region of the world known to him" as a personal domain for his unilateral physical dynamism.

The upshot is that as we come to the heart of his theory of right we confront Fichte's materialism – in two senses: Fichte binds together the materiality of the body, as the essential medium for externalized human agency, and the materialism of a fundamentally economic orientation, as the dynamic agent strives to possess her entire known world in order to bring it into the ambit of her personal causal agency. (Nota bene: The second sense of "materialism," conforms to Marxist usage, the position that human interests are fundamentally economic.) The direct linkage of the two materialisms is captured in Fichte's distillation of his two basic principles of original right: "1) the right to the continued existence of the absolute freedom of the body ... 2) the right to the continued existence of our free influence within the entire sensible world" (119) – which we therefore claim as our property. The two linked materialisms, the material body laying claim to the entire sensible world, epitomize Fichte's conception of rightful externalized human freedom: "the absolute freedom of the body," realized as "our free influence within the entire sensible world." External freedom is economic freedom, our freedom to manipulate those given objects which we possess, our freedom to expand our property, according to our individual wills. The core external fulfillment of our free nature lies in our unfettered activity as self-interested economic agents. And since our species is characterized as essentially materialist, the economic sphere is elevated as the essential arena for externalized, actualized human freedom.

Because original right is individualist, materialist, possessive and infinite it is inevitably overlapping, inevitably conflictive. Once the human race is revealed as fundamentally economic and individualistic, primarily concerned with our particular relations to objects, our relation to other humans becomes secondary, and conflictive. The others in our community stand revealed as rivals, each competing over his rightful claim to exercise a causal agency upon the entire known world. In concept, Fichte allows that a reciprocal horizontal acceptance of our delimited claims upon private property could provide a solution to the conflict inherent to original right, could elicit an "equilibrium of right" achieved when "property is grounded in reciprocal recognition, and such recognition is conditioned by mutual declaration" (130). However, this hypothetical accomplishment of a mutual horizontal two-party equilibrium cannot be actualized. The human race cannot arrive at a secure self-discipline, unaided, since our kind cannot project any achieved equilibrium into the future.

> But their mutual security does not depend only on the fact that they agree to a rightful state of affairs between themselves; rather it depends on the fact that in all their future free actions they will govern themselves in accordance with this agreement. Therefore this agreement presupposes that each trust the other will keep his word, not merely now and again, or when it seems beneficial for him to do so .... (137–8)

We need an honesty in our declarations, which we can trust, in order to arrive at an effective equilibrium. But given the pervasive self-interested materialism it is not possible for any apparent honesty and trust to be relied upon, deceit is always possible, a possible future violation our equilibrium always looms before us. The conflictive nature of original right cannot be overcome on a horizontal, two-party basis. Rather "what is needed is an irresistible coercive power that will punish the violator" (146). The Hobbesian problematic of "insecurity and war of all against all" (154) is solved by the Hobbesian antidote: the overwhelming, unitary power of the Leviathan. Assured, universal and impartial coercion can only be delivered by a supremely powerful third party, viz., state authority, which will "operate with mechanical necessity" (142) to enforce lawful property relations.[2]

2 Once and Future Democracy?

Fichte's nested conception of 1) the core dynamic, economic freedom, 2) circumscribed by countervailing positive law, 3) as enforced by the overwhelming coercive power of the state authority is in turn, 4) framed by two, once and future, instances of substantial political self-rule performed by the populace as a whole: the original free self-subjection beneath the "supreme power" (106) and the adjudication between the opposed claims of the executive and the ephors, in the wake of an "interdict."

In the synoptic #8, Fichte contends that along with the core freedom realized in the economic sphere, the universal subjection to the coercive power which secures that sphere is itself a crucial instance of achieved human freedom. The contention elicits a uniquely emphatic endorsement of the primacy of freedom in the political context:

> [I]n and through such subjection, all the freedom that properly belongs to me in my sphere, in accordance with the law of right, is secured.
>
> Unless this condition is met, I cannot rationally subject myself to such an authority, and the law of right gives no one a right to demand that I do so. Thus I must be able to judge for myself whether this condition is met. My subjection of myself to the authority is conditional upon the possibility of this judgment; such subjection is impossible and contrary to right if such a judgment is not made. Therefore, above all else, I must subject myself with complete freedom. (102)

Here Fichte insists upon the fulfillment of both our rational and practical self-rule in the political context, both "I must be able to judge for myself" whether "through such subjection, all the freedom that properly belongs to me in my sphere, in accordance with the law of right, is secured," then following upon that judgment, "I must subject myself with complete freedom." His insistence, while not explicit, involves an acknowledgment of the democratic ideal: the entitlement, enjoyed by all citizens, to rule themselves intellectually and practically, in the political context.

Nevertheless, the harvest of this unique instance of independent judgment and free self-rule is the total transference of both judgment and rule, since the citizenry, in order to escape conflict over competing property claims, "must unconditionally subordinate their physical power and their right to pass judgment, i.e. all their rights, to that third party" (101). The object of the subordination is in order that "all the freedom that properly belongs to me in my sphere … is secured" – with "the freedom that properly belongs to me" being the economic liberty to exercise our unilateral efficacy upon our private property.

This singular, deliberate instance of autonomous judgment and self-rule involves the willing exchange of our future political freedom for material freedom. The citizen knowingly gave up his power of judgment, i.e., his freedom of the intellect in relation to the political order, and his capacity to act upon that judgment freely, to direct himself accordingly, in order to establish dependable coercive authority – so that he may securely pursue freedom in the economic sphere. There is no continuity between the grounding political self-subjection and any political agency since our appropriate external free agency is not political. Instead, the fulfillment of our rightful economic freedom demands the willed abrogation of our political freedom.

While this "one time" event lies, we are told, in the past, the operation of a rightful polity is also framed in the future by the possibility of substantial political power being conferred upon the populace as a whole during a "people's tribunal," when the citizenry are gathered to adjudicate between the rival claims of the magistrates and the ephors. While Fichte rejects the separation of powers, viz., the role of the judiciary as a check upon the excesses of the executive, he does recommend the installation of a permanent ephorate, "to serve as a counter-weight to the executive authorities, who have been endowed with superior power" (177). The ephors do not enjoy positive power, as this would undermine the essential unity of the surpassing executive power, rather they claim the negative power of challenging the executive, in the event of either of the two miscarriages which Fichte allows for. It is the task of the ephors to identify the lapse, then issue a "state interdict" which serves "to suspend public power completely" (172). The result is a fundamental crisis of authority, with the two competent, empowered, positive and negative bodies in direct conflict, and a sudden power vacuum into which the assembled populace is forced. They must convene, and declare the loser between the ephorate and the magistrates. Thus secure right will be restored – but in a drastic manner: The loser will be accused of "high treason" (174), for which the magistrates will be banished.[3]

Although the "people's tribunal" (188) involves the exercise of real power, it is not a situation of positive political agency, as when citizens actively promote their own myriad conceptions of proper self-rule, but only the limited assignment of either concurring with the negation administered by the ephors, or else negating the negation and siding with the executive. More telling, Fichte characterizes the collapse of authority as "the greatest misfortune that could befall them" (173) – not a fortunate opportunity for the citizens to advance their rightful will, but a traumatic rupture which they must resolve promptly in order to return to their preferred apolitical economic activities.

Nevertheless – and surprisingly, given the pessimism evidenced in connection with the failure of the equilibrium of right – Fichte here displays great faith in the citizenry. He avers that this "momentous legal proceeding," brought about by a breakdown between the two wise and practiced political bodies, will prove "very easy to decide" and "will always be answered with complete unanimity" (179), and so "right, and only right, will infallibly and necessarily prevail" (180). But is it plausible that "right, and only right, will infallibly and necessarily prevail" in such a drastic situation? Can a "people's tribunal" operate without presuming upon honesty and trust? Is the apolitical circumstance that the populace consigns itself to during the normal life of the polity compatible with the extraordinary political competence demanded by an abrupt constitutional crisis, during "the greatest misfortune that could befall them?"

Perhaps the explanation for the implausibility of the people's tribunal lies in Fichte's closing assurance that "the ephorate will never have to exercise its authority because the executive power will always be just; there will never be any need to consider an interdict or a people's tribunal" (186). It turns out that "all these provisions have been set up, not to be implemented, but to make the situations in which they would have to be implemented impossible. It is precisely where these provisions have been set up that they are superfluous, and it is only where they have not been set up that they are necessary" (187). The true purpose of the daunting prospect of a people's tribunal is that it should not be actualized, that is, to encourage the skill and secure the power of the magistrates, and encourage them to negotiate with the ephorate (175), rather than risking an interdict. The implausibility of the popular assemblies is not a problem – because these assemblies will not take place; "there will never be any need to consider an interdict or a people's tribunal." Perhaps Fichte presents this instance of actualized popular power as drastic and implausible as possible in order to press the magistrates into political competence?

Given that the purpose of Fichte's dramatic vision of a future instance of a universal, collective exercise of political power is to remain hypothetical, to block the actualization of universal political power, then it proves to be the case that the function of both of the instances of substantial universal self- rule which Fichte envisions, both the past "one time" event of our freely chosen "unconditional subordination" and the future threat of popular assemblies, is to reinforce the power of the executive, and thereby foreclose the actualized self-rule of the citizens in the present.

The core element in Fichte's political theory is his materialism: his guiding supposition that our embodied species is essentially focused upon the self-interested, individualist, causal manipulation of private property, and seeks to expand that property aggressively. This is the efficacy that he advances as the proper fulfillment of human freedom in the sensible world. His nested theory is built up around his philosophical anthropology, this pessimistic vision of human nature. One result is an inverse relation between economic freedom and political freedom. Because Fichte holds that our external freedom is properly fulfilled in the economic sphere he does not address the question of whether or how our freedom might be fulfilled the political sphere. More to the point, it is due to the intensity of our self-interested materialism that our horizontal interactions in the economic sphere cannot be sustained, honesty and trust cannot be projected into the future, and we must subject ourselves to the surpassing coercive order. In fact, the thrust of Fichte's exposition of the origin of state authority is to encourage his audience to willingly forfeit the freedom of political judgment and self-rule in order that they may enjoy a secure economic liberty.

It may be objected that this consideration of the *Foundations of Natural Right* is anachronistic, that I am looking for a species of freedom, political freedom, which was simply not to be found in Jena during the last decade of the eighteenth century, and therefore my complaint is inappropriate, unfair. The retort is valid insofar as the culture and institutions of democracy were simply not present. But against this I submit that the *Foundations of Natural Right* is itself an impressive instance of externalized political freedom: a rational, argued, political document which is being advanced in public, positioned more or less horizontally before an audience of free and rational beings, positioned horizontally next to the alternate contemporary theories of the political order advanced by Erhard, Maimon, and Kant, which Fichte cites in his introduction. As an instance of externalized freedom in the sensible world is Fichte's philosophy of right to be understood as an instance of his causal efficacy in relation to given objects? I think not. Rather, as public text and public philosophy, it has more to do with the elevated notion of human community found within his opening "deduction of the concept of right." Yet Fichte's text is not merely conceptual, it is actualized, and is (or was) efficacious in the sensible world. Perhaps it is a product which needs to theorize its own production?

Notes

1 All quotes from J.G. Fichte, *Foundations of Natural Right*, ed. Frederick Neuhouser, trans. Michael Bauer (Cambridge: Cambridge University Press, 2000). Pagination cites the I.H. Fichte edition.

2 On Fichte's resolution to coercion, see Robert R. Williams, "The Displacement of Recognition by Coercion in Fichte's Grundlage des Naturrechts," in *New Essays on Fichte's Later Jena Wissenschaftslehre*, ed. Daniel Breazeale and Tom Rockmore (Evanston: Northwestern University Press, 2002): 47–64.

3 The modern theory of the ephorate as an occasional body set up to intervene "during times of interregnum and peril" begins with Johannes Althusius' *Politica* (1614), chapters 18 and 38. A more proximate instance of this doctrine is found in Rousseau's similar case for an occasional "tribunate" in his *Social Contract* (1762), book IV, chapter 5. Rousseau cites the ephors of Sparta as an instance of a tribunate.

Chapter 9

The "Mixed Method" of Fichte's *Grundlage Des Naturrechts* and the Limits of Transcendental *Reellephilosophie*

Daniel Breazeale

Fichte's *Grundlage des Naturrechts* opens with a provocative and uncompromising series of declarations and claims: the *Wissenschaftslehre* is to be sharply distinguished from virtually all preceding philosophies, inasmuch as it is grounded in a clear insight into the reflexive structure of *Ichheit* itself, in which subject and object, ideality and reality, are originally and synthetically united in the sheer and spontaneous self-assertion of the I. The method of transcendental philosophy consists in a complete description of the various, necessary acts of the I. The "genetic" character of this description, in which each of the described acts of the I is recognized to be the condition for the possibility of a previously described act, and hence a condition necessary for the absolutely and originally posited unity of self-consciousness itself, constitutes a pure, transcendental "derivation" or "deduction" or "proof" of the entire series of such acts, as well as of the products of the same (that is, the world "for us").

In the spirit of the age, Fichte proclaims that the *Wissenschaftslehre* will recognize no "privileged truths" and commits himself to the principles of "equality and liberty" – namely, the "equality (*of reasons* [*Gründe*])" and the "liberty (to express opinions *supported by reasons*)."[1] The guarantee that the *Wissenschaftslehre* will remain true to this proclamation is its rigorous adherence to a "strict method" of proof and derivation. Fichte, however, wrote no "Discourse on Method," or rather, he wrote *several*, including such metaphilosophical works as *Ueber den Begriff der Wissenschaftslehre*, the lectures "Ueber den Unterschied des Geistes und des Buchstabens in der Philosophie," the two "Einleitungen" to the *Versuch einer neuen Darstellung der Wissenschaftslehre*, and the *Sonnenklarer Bericht*. The problem for the student of the *Wissenschaftslehre* is that the methodology outlined in these texts does not always appear to be the *same*, nor does the method – or rather, the methods – of philosophizing that Fichte actually employs in his "scientific" writings always correspond to *any* of his explicit methodological pronouncements. The following remarks are intended as a contribution toward the larger task of clarifying and, insofar as possible, making coherent the methodology and methods of the early *Wissenschaftslehre*.

In order to accomplish the requisite derivation of the complete series of reason's (that is, of the I's) self-constitutive acts, the transcendental philosopher must elevate himself from the standpoint and presuppositions of ordinary life and "attend to what remains." He must perform an act of global "abstraction," followed or accompanied by a series of self-conscious "reflections." When he does this, we are assured, he will be able, for the first time, to detach the necessary (and hence *a priori*) acts of the I from the "products" of the same – namely, the "things" of ordinary experience – and will then be able to *observe* and to *describe* the former in isolation from the latter. Since the universal criterion of "reality" is the feeling that one is compelled to present or expound (*darstellen*) something in a certain specific way, it follows that when the philosophical observer finds himself similarly compelled by the objects of his observations (the pure, self-constitutive acts of the I), he is then entitled to attribute a certain "reality" to these acts themselves – and hence to his own "description" of the same. This, according to Fichte, is one of the most important differences between the *Wissenschaftslehre* and other philosophies. For whereas the majority of philosophers have been content to employ mere ratiocination in order to analyze and to combine mere thought-entities or "concepts," the transcendental philosopher derives – and thereby "proves" – *his* "concepts" by grounding them in pure observations (intuitions) of something that is not a concept at all: the series of those necessary acts by means of which the I constitutes itself *as* an I, for itself.

Such a method of pure, inner observation might appear to have much in common with quasi-Cartesian "introspection" or with what has been called "armchair psychology." The crucial difference, at least in Fichte's own eyes, is that the distinctive "objects" of transcendental reflection or intuition are not passively received, empirical "facts of consciousness" or objects of inner sense, but are those pure *acts* that must occur if any self-consciousness whatsoever is to be possible. For the philosophical observer, these are always *acts of thinking*, inasmuch as they represent *what else one has to think* in order to "think the I." Transcendental philosophy requires not only that the philosopher make the effort required to think these necessary thoughts, but, at the same time, that he actively observe his own activity in doing so. This is why transcendental philosophy must never be confused with psychology.[2]

Inasmuch as its proper object is this series of constitution acts, and inasmuch as it "derives" the genetic series of the same by a method of abstraction and reflection, the method of the *Wissenschaftslehre* has obvious parallels with that of Husserlian phenomenology. To this extent, therefore we may describe Fichte's method as "phenomenological." But his own favorite term for this method, at least during the period he was writing the *Naturrecht*, was "synthetic," a term he employs to emphasize the *ampliative* character of the knowledge produced in this way. The results established by the *Wissenschaftslehre* are certainly not derivable by mere analysis or inference from the concepts and principles with which the science begins. They are grounded upon actual intuitions, and hence are able to extend our knowledge. Moreover, since the intuitions in question follow upon an act of complete abstraction from experience, they are not empirical but "pure," and propositions grounded upon them are therefore universally valid (*allgemeingültig*) and "necessary." I will therefore call the philosophical method just described the phenomenological/synthetic method.[3]

Because it employs such a descriptive method, Fichte describes the *Wissenschaftslehre* as a "history" – or sometimes a "pragmatic history" – "of the human mind."[4] Such a history, of course, can claim to be accurate only insofar as the philosopher does not freely invent concepts and arguments, but finds himself *compelled* to describe the acts of the mind in precisely the manner and in precisely the order in which he observes them. He observes not merely *that* the I *does* act in a certain way, but also that it "*must* act in this determinate way"; and thereby he becomes "the observer of a real [*reellen*] thinking by his own mind."[5] This, and this alone, provides the justification for describing the *Wissenschaftslehre* as a "*Reellephilosophie*," in contrast to the kind of "*Formularphilosophie*" that merely makes inferences from arbitrarily selected or invented "thoughts."

This general distinction between "real" philosophy" and "formulaic" philosophy also applies to the philosophical science of right, or *Naturrecht*. To claim that the *Grundlage des Naturrechts* is a "real philosophical science" is to maintain that the fundamental concepts and principles of this science are "original," in the sense that they are based upon direct observations of certain determinate acts of the I, which, in turn, are conditions necessary for the possibility of self-consciousness. Thus, writes Fichte, "The philosopher has to describe [a certain] determinate action with respect to its form,[6] as well as to describe what emerges for reflection in this acting. By doing this, he simultaneously provides proof of the concept's necessity, determines the concept itself, and shows its application."[7]

This reference to the "application" or "applicability" of juridical concepts introduces a serious ambiguity into Fichte's claim that his *Rechtslehre* is a "real philosophical science." For as the work advances, the author appears to slide from his original claim (namely, that the *Naturrecht* is a "real" science because its object, while *a priori*, is given to philosophical reflection as an original act of the I) to the quite different claim that the "reality" of this science is demonstrated by the fact that the concepts deduced therein can be successfully "applied" to the sensible world and to the embodied human community. I will return to this point at the conclusion of my paper.

We have now described, in brief, the distinctive method of any "true" or "real" philosophy, and no one who finds himself unable to execute this difficult feat of abstraction and reflection is qualified, according to Fichte, to pass judgment on the claims made by or on behalf of such a philosophy. (Fichte himself referred to the talent or "knack" required for engaging in this sort of reflection as "philosophical genius"[8] or "spirit in the higher sense,"[9] and, to the consternation of friend and foe alike, was not in the least shy about accusing his critics of lacking this talent altogether.[10])

As we have already noted in passing, there is more to Fichte's phenomenological/synthetic method than merely reporting on what one happens to discover when one abstracts from ordinary, empirical consciousness. In order for philosophical reflection to obtain an *object*, the philosopher has to *think* – and think hard; for what he is trying to "observe" are those acts of positing that are conditions for the possibility of the originally posited act of pure self-positing. In order to move beyond this bare concept of the I as subject-object, the philosopher must make the considerable intellectual effort required to raise it to clear consciousness, which means that he has to ask himself: what else do I – and since I have already abstracted from everything that distinguishes me from anyone else, what else does any rational subject (that is, any finite I) – have to think in order to "think the I?" The "acts" that become the object of philosophical intuition are precisely these acts of necessary thinking. Hence the transcendental philosopher has to play a *dual role*: on the one hand, he must remain the "observer" of those necessary (and therefore "real") acts that are required for the self-constitution of subjectivity and hence condition the possibility of any experience whatsoever. So considered, the philosopher becomes, in Fichte's words, a "spectator" in the theater of his own mind.[11] On the other hand, he must also take the stage and assume the role of stand-in for the real star of the production: the pure I or pure reason itself.[12] It is in this role that he must actively "seek out" whatever "must be thought" in order to "think the I," and then he must actively "think it," as well as everything that "follows from" such thinking, in the sense of being a condition for the possibility thereof. When he engages in such pure thinking, he is necessarily guided by the laws of the same, including the familiar principles of logical analysis and inference (*modus ponens*, *modus tolens*, and the rules of syllogistic reasoning).[13]

When we turn from an account of the method of philosophical observation (which is all that Fichte stresses in his introduction to the *Naturrecht*), and consider the kind of *thinking* that must accompany, and is indeed presupposed by, the latter, it quickly becomes obvious that the actual method (or "methods") of philosophizing employed by Fichte in all of his Jena period works, including the *Naturrecht*, is quite a bit more complex than his own quasi-phenomenological account of "real philosophical science" would suggest. In fact, the *Naturrecht* contains very little in the way of a "history" of the necessary acts of the I, and an enormous amount of sheer conceptual analysis, logical inference, dialectical argumentation, and empirical description.

Once the necessity of a particular "synthesis" (or act of synthetic thinking) has been established, the task of philosophy is then to *analyze* or to *explicate* [*erörtern*][14] the new concept or principle grounded thereupon, in order to determine what is "contained therein" [*gehört dazu*].[15] Not only can we analyze or explicate previously established concepts; we can also draw *inferences* [*Folgerungen, Schlüsse*] from previously established propositions or theorems.[16] *Corrollaria* established in this manner may, in turn, be incorporated into formal, syllogistic arguments.[17] A particularly favored mode of "indirect inference" employed throughout the *Naturrecht* is the one based upon the logical principle, "If the ground of something ceases to exist, then what it grounds also ceases to exist,"[18] which is, I take it, nothing more than a somewhat opaque formulation of the principle of *modus tolens*: if not A, then not B.[19] Straightforwardly deductive or syllogistic arguments also abound in the *Naturrecht*, particularly, though not exclusively, in the later portions of the same, for example in Fichte's formal proof of the necessity of consent to the so-called "transfer contract."[20]

Before proceeding any further in our examination of the modes of inference employed in the *Naturrecht*, a word of caution may be in order, for it is all too easy to be misled by Fichte's use of the terms "analysis" (or "analytic") and "synthesis" (or "synthetic") to designate different aspects of his own philosophical method. The *Wissenschaftslehre* as a whole may be described as an "analysis" of pure subjectivity or of the "concept of the I," and hence as an *a priori* "deduction" or "derivation" of the conditions of the same. This, however, by no means implies that the method of such an "analysis" or deduction is itself purely "analytic." When Fichte asserts, at the conclusion of the First Main Section of Part One, that he has now deduced the *Aufforderung* "by mere analysis" of the act of positing oneself as an individual,[21] this does not imply that the proof in question is a matter of mere *conceptual* analysis. On the contrary, a "real" philosophical analysis of the necessary acts of the I requires a genuinely *synthetic* method of proof: namely, the "phenomenological/synthetic" method described above, which is also the method actually employed by Fichte in the first paragraphs of the *Naturrecht*.[22] Yet there is more to Fichte's synthetic method than mere abstraction, observation, and description. The *Wissenschaftslehre* also involves a kind of synthetic *thinking*, to a consideration of which we now turn.

By far the most innovative, as well as the most frequently employed mode of inference in Fichte's *Naturrecht* is what might be described as the "dialectical" or "proto-dialectical" method of proof. This method, which was perfected in Part Two of the *Grundlage der gesamten Wissenschaftslehre*, proceeds by explicitly thematizing a contradiction (or, alternatively, a vicious circularity) implicit in some previously derived set of propositions, and then "seeking out" [*aufsuchen*] some "higher principle" that allows one to avoid the objectionable contradiction and is *therefore* declared to be "necessary." Unlike conceptual analysis, logical inference, or syllogistic reasoning, this "dialectical" method is *synthetic*, in the sense that the new principle that resolves or dissolves (Fichte usually says "*hebt*" or sometimes "*aufhebt*") the contradiction in question is not "contained" in and thus cannot be analytically derived from the set of concepts and propositions that precede it. Furthermore, since it is not derived from experience, but is instead a product of pure thinking, this new principle can be called "*a priori*." As such, it represents a synthetic *a priori* extension of our knowledge. In order to distinguish this type of synthetic argument from the previously discussed "phenomenological/synthetic" type I will refer to it as Fichte "dialectical/synthetic method."

Despite the fact that Fichte employed this dialectical method of derivation in all of his Jena-period writings, he never formulated it explicitly or indicated how it is to be related to his phenomenological method or to the methods of ordinary conceptual analysis and logical inference. We must therefore resort to specific examples in order to understand the method in question. For present purposes, one such example will have to suffice. In §8 of the *Naturrecht* Fichte remarks that one can trust another person to subject himself to the law of right only if one possesses foreknowledge of all his future actions, since only this can confirm the sincerity of his subjection to the law and warrant our trust in him. Such experience, however, already presupposes that he does in fact subject himself to the law and recognizes that I do so as well. In other words, it presupposes the very trust it is supposed to make possible. Thus, comments Fichte, "we are caught in a circle," which means that we must here "proceed in accordance with the synthetic method," since otherwise we would be "entangled in an irresolvable" and "obvious contradiction."[23] We can eliminate this contradiction by "synthetically uniting" the contradictory elements "in accordance with the method demonstrated [*erwiesen*] in the *Wissenschaftslehre*," and the *only* way to combine the thought of a confidence-based, mutual restoration of freedom with the thought of all possible future experience, is by thinking of a *third party* as the guarantor of the agreement.[24]

No sooner, however, have we made this "synthetic" advance in our argument than another contradiction becomes explicit: namely, that between my original freedom to judge and to enforce the proper limits of my own free actions and my (postulated) total alienation of my freedom to do these things to a third party. This contradiction, which Fichte explicitly formulates in terms of a "thesis" and its "antithesis," is in turn "canceled" [*gehoben*] by a new, synthetic proposition: namely, that my alienation of my freedom to this third party must itself be accomplished with complete freedom.[25] By repeated application of this same dialectical/synthetic method of argument, Fichte ultimately derives both the necessity and the necessary determinacy of the social contract and of the kind of political arrangement it requires – that is, a commonwealth.

With the introduction of the concept of a commonwealth, Fichte claims to have solved the problem before him "in accordance with a strict method [*nach strenger Methode*]," and he obligingly summarizes his "proof" in quasi-geometrical terms: The *problem* is *to find* a kind a willing that is necessarily identical to the common will. Let us call the will that we are seeking [*der zu suchende Wille*] "X," and then let us "solve for" X.[26] X, of course, turns out to be the common will, as embodied in the *Staatsbürgervertrag*, which, in turn, harbors internal contradictions of its own, contradictions that can be eliminated only be providing a full account of the authority and constitution of a "just state."

At every step of Fichte's deduction of the social contract and the *Rechtsstaat*, one encounters new contradictions that cannot be analytically resolved, fresh *problems* to be solved and *challenges* to be met.[27] It must be emphasized that no algorithm is available for solving such problems. To say, as Fichte does, that an appropriate solution is something we have to "seek out"[28] is to say that every such problem must be dealt with in its own terms and that each requires a fresh exercise in *creative problem solving.*

Nor can we resort to past or present experience as a guide in such cases, for here we are still within the realm of pure reason[29] – or, if one prefers, of pure "reasons" – and must therefore seek our solution in the pure realm of *imaginative thinking*.

Anyone who has ever tried to construct a proof in geometry, to solve a mystery, or, indeed, to demonstrate a philosophical proposition is surely acquainted with the kind of "power" presupposed by Fichte's dialectical/synthetic proofs. But such a person will also be acquainted with another, problematic feature of all such "solutions" or "proofs," one that Fichte steadfastly refused to recognize. I am referring to the problem of *necessity* or "*uniqueness*."[30] It is one thing to construct or to imagine a "workable" solution to a problem or an ingenious way of avoiding a theoretical contradiction by introducing a new, synthetic principle, but it something else altogether to claim that the solution in question is the *only possible one*. This, however, is precisely what Fichte does claim for his own dialectical/synthetic proofs[31] – and indeed, what he must claim, if his conclusion, at the end of Part One of the *Naturrecht*, is to be warranted: namely, that "the entire mechanism described here is *necessary* if a rightful relation among human beings is to be realized."[32] This too is a problem to which I shall return.

I cannot, however, conclude this inventory of the various types of argument and evidence employed in the *Naturrecht* without mentioning one that is particularly prevalent in Part Two, though it can also be found in Part One: namely, straightforward appeal to the "facts of experience." Given Fichte's own philosophical manifestos, this is perhaps the last thing one would expect to encounter in a treatise written "in accordance with the principles of the *Wissenschaftslehre*," and the author himself betrays a certain amount of unease on this point. Nevertheless, at several critical junctures in his argument, he appeals directly to the facts of experience or to "nature" itself, not simply for assistance in "gaining a hearing for reason,"[33] but in order to advance his overall deduction, particularly his proof of the "applicability" of the concept of right and his demonstration of the application of the same.

Though the most notorious examples of this practice are unquestionably to be found in the First Appendix to Part Two, in which Fichte's *a priori* deduction of juridical laws pertaining to marriage and child-rearing are inextricably interwoven with flat declarations on his part concerning the distinct empirical "natures" of men and women, there is no lack of examples of such an appeal to nature elsewhere in the treatise. His defense, for example, of the social welfare functions of the state depends, first of all, on the transcendentally problematic claim that "nature has destined human beings for freedom,"[34] and secondly, upon a series of all-too-specific claims concerning the "natural needs" of such beings, the various ways in which these needs can – and must – be met, etc. At one point in this portion of his argument, Fichte himself calls attention to the "wholly empirical character of the present investigation" and declares his intention simply to rely upon the facts of the matter without any further "deduction" thereof.[35] In the absence of such a deduction, he then proceeds, in Part Two, to ground a series of "necessary" rights and laws upon a series of "whole empirical" claims, on the principle that "anything whose non-existence would make every relation of right impossible is absolutely valid as a matter of right."[36] In this manner he manages to deduce the "absolute necessity" of such things as door locks, passport portraits,[37] and requiring hunters to exterminate caterpillars. There is, I take it, no need to further belabor the point.

Though Fichte does not provide any *a priori* deduction of the empirical facts he appeals to in the *Naturrecht*, he at least suggests that such a deduction is possible, if only "in principle." Thus, in §3, he assures his readers that transcendental philosophy is fully capable of confirming the necessity of a "world such as ours" – not just the necessity of a "world *überhaupt*," but the necessity of "*all the particular objects in nature* and the necessary classification of the same."[38] Similarly, in §6, in the course of deducing certain empirical features of the human body and external world – including "light," "air," and "coarse matter" – Fichte remarks that "since free beings, as such, are to exist in community in the world, the world must be constituted in *just this way*."[39] But his most notorious effort to provide an *a priori* deduction of certain concrete features of the natural world comes at the beginning of the First Appendix, where he prefaces his deduction of "family right" with a non-juridical deduction of the "natural" differences between the sexes and of marriage itself as a "natural" and "moral" institution.[40] Despite his concession that "such a deduction does not really belong here," he nevertheless recognized that his innovative application of the law of right to marriage was utterly dependent, not only on his preceding deduction of the law of right and of the *Rechtstaat*, but also upon a quite specific characterization of the "natural" differences between the sexes. This means that the universality and necessity of his doctrine of domestic right depends, in part, upon the ability of the *Wissenschaftslehre* to provide an *a priori* deduction of the differences in question.

It is an understatement to remark that what we find in this section of Fichte's text does not exactly inspire confidence in the ability of transcendental philosophy to accomplish the task at hand. Without denying that there are significant biological differences between men and women, it is still discouraging to see a thinker of the first rank found an entire theory of family right upon propositions as dubious as the claim that "woman necessarily wants the love of some man," whom she must "necessarily believe to be the most lovable of his sex," or that "lasciviousness [*Wollust*] is contrary to a woman's nature."[41] My point here is not to have a cheap laugh at Fichte's expense, but simply to issue an admonitory warning against tying the fate of transcendental philosophy so closely to such utterly *a posteriori* – and easily falsifiable – claims. At this point, however, I have already begun to formulate my conclusions.

As mentioned above, Fichte's claim to have established the doctrine of right as a "*reelle philosophische Wissenschaft*" harbors a significant ambiguity. On the one hand, the *Wissenschaftslehre* can be described as a *Reellephilosophie* precisely because it claims to be a *descriptive* science or "pragmatic history" of those necessary acts through which the mind "constitutes" or "constructs" itself and its world. Such a science is "real" because the "acts" in question (and the "necessary ways of thinking" corresponding thereto) *really* do occur, and occur necessarily, whenever one tries to "think the I." This is a "reality" that anyone – or at least anyone with the requisite philosophical talent – can directly demonstrate for himself by actually *doing* what Fichte demands: thinking the I and paying attention not only to what one *actually does*, but also to what one *has to do* in order to accomplish this. The *Wissenschaftslehre* is a "real" science because it describes a "real" object. The evidence that these acts are "real" and not just fabricated by the philosopher is that they can be directly "observed" or "intuited." This is the criterion of *Reellephilosophie* advanced in the introduction to the *Naturrecht* and also describes the philosophical method employed in the first paragraphs of that work, up to and including the derivation of the *Aufforderung*, the other, and the articulated human body.

In the later portions of the *Naturrecht*, however, the author appears to be proposing quite a different justification for the claim that his *Naturrecht* is a "real philosophical science." The "reality claim" now seems to be based not upon Fichte's strict employment of the phenomenological/synthetic method, but upon the fact that this doctrine can be successfully *applied* to the "real," which is to say, to the "sensible" world. Accordingly, in the Third Main Division of Part One, devoted to the "Systematic Application of the Concept of Right," Fichte maintains that it is not sufficient for a "real" [*reelle*] doctrine of right simply to provide an *a priori* derivation of the proposition that the right of coercion is conditioned by the other's voluntary subjection to the law of right; instead, "since we are propounding a real and not merely formal doctrine of natural right," we must also explain *that* and *how* this theoretically demonstrable limit of the right of coercion can *actually* be "discovered and determined in *applying* the law."[42] Whereas a purely formal doctrine of natural right is concerned merely with the "thinkability" of the concept of right, a *reelle Rechtslehre*, such as Fichte's, absolutely must explain and demonstrate how this concept "can be applied."[43] The synthetic principle according to which the purely formal law of right is able to determine materially the scope of each person's right is therefore to be "confirmed" [*bewährt*] by showing its "general applicability" to my own body, that of the other, and our respective property.[44]

Nor is it enough for the *Naturrecht* to deduce the "general applicability" – in principle – of juridical concepts to the realm of sensible experience; it must also *confirm* this conclusion by *actually applying* these principles. It appears, therefore, that Fichte considered his own finely-grained "applications" of the principles of right to the empirical world to constitute important corroborating evidence for the claim that the *Naturrecht* is a "real philosophical science" – in the sense that it "really" applies to the "real" world.

It is noteworthy that the "foundational" portion of the *Wissenschaftslehre*, whether in its 1794/95 version or in its 1796/98 version, *nova methodo*, includes nothing comparable to the "demonstration of applicability" that is such a central feature of the *Naturrecht*. And yet these "foundational" treatises are the paradigmatic instances of "*Reellephilosophie*," in the sense of a "pragmatic history of the human mind." The "reality" of Fichte's account of the self-constitution of self-consciousness stands in no need of a separate deduction of its applicability to "external objects"; its reality is *guaranteed* by its *descriptive*, phenomenological/synthetic *method*. The fact that the *Rechtslehre does*, in Fichte's view, require such an additional "deduction of the applicability" of juridical concepts therefore points to and reflects significant differences between the methodology of these two philosophical sciences, as well as between the "objects" of the same.

"The *complete object* of the concept of right," according to Fichte, is "a *community of free beings as such*"[45] – that is to say, the real community of sensible beings interacting in a material world. The latter, however, unlike the "object" of the *Grundlage der gesamten Wissenschaftslehre* and the *Wissenschaftslehre nova methodo*, lies well beyond the sphere of pure, self-constituting subjectivity, which is the *only* sphere that lends itself to the direct, phenomenological/synthetic method of demonstration. This, I suggest, is why Fichte had to abandon the phenomenological method very early in the *Naturrecht* for the dialectical method.[46]

The problem, of course, is that once one abandons the phenomenological method, the "reality" of his *Rechtslehre* is no longer automatically guaranteed, which is why a separate, dialectical deduction of the applicability – and hence of the "reality" – of the pure principles of right is now required. Perhaps it was Fichte's sensitivity to this issue that led him, on several occasions in the later portions of the *Naturrecht*, to suggest a way in which the "intuitive" method of fundamental philosophy might be applied to or combined with the dialectical mode of derivation. Thus, for example, he suggests that his dialectical deduction of the "protection contract" can be made "intuitive" (*anschaulich*)[47] if one imaginatively places oneself in the position of the contracting individuals, while simultaneously "observing" how one would necessarily act in such circumstances. In order to appreciate how the contract as a whole (and hence the general will) can arise, Fichte exhorts his reader, "let us see with our own eyes how it comes to exist" by adopting the perspective of an "observer" of an imagined individual as he negotiates the social contract.[48] Such a "thought experiment," however, is in no way comparable to the kind of direct *a priori* intuition demanded by the phenomenological/synthetic method and does nothing to ameliorate the difficulty we are presently exploring nor to guarantee the "reality" of a theory constructed by the method of *a priori* dialectical reflection.

Let us consider this issue more closely. If the "reality" of the pure doctrine of right is supposed to be demonstrated, as Fichte appears to have believed, by its *application* to the sensible world, then, in order to maintain the larger claim concerning the *a priori* necessity and "reality" of such a doctrine and of such an application, one must also commit oneself to the thesis that the sensible world in its entirety is both necessary and *a priori*. Otherwise, one would have to concede that a theory of right can be "real" only to the extent that it is *not* completely *a priori*.

There is, of course, another option: namely, to concede the irreducible contingency of the sensible world while strictly separating the pure transcendental doctrine of right from the application of the principles of the same and basing the "reality claim" for this doctrine purely upon its *method of a priori description* and not upon its possible application to experience. All questions concerning the latter would belong to the non-transcendental science of "politics" and not to the pure science of natural right. In this manner, one could distinguish between the *Wissenschaftslehre in sensu stricto* and other "philosophical sciences," including the science of natural right. Whereas the former would have to confine itself scrupulously to the realm of pure subjectivity (a realm that extends to and includes the deduction of the recognition of one individual of and by another as a condition necessary for the possibility of self-consciousness) and would have to proceed by the "strict" phenomenological/synthetic method,[49] the latter, less "pure" philosophical sciences could employ a more "mixed" method, including appeals to the evidence of experience. To use the terminology employed in the fourth of Fichte's lectures *On the Scholar's Vocation*, only the first portion of the 1796/97 *Grundlage des Naturrechts* would provide us with genuinely "philosophical" knowledge, whereas the rest would be devoted to "philosophical-historical" knowledge. If would follow, of course, that we could not advance the same claims concerning the "necessity," "universality," and "reality" of a philosophical-historical science that we could advance concerning the *Wissenschaftslehre* proper. It is tempting to postulate that this is what Fichte meant to suggest when he titled his book *The Foundations of Natural Right, in accordance with the Principles of the Wissenschaftslehre*, rather than something such as "System of the *Wissenschaftslehre*, Part Two: Doctrine of Right" – a hypothesis that may also appear to be supported by his occasional efforts, in his *Foundations of Natural Right*, to distinguish the sorts of questions appropriate to "natural right" from those appropriate to "politics."[50] But even if he meant to endorse such a distinction, it is undeniable that he violated it more often than he observed it in his own treatise on the subject.[51]

Many of the first readers of the *Naturrecht* took exception to Fichte's efforts to "deduce" *a priori* various features of the sensible world as necessary for a relationship of right (and ultimately, for the very possibility of self-consciousness). One such reader, an anonymous reviewer,[52] had the temerity to challenge not only Fichte's *a priori* deduction of light and air, but even to quote his boastful promise that the *Wissenschaftslehre* could, in principle, provide an *a priori* deduction of every single object in the sensible world. Fichte's response to this critic, a response that was at least to some degree provoked by what he took to be the insulting and derisive "tone" of the offending review, was to dig in his heels and reiterate his original claim. In his *Annalen des philosophischen Tons*, written in response to this review, Fichte insisted that the distinction between *a priori* and *a posteriori* is just a distinction between two different perspectives on one and the same thing and that *everything* we experience can be looked at from either perspective. Summarizing the general conclusions of his philosophy, he maintained that "man receives nothing from without," but that "he cannot exist for himself unless *a specific system of other things* [that is, the system of experience in its entirety] also exists for him." Thus, when man "discovers himself" he also discovers this "system of experience." If we attend merely to the empirical process of "discovery," then *all our knowledge*, including pure philosophical knowledge, is *a posteriori*. But if we attend, instead, to "the fact that *everything is necessarily grounded in one's nature*, then the same things are *a priori*."[53]

From the perspective of the *Wissenschaftslehre*, these remarks are not particularly controversial. What *is* problematic is the implicit claim (if, indeed, there is such a claim) that transcendental philosophy can *actually deduce*, *a priori*, the most specific objects of experience and the most specific laws governing the same. It is, after all, one thing to derive the necessity of positing some medium of communication between one free individual in the sensible world and another (as a condition necessary for the possibility of the *Aufforderung* and a relation of right) and something else entirely to claim to have provided an *a priori* deduction of the necessity of precisely *three* specific media: crude matter, air, and light.[54]

This points to a further ambiguity, not only in the *Naturrecht*, but in Fichte's entire Jena project. On many occasions the claim that the domain of what is *a posteriori* is coextensive with that of what is *a priori* can be interpreted to mean that philosophy can demonstrate *a priori* the necessity of certain general features of experience for the possibility of the same, as well as the necessity of a field of brute contingency ("the original limits of the I") with respect to the determinate contents of experience. Even if it can be somehow demonstrated *a priori* that this latter field of contingency must be thought of as grounded, *a priori*, in the same "supersensible ground" (or "pure I") that provides the ultimate foundation for empirical subjectivity, it can also be demonstrated that every finite I – and every finite philosopher – is always constrained by those "incomprehensible boundaries, within which we simply find ourselves to be confined": namely, the *Anstoß* (or manifold of "original feelings"), the *Aufforderung*, and the moral law.[55] Thus, even the most ambitious system of transcendental philosophy would still have to renounce any intention to "explain" – that is, to deduce in its full determinacy – one of the most striking and undeniable features of mundane experience: namely, the radical contingency of the same with respect to its material determinacy or *Bestimmtheit*.

To claim any more than this, to claim – as Fichte at least appears to claim on a very few occasions[56] – that the *Wissenschaftslehre* can actually provide a universally valid, *a priori* deduction of every single feature of *a posteriori* experience, is to expose transcendental philosophy to a challenge similar to the one issued more than a century ago by Josiah Royce: that is, to explain precisely why the world that I posit is one that "has a belt of asteroids between the orbits of Mars and Jupiter," or to deduce the part played by the Silurian period in my moral world order.[57] If these are the kinds of questions the *Wissenschaftslehre* is supposed to answer, then they are, of course, devastating to Fichte's entire project, inasmuch as they are obviously unanswerable.

In my opinion, however, the *Wissenschaftslehre* should by no means be expected to provide us with such knowledge. That Fichte himself should have, on occasion, been partly responsible for encouraging precisely this misconception of his own project is an historical fact that cannot be denied, though most of the offending passages can be interpreted in a manner consistent with a more modest conception of the task and scope of transcendental deduction. Here again we are reminded of how important it is to interpret all of Fichte's texts (or at least all of the texts of a particular period) – not to mention all of his specific claims – with constant reference to one another, to understand the parts in the context of the whole, and to illuminate the "letter" of the *Wissenschaftslehre* with the light of the "spirit."

There are numerous other issues that might be discussed in the context of the preceding examination of the "mixed method" of the *Naturrecht*. Foremost among these is a problem that might be described as the Achilles heel of post-Kantian philosophy as a whole: namely, the problem of establishing and assessing the claims to "necessity" and "uniqueness" that seem to be such an integral part of the entire tradition of German idealism. I have briefly alluded to this problem, if only in passing, in the course of my consideration of Fichte's synthetic method and of the differences between the phenomenological and dialectical varieties of the same. Any adequate consideration of the issues involved would, however, require a separate inquiry.

I will instead conclude with what is intended to be a provocation for further research on this topic: that is, with the bare assertion that the dialectical/synthetic method is quite unable to sustain claims of necessity and uniqueness made on its behalf and that the phenomenological/synthetic method can at most *postulate* necessity and universality for its claims. One of the questions, I submit, that anyone who considers taking the early *Wissenschaftslehre* seriously as a living philosophical project would do well to ask is this: what happens if we simply abandon such claim? Can transcendental philosophy surrender its claim to *Allgemeingültigkeit* without surrendering its very soul?

Notes

1 GNR, GA, I/4: 76 (FNR: 245). All translations in this chapter are by the author.
Abbreviations:
SW = *Johann Gottlieb Fichtes sämmtliche Werke*, ed. I.H. Fichte, 8 vols (Berlin: Viet and Co., 1845–46); reprinted, along with the three volumes of *Johann Gottlieb Fichtes nachgelassene Werke* (Bonn: Adolphus-Marcus, 1834–35), as *Fichtes Werke* (Berlin: de Gruyter, 1971);
GA, = *J.G. Fichte-Gesamtausgabe der Bayerischen Akademie der Wissenschaften*, ed. Reinhard Lauth, Hans Gliwitzky and Erich Fuchs (Stuttgart-Bad Cannstatt: Frommann-Holzboog, 1964ff.);
BWL = *Ueber den Begriff der Wissenschaftslehre* (1794);

GWL = *Grundlage der gesamten Wissenschaftslehre* (1794/95);
GNR = *Grundlage des Naturrechts* (1796/97);
FNR = *Foundations of Natural Right*, ed. Frederick Neuhouser, trans. Michael Baur (Cambridge: Cambridge University Press, 2000);
WLnm[H] = *Wissenschaftslehre nova methodo* ("Halle Nachshrift," 1796/97);
WLnm[K] = *Wissenschaftslehre nova methodo* ("Krause Nachschrift," 1798/99);
APT = *Annalen des philosophischen Tons* (1797);
SS = *System der Sittenlehre* (1798);
EPW = *Fichte: Early Philosophical Writings*, ed. and trans. Daniel Breazeale (Ithaca, NY: Cornell University Press, 1988).

2 Fichte's rejection of what would today be called "psychologism" begins with his criticism of Platner and continues in his famous criticism of the effort of Schmid and others to base philosophy upon an appeal to the "facts of consciousness." It becomes even more explicit and pointed in his writings of 1799–1801. See, e.g., "Antwortschrieben an Herrn Professor Reinhold" (1801), GA, I/7: 296–7, and "Aus einem Privatschreiben" (1800), where Fichte notes that unlike psychology, which deals with "facts of consciousness," which one simply discovers to be the case, the *Wissenschaftslehre* deals with that "what one discovers to be the case only when one discovers oneself" (GA, I/6: 387n.).

3 See Breazeale, "Fichte's *nova methodo phenomenologica*: On the Methodological Role of 'Intellectual Intuition' in the Later Jena *Wissenschaftslehre*," *Revue Internationale de Philosophie* [Brussels], No. 206 (1998): 587–616.

4 Fichte famously describes the *Wissenschaftslehre* as a "pragmatic history of the human mind," or simply as a "history of the human mind." As I have shown elsewhere, this phrase is to be understood in a manner consistent with the above description of the method of the *Wissenschaftslehre*. A "history of the human mind" is a *genetic* account of self-constitution of the I in the form of an ordered *description* of the various acts of thinking that are presupposed by the act of thinking the I. Though the phrase "history of the human mind" does not occur in GNR, it does occur in the preface to a student transcript of Fichte's lectures on the "Philosophical Science of Right" from the Winter Semester of 1795/96 (his first lectures on the subject). See GA, IV/3: 60.

For a detailed examination of this topic, see Breazeale, "What is a 'Pragmatic History of the Human Mind? Some Methodological Remarks on Fichte's Jena Project," in Fichte: *Crença, imaginaçãi e temporalidade*, ed. Fernando Gil, Viginia López Dominguez, and Luisa Couto Soares (Porto: Campos das Letras, 2002): 89–108 and "Fichte's Conception of Philosophy as a 'Pragmatic History of the Human Mind' and the Contributions of Kant, Platner, and Maimon," *Journal of the History of Ideas*, 62 (2002): 685–703.

5 GNR, SW, III: 5; GA, I/3: 316 (FNR: 7).

6 That is, transcendental philosophy describes how each new act is related to all of the preceding acts it has described. This "genetic" method of derivation is what produces the systematic "form" of such a philosophy.

7 GNR, SW, III: 8; GA, I/3: 319 (FNR: 9).

8 GNR, SW, III: 5; GA, I/3: 316 (FNR: 6).

9 See the second of Fichte's three lectures "Ueber den Unterschied des Geistes und des Buchstabens in der Philosophie," GA, II/3: 323–33 (EPW: 199–208).

10 The *Naturrecht* is particularly rich in *ad hominem* attacks on critics and unsympathetic readers. Even Fichte's friends and supporters complained about the *tone* in which he criticized anyone who criticized or professed to be unable to understand the *Wissenschaftslehre*. See Reinhold's remarks on this topic in his 14 February 1797 letter

to Fichte (GA, III/3: 51).

11 *Eigne Meditationen/PractischePhilosophie*, GA, II/3: 70. See too WLnm (K): "The *Wissenschaftslehre* itself does not generate any new cognition. It merely observes the human mind in its original generation of all cognition" (GA, IV/3: 480 [FTP: 380]).

12 Whereas the "formulaic philosopher" is conscious only of his own thinking (and hence only of the acts of his own individual I, the "real [*reelle*] philosopher," by virtue of the act of abstraction with which he begins, is able to become the observer of the necessary operation of "Vernunft überhaupt," according to its own inner laws (GNR, SW, III: 5–6n.; GA, I/3: 316n. [FNR: 7n.]).

13 This does, of course, raise a certain problem of circularity, since philosophy not only has to employ these laws and principles, but is also supposed to "deduce" or "prove" the universal validity of the same. Fichte was clearly aware of this problem, and hence of a certain, unavoidable circularity in his own – indeed, in any – philosophical method. See Breazeale, "Circles and Grounds in the Jena *Wissenschaftslehre*," in Daniel Breazeale and Tom Rockmore (eds), *Fichte: Historical Contexts/Contemporary Controversies* (Atlantic Highlands, NJ: Humanities Press, 1994): 43–70.

14 Thus, for example, after having established, in the second theorem of the *Naturrecht*, that a finite being cannot ascribe to itself free efficacy in the sensible world without ascribing the same to others and thus presupposing their existence, Fichte describes the next task as that of *analyzing* this proposition, in order to *explicate* [*erläutern*] and *clarify* what has already been established (GNR, SW, III: 35; GA, I/3: 344 [FNR: 34]). See too §14, where, once the synthetic principle of the law of coercion has been proposed, Fichte's next step is to "*analyze* it in order to *clarify* it" – and to continue the analysis until the concept of a law of coercion "is fully exhausted" (GNR, SW, III: 141, 145; GA, I/3: 426, 429 [FNR: 126, 130]).

15 GNR, SW, III: 93; GA, I/3: 390 (FNR: 86–7). See too §12, in which Fichte "analyzes" the claim that the concept of the formal freedom of a being outside of me prescribes the quantity of the material self-limitation I must impose upon my own freedom and concludes that this proposition "contains" three distinct elements (GNR, SW, III: 122; GA, I/3: 412 [FNR: 111]). Note also that Part Two begins with an explanation of the need to "analyze, and with greater care than has been necessary up to this point, the concept of a contract in general" (GNR, SW, III: 191; GA, I/4: 5 [FNR: 165]). This analysis is intended to provide the "premises" for an examination of the concept of the *Staatsbürgervertrag*.

See too GNR, SW, III: 85; GA, I/3: 384 (FNR: 79), where Fichte announces that "our path now leads us to an explication [*Erörterung*] of the *inner* conditions of such reciprocal interaction." See too the long section, "Von der bürgerlichen Gesetzgebung," in Part Two, which commences with the claim that all we need in order to exhaust the topic of civic legislation is a "complete explication" [*vollständig erörtern*] of the previously described contract (GNR, SW, III: 210; GA, I/3: 20 [FNR: 183]). As Fichte explains in BWL, to "explicate" a concept scientifically is "to assign it a place" in relation to other concepts (GA, I/2: 127 [EPW: 113–14]).

16 GNR, SW, III: 35; GA, I/3: 344 (FNR: 34).

17 See for example, the strictly deductive "proof" (*Beweis*) in §14, of one of the corollaries of the principle of the law of coercion: viz., that each person must exercise as much care not to violate the rights of others as he does to prevent his own rights from being violated. This proof consists in showing how the corollary in question follows logically from propositions that have been previously established (GNR, SW, III: 143; GA, I/3: 428 [FNR: 128]).

Or see Fichte's comment, in §7, that his deductive proof [*Erweis*] of the external conditions for the possibility of a community of free beings "is based solely on the presupposition of such a community, which is itself grounded on the possibility of self-consciousness," and that "all the conclusions up to this point have therefore been derived [*abgeleitet*], by way of mediate inference [*mittelbare Schlüsse*], from the postulate "I am I" (GNR, SW, III: 85; GA, I/3: 384 (FNR: 79]).

18 GNR, SW, III: 252; GA, I/4: 53 (FNR: 220).

19 Since, for example, the right to continue to possess acquired property depends upon clearly designating the boundaries of the same, if one allows such visible markings to deteriorate, one thereby forfeits one's property rights; or, since the relation of right depends upon the civil contract, a violation of the latter cancels the former (GNR, SW, III: 135, 194; GA, I/3: 422 and I/4: 7 [FNR: 122 and 168]).

For other instances in which Fichte explicitly employs this same principle of inference, see SW, III: 235, 252, 324, 342, and 364; GA, I/4: 39–40, 53, 112, 127, and 146 (FNR: 205, 220, 280, 296, and 315–16).

20 Since (major premise) the law of right cannot be applied unless a public authority is established, and since (minor premise) such an authority can be established only by transferring it to particular persons, then (conclusion) there is a right to coerce everyone to consent to such an arrangement – assuming of course that we have previously established the necessity of entering into a relationship of right with others (GNR, SW, III: 164; GA, I/3: 443 [FNR: 145]).

See too the "clarifying syllogism" at the end of §3, which purports to "deduce" the concept of right from the concept of an individual and to "prove," from the mere concept of a rational being, that such a being cannot assume the existence of others without also assuming that he stands with them in a relationship of right (GNR, SW, III: 44–52; GA, I/3: 351–8 [FNR: 42–9]).

21 GNR, SW, III: 51–2; GA, I/3: 357–8 (FNR: 48–9).

22 See too Fichte's comment at the beginning of the Second Main Division of Part One, dedicated to the deduction of the human body, that "our task here is to analyze the action indicated above [that is, the action of allocating to oneself an external sphere of freedom], to see [*zu siehen*] what actually happens [*geschiet*]" (GNR, SW, III: 57; GA, I/3: 370 [FNR: 53]).

23 GNR, SW, III: 98–100; GA, I/3: 394–5 (FNR: 91–2).

24 GNR, SW, III: 100; GA, I/3: 395–6 (FNR: 92–3). For other explicit "thesis/antithesis" formulations of the synthetic method of proof, see GNR, SW, III: 237, 260; GA, I/4: 41–2 and 59–60 (FNR: 206–7 and 226–7).

25 GNR, SW, III: 102; GA, I/3: 397 (FNR: 94).

26 GNR, SW, III: 151–2; GA, I/3: 433–4 (FNR: 134).

27 For some additional examples of Fichte's dialectical/synthetic mode of proof, see GNR, SW, III: 116–17, 169–70, 177, 181–2, 201, 260, and 379; GA, I/3: 407–8, 447–8, 453, and 456–7; GA, I/4: 12, 59–60, and 159–60 (FNR: 106, 149–50, 155–6, 159–60, 174, 226–7, and 329). The famous "deduction," in §§5 and 6, of the human body and of the two organs of the same – as well as the corresponding deduction of the various external "media" through which these organs can be affected – also contains many examples of "dialectical" inference of the sort described above.

Consider too the case of *money*, the necessity (and determinate character) of which Fichte "derives" from the contradiction between (1) the civil guarantee that once a citizen has fulfilled his duties of protection and support with regard to the state he has an absolute, unrestricted right to the remainder of his possessions and (2) the state's absolute right to appropriate the products of each citizen's labor in order to make possible the exchange of goods, thereby allowing everyone to live off his own labor. The property right seems to be contradicted by one of its immediate implications. Here again we are forced to "seek out" a solution and thereby to demonstrate the *necessary* introduction by the state of legal tender, which allows the state to control the substance of its citizens" possessions, but not the form thereof (GNR, SW, III: 237–8; GA, I/4: 41 [FNR: 207]).

28 GNR, SW, III: 248; GA, I/4: 50 (FNR: 216).

29 See Fichte's claim to have deduced the necessity of the ephorate, not from any appeal to experience, but "aus reinen Vernunft" (GNR, SW, III: 171–2n.; GA, I/3: 449n. [FNR: 151n.]).

30 I am indebted to Kevin Zanelotti for this way of describing the problem in question.

31 See e.g., Fichte's claim that his dialectical argument demonstrates that expulsion is "the only possible punishment" for magistrates convicted of betraying their public trust (GNR, SW: 177; GA, I/3: 453 [FNR: 155–6]).

32 GNR, SW, III: 185; GA, I/3: 459 (FNR: 163), emphasis added.

33 See GNR, SW, III: 281; GA, I/4: 74 (FNR: 244): "It is sometimes necessary to gain a hearing [*Gehör zu verschaffen*] for reason by appealing to experience." It is, of course, more often the case that an "appeal to experience" is intended to denigrate and discredit the claims of reason. Indeed, Fichte takes note of this fact when he comments that his own students have criticized his principle that it is *absolutely necessary* that no guilty party *ever* go uncaught and unpunished in a *Rechtstaat*. He explains their resistance on this point as based upon too close an acquaintance with the practice of *actual* ("ordinary") states and insufficient appreciation of what is required by the *concept* of a just state. See GNR, SW: 301; GA, I/3: 91–3 (FNR: 261–3).

34 GNR, SW, III: 211; GA, I/4: 21 (FNR: 184).

35 GNR, SW, III: 232; GA, I/4: 37 (FNR: 202).

36 GNR, SW, III: 235; GA, I/4: 39–40 (FNR: 205).

37 This requirement is singled out for ridicule by Hegel in the Preface to his own *Rechtslehre*. See Hegel, *Grundlinien der Philosophie des Rechts*, in *Werke in zwanzig Bänden*, ed. Eve Moldenhauer and Karl Markus Michel (Frankfurt: Suhrkamp, 1970), Bd 7: 25 (*Outlines of the Philosophy of Right*, ed. Allen W. Wood, trans. H.B. Nisbet [Cambridge: Cambridge University Press, 1991]: 21).

38 GNR, SW, III: 40; GA, I/3: 348 (FNR: 38).

39 GNR, SW, III: 73; GA, I/4: 374; (FNR: 68).

40 GNR, SW, III: 305; GA, I/4: 96 (FNR: 265).

41 GNR, SW, III: 347, 312, 333; GA, I/4: 131, 101, and 119 (FNR: 300, 270, and 288).

42 GNR, SW, III: 95; GA, I/3: 392 (FNR: 89), emphasis added.

43 GNR, SW, III: 100; GA, I/3: 395 (FNR: 92).

44 GNR, SW, III: 136; GA, I/3: 423 (FNR: 123).

45 GNR, SW, III: 9; GA, I/3: 320 (FNR: 10).

46 Interestingly, the situation was just the reverse in the *Grundlage der gesamten Wissenschaftslehre*, where Fichte employed the dialectical/synthetic method only until he had "deduced" the *Schweben des Einbildungskrafts* and the occurrence of the *Anstoß*, following which he was able to pursue the more direct, phenomenological/synthetic method for constructing his *a priori* "history of the human mind."

47 GNR, SW, III: 202; GA, I/4: 13 (FNR: 175).

48 GNR, SW, III: 204; GA, I/3: 15 (FNR: 177).

49 Note that this hypothetical prescription accurately describes the actual content and method of the 1796/98 WLnm.

50 See GNR, SW, III: 163, 173, 176, 286, 291, 367; GA, I/3: 442, 450, 452, I/4: 80, 8–5, and 148 (FNR: 144, 152, 155, 249, 253–4, and 318). The relationship between the pure

science of right and politics is also discussed in Fichte's 4 July 1797 letter to Reinhold.

51 This attractive hypothesis is, however, belied both by Fichte's various accounts of the systematic structure of the *entire Wissenschaftslehre* – of which the doctrine of natural right is an integral part, along with theoretical philosophy, practical philosophy (or ethics), and the philosophy of religion. See, for example, the "Deduction of the Subdivisions of the *Wissenschaftslehre*" at the conclusion of WLnm, as well as the "Hypothetical Division of the *Wissenschaftslehre*" in Part III of the first edition of BWL.

Also relevant to a consideration of the systematic structure of the Jena *Wissenschaftslehre* is a letter that Fichte wrote Franz Willhelm Jung, 3 November 1798, in which he discusses the plan of lectures he proposed to follow if appointed to a projected post in a new university to be established in the occupied Rhineland. In doing this, he also illuminates his conception of the systematic interrelation between the various philosophical sciences. Here, for example, he distinguishes between *Wissenschaftslehre* (which is the name reserved exclusively for the science dealing with the "foundations of transcendental philosophy") and the doctrines of right and ethics [*Rechtslehre, Sittenlehre*], and distinguishes all three of these sciences from aesthetics and the philosophical doctrine of religion. See GA, III/3: 156.

52 The reviewer was actually G.E. Schulze, and the review in question appeared in the *Göttingische Anzeigen von gelehrten Sachen* in December of 1796. For more on this see EPW: 337–40 and GA, I/4: 285–91.

53 APT, SW, II: 478; GA, I/4: 310 (EPW: 352), emphasis added. A similar claim occurs in WLnm: "When the I thinks of itself in the act of synthetic thinking just described, it also thinks of its consciousness as a whole and of its experience in its entirety. Therefore, it simultaneously thinks of what is intelligible and of what is empirical (or of what is '*a priori*,' in the Kantian sense of the term, and of what is '*a posteriori*'): these are one and the same, simply viewed from two different sides" (WLnm(K), GA, IV/3: 481 [FTP: 381]). See too WLnm(H), GA, IV/2: 197 (FTP: 381).

54 A similar ambiguity haunts Fichte's claim, *contra* Reinhold, that all experience is not merely *conditioned by*, but also *determined* [*bestimmt*] *by* the I. This does not necessarily imply that transcendental philosophy can deduce *a priori* all the "determinations" in question.

55 This point is perhaps most clearly stated in *Ueber den Grund unseres Glaubens in einer göttliche Weltregierung* (1798), SW, V: 184; GA, I/5: 353 (IWL: 149). But see too the admission, from WLnm(H), "That I am precisely this individual is not something that follows from reason" (GA, IV/2: 263–4 [FTP: 470]) and the similar comment in SS: "That I am this or that specific individual is a contingent matter, and thus something that has an empirical origin" (SW, IV: 254; GA, I/5: 229). For further discussion of this point, see Breazeale, "Check or Checkmate? On the Finitude of the Fichtean Self," in Karl Ameriks and Dieter Sturma (eds), *The Modern Subject: Conceptions of the Self in Classical German Philosophy* (Albany: State University of New York Press, 1995): 87–114, and "Fichte's Abstract Realism," in Michael Baur and Daniel O. Dahlstrom (eds), *From Transcendental Philosophy to Metaphysics: The Emergence of German Idealism* (Washington, DC: Catholic University of America Press, 1999): 99–115.

56 See Fichte's claim, in a footnote to §5 of the first edition of BWL that "it can be *strictly proven* [*streng erweisen läßt*]" that the scientist himself has imposed upon nature all those laws, *including the most specific ones*, that he believes he learns from observation of nature, and that all of these laws – the most *specific*, as well as the most general, the construction [*Bau*] of the *smallest* blade of grass, as well as the movements of the heavenly bodies – *must be derivable in advance* from the first principles of all human knowledge" (BWL, SW, I: 64n.; GA, I/2: 135n. [EPW: 121n.], emphasis added). Even this claim is susceptible

of a stronger and a weaker (and less plausible) interpretation, though it certainly lends itself to the latter. This, I suggest, is precisely why Fichte chose to eliminate this remark from the second, 1798 edition of BWL.

57 Josiah Royce, *The Spirit of Modern Philosophy* (Boston and New York: Houghton, Mifflin, and Company, 1892): 167.

Chapter 10

An Aesthetics of Influence: Fichte's *Foundations of Natural Right* in View of Kant's Third *Critique*

F. Scott Scribner

In the first corollary to the Fifth Theorem (s6) in the *Grundlage des Naturrechts*, Fichte acknowledges that one of philosophy's most vexing problems is to understand "how we come to transfer the concept of rationality onto some objects in the sensible world and not others" (SW, III: 80). What is it precisely that makes possible our recognition of another rational being as such? What is at stake, Fichte warns us, is the very "applicability" of the principle of right (SW, III: 81).

In the GNR, Fichte does not merely deduce the transcendental necessity of intersubjective recognition; he goes on to explain how this dynamic actually occurs in empirical terms.[1] Fichte intends to explain how the figure or percept of the other empirically produces a recognition of right.[2] In fact, he offers at least two related empirical accounts. The first explanation occurs in the discourse of "subtle matter," which I have elaborated elsewhere.[3] The second, parallel account, which is the subject of this paper, offers an explanation of intersubjective recognition in terms of an aesthetics, and shows how such an aesthetics in best understood in terms of Fichte's engagement with Kant's *Critique of Judgment*.[4]

I contend that Fichte's description of the power of the influence of the human form in intersubjectivity is a radicalization of Kant's account of the empirical basis of the judgment of taste in the *Critique of Judgment* in which an empirical interest in the beautiful prepares the way for rational accord (cognitive agreement).[5] The percept of the human form, as an empirical sign of freedom, establishes an aesthetic consciousness which makes recognition as such possible. I will argue that, for Fichte, the recognition of another rational being emerges as an experience of the beautiful. It is a recognition of the indeterminateness of the human form as sign or symbol of the supersensible, which produces within the observer something like a harmony of the faculties – a harmony Kant described in terms of aesthetic judgment.[6] Finally, through an exposition of Fichte's own interpretation of *sensus communis*, I show that Fichte indeed understands the human form as an empirical sign of freedom, not merely by analogy to Kant's judgment of the beautiful, but explicitly in these terms.

1 Recognition and the Aesthetics of Immediacy

In the same section in which Fichte develops an account of intersubjective influence through subtle matter, he also invokes what I understand to be a Kantian styled aesthetics in which he outlines *the power of the percept of the human body as an empirical sign of freedom.*[7] In speaking of the percept of the human form, Fichte asks, "when you saw this figure (*Gestalt*) you had to take it necessarily as the representation of a reasoning being in the sensible world, if you are a reasoning being. How is this possible?" (SW, III: 80–81). In other words, how do we come to recognize another being as a rational being?

While one might be tempted to think of the other simply as a hypothetical other, as the effect of a transcendental deduction of the possibility of freedom, and thus as an intellectual construct, it should be emphasized that here Fichte is clearly dealing with the phenomena of immediate perception. And it is this perception which makes the consequent conceptualization possible. After all, Fichte designates the skin (that is, "touch") as "the first and most important organ" (SW, III: 83). He explains, "all of these things," "the skin," "the eye," "the expressive face," "– not considered in isolation, the way philosophers split them up, but rather in their amazingly grasped connection, as given to the senses – these are what compel everyone with a human countenance to respect the human shape everywhere ..." (SW, III, 84). And Fichte even seems aware that such a description exceeds the philosophical register (read: transcendental register), strictly speaking. There is compulsion on the order of sensation. The other is given, on the order of the senses, in an immediacy and unity, anterior to any concept. The body's refusal to be subsumed by the concept, in fact, is the very ground of its immediacy.

The recognition of right entails two distinct moments that I will later detail in the Kantian terms of aesthetic judgment and teleological judgment. The first moment is that immediate percept of the human form. It is the experience of the other anterior to any conceptualization. The human form's refusal of any concept is the fundamental indication that we are indeed confronted with another rational being. And while it is not yet a full recognition of right, it is nevertheless the originary moment of a non-cognitive recognition. The second moment arises as a consequence of this failed conceptualization. Without any purposiveness inherent in this observed being, the observer is forced to supply an external concept or purposiveness. As Fichte explains, "(b)ecause it is impossible to superimpose upon a human shape any concept other than oneself, every human being is inwardly compelled to regard every other human being as equal" (SW, III: 81). The rational observer must supply his or her own concept: the concept of equality. While in the first moment the experience of the other was one of primordial recognition, here we have a clear transcendental recognition of right through the transfer of the concept of "equality."

In speaking of the human form as a "product of artifice," Fichte explains that the "faculty of judgment" grasps or unifies the whole – not through the parts, but teleologically, "as an end outside of itself" (SW, III: 78). As we noted, there are two distinct but related moments. First, the human form itself is without concept: it finds its concept outside of itself. Second, the human form or body partakes of sense or the sense world, but is fundamentally undetermined. It is in this respect that, for Fichte, the other stands, as Luc Ferry emphasizes, as an empirical sign of freedom. The human body, however, as an empirical sign of freedom, represents an antinomy: it both partakes of the sensible, causal world, and the realm of freedom. Kant, of course, designated this type of conflict as the *third antinomy* (freewill vs. determinism). We are now confronted with two related antinomies. The other antinomy is the antinomy of teleological judgment (mechanism vs. purposiveness). The body, as an empirical sign of freedom, is also determined both by mechanism and a purposiveness beyond itself.

Before we explore these antinomies in greater detail in the next section by turning to Kant more directly, it is worth emphasizing that the fundamental paradox we have stumbled upon is that the determination of a being as rational stands on an aesthetic ground. We bestow the concept of rationality, and thus equality, only on that living percept that embodies, in Kant's words, a "purposiveness without purpose." Such a tentative argument, however, demands further exposition.

2 The Kantian Foundations of Fichte's Transformation of Aesthetic Judgment: Between the Third Antinomy and the Antinomy of Teleological Judgment

Fichte's search for an empirical sign of freedom must be understood in the context of the Kantian problem of how moral freedom is possible in the phenomenal world. Of course, another way of asking this is "how is freewill possible in a world determined by causality?." Kant recognized the difficulty of such a thought in his explanation of the third antinomy in the First Critique. The third antinomy, in effect, asked how freewill would be possible in a causally determined world.

Following the lead of scholars like Alex Philonenko and Luc Ferry, I will show that Fichte believed Kant's solution to the third antinomy to be inadequate. Consequently, he would attempt to resolve the third antinomy through the antinomy of teleological judgment.[8] Such a suggestion seems to make sense since even Kant makes clear that a possible resolution to the third antinomy lies in the *Critique of Judgment's* antinomy of teleological judgment (CJ: 265–301/GS, V: 385–415). While we have already briefly explained the third antinomy, we now turn to explore the antinomy of teleological judgment.

In the *Critique of Pure Reason*, Kant argues that the world is not mechanism alone, but from the perspective of the finite transcendental subject, it is penetrated and directed by a purposiveness. Kant is *not* arguing that nature is intrinsically purposive, but rather, as finite beings, there stands a regulative ideal of reason that leads us to the idea of a conceptual totality, to the idea of a purposiveness by which we are able to attribute a coherent unified end to the varied causal mechanisms of an organism and, by extension, to nature as a whole. Teleological judgments then, are subjective, reflective judgments. Reflective and cognitive teleological judgments make use of reason's determinate concept of purpose, but apply it only subjectively. Here, nature is attributed a subjective purposiveness. Consequently, a teleological judgment (as a reflective, rather than determinative judgment), is best understood according to Kant as "a maxim imposed … by reason" (GS, V: 98; CJ: 280).

In the context of teleological judgment then, the third antinomy of freedom and causality strives towards a tentative resolution in which the theoretical claims of causality ultimately point towards the supersensible realm of freedom (which had formerly only defined the practical). Insofar as we are not infinite, but finite beings, we cannot rule out freedom, or purposiveness in nature. The theoretical postulation of an indeterminate supersensible in teleological judgment readily leads to a moral teleology (GS, V: 455; CJ: 345–6) in which the theoretical demand for a final cause is united with the moral concept of freedom.

Now the methodological advantages of resolving the third antinomy through the antinomy of teleological judgment is that by explaining how the notion of finality co-exists within the causal world, the antinomy of teleological judgment suggests that another account of the world – perhaps one of freedom – is possible (and not necessarily or truly antithetical). When one asks of the status or reality of the antinomy per se, it is an aesthetic reading that suggests that the antinomy is perhaps more perceived than real. For instance, to what extent can the principle of causality be thought of as a principle of reflective judgment?

Insofar as the principle of causality, like any transcendental condition, is constitutive of experience, such a principle stands as a very model of determinative judgment.[9] Nevertheless, the principle of causality, as a transcendental category, is wholly "regulative" in regard to experience. It does not instantiate "real" existence. Luc Ferry explains: "The principle of causality is determinative at the level of possible experience and reflective at the level of real experience."[10] The point here is that the idea of finality is invoked as a reflective judgment for at least two reasons. First, because an explanation by means of mere mechanism remains, in certain instances, highly improbable; and second, that without such reflective judgments we would be compelled to posit the epistemic reality of objects like God and the Thing-in-itself.[11]

3 The Antinomies of the Empirical Sign of Freedom

Fichte can be understood to resolve Kant's antinomy of teleological judgment by developing the notion of the articulated body as an instance of free finality in the phenomenal world.[12] Fichte will show that the body stands as an empirical sign of freedom: a free finality distinctly different from both the natural finality of an organized being, and the causality of mere mechanism.

In the *Vocation of the Scholar* Fichte is at pains to distinguish an organism, as a unity organized by the principle of finality, from mere causal mechanism. He explains: "the question remains: how to distinguish an effect produced in experience by necessity from a similar effect produced through freedom" (SW, IV: 304).[13] What he suggests is needed "is another distinguishing mark." This new distinction will be between organization and life. To be fair, these three levels or distinctions – mechanism, organization, and life – were already present in Kant. *Fichte's true innovation is in offering an empirical criterion for life*. Thus, while Kant would define life in the *Critique of Practical Reason* as the "faculty a being possesses of acting according to its representations," Fichte will attempt to describe the empirical criterion for life in the phenomenal world.[14] He does so through the notion of the articulated body.

While humanity is easily distinguishable from mere organization – like that of plants – what is required is a distinction that separates us from other animals, from other articulated bodies. At this point, Fichte is largely following the Kantian definition of living beings, as beings able to act according to representations (and having articulated bodies). What Fichte adds is the qualifying terms of determined and undetermined free movement (*bestimmte und unbestimmte freie Bewegung*) (SW, III: 79). Such a qualification is made in order to explain that while animals move by representations, and are largely a function of instinct, and thus *determined*, humanity, by contrast, moves according to representations that are the product of freewill, and are thus *undetermined*. In this sense humanity stands as pure possibility.[15]

Since the ego is not a particular essence, but is defined by act, the essence of humanity is precisely a nothingness, a *tabula rasa*, that makes possible Fichte's understanding of humanity as a power of pure possibility. Fichte writes: "Every animal is what it is, man alone is originally nothing at all; what he must be, he must become (*was er sein soll, muss er werden*) … malleability, as such, is the character of humanity (*Bildsamkeit, als solches, ist der Character der Mencheit*)" (SW, III: 79–80). Malleability then, is a description not only of the character of humanity, but also of the *mode* of humanity's indeterminate freedom. Humanity's "mode" is its malleability, and this *Bildsamkeit*, as *das Bild*, also expresses its capacity to stand as a transparency to what is transcendent to it.[16] It is this visible instance of the human body and its pure possibility in "undetermined free movement" that would seem to offer an empirical sign of freedom, and thus point to a supreme realm of moral freedom. It is in this sense that Fichte attempts to complete Kant's *Critique of Judgment*. He offers a justification or criterion for thinking the purposiveness or finality of humanity within the natural world through an analysis of the undetermined free movement of the articulated body. And it is this material body that stands as a phenomenal sign or symbol of freedom.

4 The Body as Symbol and Empirical Sign of Freedom

While an array of mechanical causes can be unified through the attribution of a specific purpose we designate as an organism, it is the *human* body, we recall, according to Fichte, which – since it cannot be attributed a specified purpose – is precisely itself a sign of the supersensible. Kant's resolution of the third antinomy through teleological judgment, allows us to understand how the body uniquely stands at the juncture between phenomenal and noumenal worlds. If we are to understand how the body stands as a symbol of freedom in its indeterminacy as the distinguishing character of humanity, Kant's account of the beautiful as the "distinguishing property of man," leads one to surmise that an investigation of the power of the human body in intersubjectivity would further demand an account of aesthetic judgment.

The human body, as a symbol of freedom and the supersensible, is a work of beauty, a purposiveness without purpose. While all bodies, of course, are not empirically beautiful, I am suggesting that for Fichte the recognition of the indeterminateness of the human form, as a symbol of the supersensible, affects within the observer something on the order of what Kant describes as that harmony of faculties known as aesthetic judgment. In other words, I am arguing that the key to understanding the body as a power of communicative summons, through its symbolic reference to the supersensible, lay in part in Kant's transition between teleological judgment and the judgment of taste. Kant himself was already profoundly aware of the intimacy of teleological and aesthetic judgment. Kant explains the intersection of these two forms of reflective judgment as follows: "Hence the object is called final, only because its representation is immediately connected with the feeling of pleasure; and this representation itself is an aesthetic representation of the finality"(GS, V: 189).[17] The human body, as Fichte articulates it however, makes the intersection of teleological and aesthetic judgment still more clear. While neither type of reflective judgments (teleological or aesthetic) are determinative (i.e., determine objects), teleological judgment is typically based on the concept of purposiveness *with* purpose, while aesthetic judgment refers to a purposiveness *without* purpose. In other words, while with teleological judgment, through the concept of nature's "subjective purposiveness" (nature's purpose for our subjective judgment) we might attribute a particular purpose to a given organism – like a snake – the aesthetic judgment of the beautiful is wholly without purpose. In Kant's words, "apart from a relation to the subject's feelings, beauty is nothing by itself" (GS, V: 218; CJ: 62–3). By contrast, teleological judgment is a reflective judgment that nevertheless makes reference to a concept. Beauty, in the instance of Kant, and the human body, in the instance of Fichte, each carry the same signifying weight as a symbol.[18] In each case the symbol signifies freedom, morality, and the supersensible. This symbol of beauty and/or the body was made possible by the rapprochement of sensible and intelligible worlds through the explanation of teleological judgment.

It must be reiterated that teleological and aesthetic judgment are both forms of reflective judgment. My point is that insofar as teleological judgment identifies the subjective purposiveness of a given organism in nature, things turn out to be much more complex with Fichte's account of the human body which – like Kant's account of beauty – is defined as a purposiveness without purpose. Here, I suggest, the two forms of reflective judgment – the teleological and the aesthetic – are intimately bound in the GNR's account of intersubjective recognition.

The initial moment of recognition is an immediacy that occurs through aesthetic judgment: the human form exhibits a purposiveness without purpose. In the second moment, however, a recognition of right occurs through teleological judgment: it arises through an application of the external concept of purposiveness. And it is here, between these two moments of reflective judgments, that the entire dynamic of recognition transpires.

The empirical component of aesthetic judgment, which occurs in the empirical percept of the human body as a sign of freedom, is itself significant. As Kant himself acknowledges, there is an empirical basis to the judgment of taste: an empirical interest in the beautiful prepares the way for cognitive agreement. An empirical interest in the beautiful leads to rational accord because, as Kant affirms, the "beautiful is what without a concept is liked universally" (GS, V: 219; CJ: 63–4). The judgment of taste allows Kant to deduce the subjective universality in which one can claim, *a priori*, a universal assent, a common bond beyond the subsumption of the particular to a universal concept. Kant calls this idea of a subjective universality to which all must assent *a priori*, a common sense, or *sensus communis*.

While Kant himself makes clear that the antinomies of teleological and aesthetic judgment are manifestations of the same fundamental antinomy, the antinomy of pure reason, this reciprocity is perhaps most clear in Fichte's articulation of the human body. As a pure nothing, the human body stands as both a material symbol of the supersensible (teleological antinomy), and like Kant's account of beauty (judgment of taste), as an entity characterized by its power to effect an aesthetic judgment.[19] The body then evinces an aesthetic of pure reflection by which one's subjective self-awareness is given universal validity as a *sensus communis* or, in the register of Fichte, as universal – as a fundamental social bond, consecrated though an awareness of one's own freedom, made possible by the percept of the body of the other.

5 Sensus Communis

Common sense (*sensus communis*) is common. It stands as the possibility of a subjective universal claim, precisely because this feeling or self-feeling results from "the free play of our cognitive powers," or attunement that occurs universally in every rational being (GS, V: 238; CJ: 88). Kant emphasizes that "it is not the pleasure, but it is the universal validity of pleasure" with which he is concerned – yet it is nevertheless feeling which remains the form or conduit of this universal communicability.

To the extent that the *sensus communis* represents the possibility of "the universal communicability of our cognition," much is at stake here for Kant. Yet, if for Kant aesthetic judgment offers "proof" of the intersubjective, and thus universal (objective) nature of subjective judgments, their origin in aesthetic feeling gives us a further foothold in attempting to understand the affective basis of the social relation. Since aesthetic judgments are non-determinative, non-cognitive judgments, what stands in for the conceptual predicate, seems to be precisely feeling (GS, V: 288). In fact, according to Kant it is the "feeling of pleasure (or displeasure)" which "serves … in place of the predicate" (GS, V: 288). In other words, I, as subject, am feeling myself. But since the very constitution of the ego is defined by the auto-affective feeling which purportedly stands as predicate, what we are dealing with in the phenomena of aesthetic feeling is a mental state already anterior to the representational structure delimited by the terminology of subject and predicate.

Yet, as many commentators recognize, the exact nature of the *sensus communis* is unclear.[20] While the *sensus communis* can on the one hand be thought of as a principle of judgment, it is nevertheless also a feeling.[21] The difficulty Kant enters into is to explain how a subjective feeling could attain a universal communicability. Kant suggests that the possibility of such a universal communicability lies in feeling. He writes, "… if cognitions are to be communicated then the mental state … must also be universally communicable. For this attunement is the subjective condition of [the process of] cognition, and without it cognition … could not arise" (GS, V: 238; CJ: 88). Affectivity is what makes cognitive communicability possible: it is the mental state or feeling which makes possible the universal assent defined by the *sensus communis*.[22] Our feeling of this attunement, the subjective condition, is what establishes a universal communicability. In other words, as stated above, if the predicate of this non-cognitive judgment is itself feeling – the feeling of pleasure or displeasure – then what is being felt is feeling itself. In more Fichtean terms, it is the feeling of feeling, that immediacy beyond the pleat of reflection – epitomized in the system of sensibility known as the body – that is the ground of that universal communicability Kant refers to as *sensus communis*. Such a claim, however, demands more explanation.

While Kant's account of aesthetic judgment is extremely insightful in helping us understand the dynamic of influence exerted by the human body in the *Aufforderung*, Kant's approach, from the perspective of Fichte, remains too limited: his account of community is not dynamic enough.[23] For Kant, as we noted, the *sensus communis* defined a common feeling, a common state that could be predicated of others universally. Yet while such a claim makes possible both knowledge and communication by establishing the universality of certain subjective judgments, it nevertheless only explains the possibility of communication, rather than the initial act or dynamic of communication which first constitutes the original moment of social interaction. The difference between Kant's and Fichte's respective approaches might be further brought to relief through the language of "faculties." As we will see, if for Kant the aesthetic powers of the imagination are ultimately demarcated by the parameters of the understanding, for Fichte the imagination is given no such bounds. Let us look then at the mental state called "aesthetic pleasure" from the perspective of the faculties.

The universality which occurs in aesthetic judgment and produces the feeling called pleasure results from the free play between the imagination and the understanding. The relation between these faculties, however, is more complex than the term "free play" would indicate. Thus, the pleasure one finds in aesthetic judgment is "the imagination's free conformity to the law" – the law of the understanding. For Kant, while a harmony is established between the imagination and understanding, the representational structure of consciousness still demands that the understanding retain its throne.

As we noted, however, Fichte's attempt to delineate a pre-representational self led him to radicalize the power of the imagination so that the understanding would no longer be the seat of transcendental spontaneity; it would now be located in the imagination.[24] Thus, if it is in the judgment of the beautiful that aesthetic consciousness (as the harmony of the faculties) arises in Kant, and thus, as a *sensus communis*, constitutes an intersubjective validity, what is the dynamic of communication that arises in intersubjective recognition for Fichte with the appearance of the human body as a symbol of the supersensible? To what extent are we to speak of an aesthetic consciousness in Fichte, and if so, how? In other words, what is the equivalent of the Kantian harmony of the faculties which, in the instance of Fichte, arises in the process of recognition with the percept of the human body? An answer to such a question, of course, would require a re-interpretation of "common sense" in more explicitly Fichtean terms.

In "The Spirit and the Letter of Philosophy" Fichte engages quite explicitly with the Kantian notion of *sensus communis* (*Gemeinsinn*). He explains his use of the term through the image of the artist. Fichte writes: "What the inspired man (*Begeisterte*) finds in his breast lies in every human breast, and his capacity is the common capacity (*Gemeinsinn*) of the whole species."[25] It is the figure (*Gestalt*) of the artist itself – and not any mere beautiful object

– which has the capacity to convey this *Gemeinsinn*, and thus signals the significance of the human form for establishing community in the work of Fichte. Ultimately then, as witnessed in the difference between the "Spirit and the Letter of Philosophy" and in the *GNR*, Fichte makes the transition from the figure of the artist as a concrete universal who, as a point of access to the absolute, conveys *Gemeinsinn*, to that point in the *GNR* in which the human body of each individual functions as a work of art. As a transparent conduit of the absolute, each human body stands, as the artist, as an incarnate work of beauty.

Of course while one might argue that some bodies are more aesthetically pleasing, more beautiful than others, such an argument misses the point. What Fichte is trying to demonstrate is that it is the percept of the human form itself, the mere recognition of another human being – in its most basic form – which effects that reflective judgment within us called a judgment of taste. Thus, Fichte suggests, it is a consequence of this recognition of another rational being, by means of the percept of the human form, that we experience an aesthetic response that Kant referred to as common sense (*Gemeinsinn*). And it is this immediate aesthetic experience, a pre-cognitive aesthetic recognition, which would seem to precede any consequential transcendental deduction of right.[26]

Notes

1 One of the more vexing questions, which, in the context of our present discussion, must be left in abeyance, is precisely the role of applicability, or the role of the empirical in Fichte's account of the transcendental deduction of right. I have argued elsewhere that Fichte's account of the transcendental is reformulated in such a way that it is with reference to experience that transcendental claims are falsifiable. See Fichte's reference (IWL: 32), as well as my work *Spirit in the Age of Technology: the Fichtean Imagination and the Medium of the Social* (dissertation, State University of New York, Binghamton, 2001). Robert R. Williams also addresses this issue in his work, *Recognition: Fichte, Hegel, and the Other* (Albany: State University of New York Press, 1992): 37–43.

2 Fichte uses both German terms *Gestalt* and *Gesicht*. The German word *das Gesicht* has a multivalent meaning. It implies both the face and the look. Such an account which seeks to explore the influence of another, anterior to any transcendental account, particularly in the discourse of "the face," would seem to have much in common with the project of the twentieth century French Philosopher Emanuel Lévinas. See for instance my work, "Lévinas Face to Face with Fichte," in *The Southwest Philosophy Review*, 16:1 (2000): 151–60.

3 See my article "The 'Subtle Matter' of Intersubjectivity in the *Grundlage des Naturrechts*," in Daniel Breazeale and Tom Rockmore (eds), *New Essays on Fichte's Later Jena* Wissenschaftslehre (Evanston: Northwestern University Press, 2002).

4 An index of the importance of the Kant's *Critique of Judgment* for Fichte's larger philosophical project is provided by the following remark. Fichte writes in *Concerning the Concept of the Wissenschaftslehre, or of So-Called Philosophy*: "The author remains convinced that no human understanding can be advanced further than that boundary on which Kant, especially in the *Critique of Judgment*, stood ..." (EPW, 95).

5 See CJ, s41. My citations from Kant's *Critique of Judgment* are from his *Gesammelte Schriften*, ed. Königlich Preussischen Akademie der Wissenschaften (Berlin and Leipzig: de Gruyter, 1922). The citation is abbreviated as GS, followed by volume and page number. I have generally cited the following translation, with only minor changes: the *Critique of Judgment*, trans. Werner S. Pluhar (Indianapolis/Cambridge: Hackett Publishing Company, 1987). Abbreviated as CJ. Now although Kant will argue that while empirical interest in the beautiful – as a form of sociability – prepares the way for intellectual, cognitive assent, he insists that such empirical deductions should not be conflated with transcendental ones. For Fichte, however, we recall, the very validity of the transcendental claim will depend upon the falsification (or, non-falsification) of the empirical proof (IWL, 32). In this sense, for Fichte, the articulation of the actual grounds of intersubjective influence is of great consequence.

6 Luc Ferry also uses the terminology of both sign and symbol to describe Fichte's notion of the articulated body. See Luc Ferry, *Political Philosophy 2: The System of the Philosophies of History*, trans. Franklin Philip (Chicago: University of Chicago Press, 1992): 163. While some might argue that the body cannot be both sign and symbol, specifically, that the human body, as an empirical sign of freedom, cannot also stand as symbol in the Kantian sense, Fichte does intend the body to be precisely this very site of contradiction. As I will argue (following Ferry), the body stands as the site of a dual antinomy. It stands as a possible unity of teleological and aesthetic judgment. In the Third Critique, Kant argues that the beautiful stands as a symbol of the morally good (s41–2). As he explains, a symbol is offered as an analogy of an idea of pure reason, like freedom, "to which no sensible intuition can be adequate." The articulated body for Fichte is not a mere instance of the beautiful, but from the perspective of an aesthetic account of intersubjective recognition, the body itself catalyzes a judgment of taste. To the extent that the human body marks the experience of the beautiful, it can be said to "symbolize" morality. The paradox, of course, is that to the extent that it stands as an *empirical* sign of freedom, it would seem to break with a strict Kantian understanding of symbol.

7 Luc Ferry emphasizes Fichte's understanding of the body as an empirical sign of freedom in his work. Ferry's interpretation of Fichte's relation to Kant's aesthetics was crucial in shaping my own understanding of Fichte's notion of subtle matter within the framework of Kantian aesthetics.

8 Ibid.

9 Ferry: 154.

10 Ibid.: 155.

11 Ibid.

12 Ibid.: 167

13 Cited in Ferry: 164.

14 Ibid.

15 Fichte explains: "Its articulation ... must be incomprehensible in any determined conception. ... There must not be a determinedness (*Bestimmtheit*) of articulation, but an infinite determinability of articulation; not a development, but a developability ... A rational observer of the human body can unite its parts in no conception except in the conception of a rational being like himself, or in the conception of freedom given to him in his self-

consciousness. He must subsume the conception of his own self to his contemplation of that other human body, because that body expresses no conception of its own … every animal is what it is; man alone is originally nothing at all" (SW, III: 80).

16 This description of humanity in terms of a malleable image is quite suggestive in view of Fichte's later articulation of the imagination in terms of a metaphysics of imaging. In the last period of his thought Fichte describes the height of the moral achievement of an individual in terms of one's ability to stand as a transparent image or conduit of the absolute.

17 Emphasized and cited in Paul Guyer's *Kant and the Claims of Taste* (Cambridge: Harvard University Press, 1979): 68.

18 See note 6.

19 While we suggested earlier that Kant was aware of the intimacy of aesthetic and teleological judgments, insofar as the judgment of finality was linked to the feeling of pleasure (GS, V: 189), I am certainly not suggesting that there is an unproblematic relation between the two forms of judgment. In fact, following Philonenko and Ferry in suggesting that Fichte hoped to unify Kant's teleological and aesthetic judgment through the notion of the empirical sign of the human body, is not to claim that Fichte was altogether successful in undertaking such a task.

20 Donald W. Crawford emphasizes this in his work *Kant's Aesthetic Theory* (Madison: The University of Wisconsin Press, 1974).

21 While Crawford emphasizes that the *sensus communis* can be understood as a feeling, Guyer seems less convinced. For insight into this contentious point see Crawford and Guyer.

22 Although Fichte typically uses the German word *Gefühl* rather than *Affectivität*, his notions of self-feeling and the *Anstoss* would seem also to convey the idea of mutual influence in terms of affection. For instance, Michel Henry uses the terminology of hetero-affection and auto-affection to describe the emergence of the cogito in ways not unlike Fichte's. See Michel Henry's, *The Genealogy of Psychoanalysis*, trans. Douglas Brick (Stanford: Stanford University Press, 1992).

23 As a limited analysis of the possible empirical basis of Fichte's account of the transcendental deduction of right, read in terms of an aesthetics, it is beyond the scope of this work to confront the terminology *Auffordering* and *Anerkennung* in any direct or detailed manner.

24 Rudolph Makreel emphasizes this point in his article "Fichte's Dialectical Imagination," in *Fichte: Historical Contexts/Contemporary Controversies* (New Jersey: Humanities Press, 1994): 7–16.

25 Cited from J.G. Fichte's "On the Spirit and the Letter of Philosophy, in a Series of Letters," trans. Elizabeth Rubenstein, in David Simpson (ed.), *German Aesthetic and Literary Criticism: Kant, Fichte, Schelling, Schopenhauer, Hegel* (Cambridge: Cambridge University Press, 1984): 88.

26 It is an open question whether aesthetic recognition merely precedes the transcendental level, or the transcendental in some way remains dependent upon it. Again, while one might be tempted to assert that a transcendental deduction of right, as a deduction of the very conditions of the possibility of right, need not be concerned with empirical matters, at minimum, two factors deeply complicate such a view. First, Fichte's assertion that the transcendental claims are in part dependent upon empirical results, at least from the perspective of falsifiability (IWL: 32), would seem to offer an important place for the empirical within his admittedly largely transcendental understanding of philosophy. Second, one would have to explain Fichte's attempt to offer, in addition to his deduction

of right, the empirical intricacies of recognition both in terms of "subtle matter" and his account of aesthetics I have offered in the foregoing chapter.

Chapter 11

Fichte's Theory of Gender Relations in his *Foundations of Natural Right*[1]

Bärbel Frischmann

Fichte's theory of gender relations, as developed in his *Foundations of Natural Right According to the Principles of the Wissenschaftslehre* and also maintained in the *Sittenlehre*, is not only philosophically and historico-culturally interesting; it is also a doctrine that draws the attention of feminist philosophers.[2] Up to the present day, the fundamental discussion among feminists centers around two problem areas, which are also important in Fichte's theory of gender. The first deals with the adequate, descriptive formulation of the terms, "man" and "woman," and raises the question as to whether the similarities (postulate of identity) or the distinctions (postulate of difference) between the sexes should be emphasized more than the other. At the same time, the epistemological place of the gender-question has to be defined: are the naturally given conditions or the socio-cultural ones to be clarified, or are the central terms "man" and "woman" only constructs discussed in the orientation of each respective praxis of life? A second problem area concerns the clarification of the normative goals that are supposed to be achieved through the struggle for women. This discussion of normative goals is frequently raised within the framework of the universalism-particularism debate. The subjects of this debate are, on the one hand, whether principles such as the political equity of autonomous citizens as well as legal equality are universalizeable rights; and, on the other hand, whether the concretely diverse situation of the particular person can be sufficiently accommodated.

In his doctrine on the marital right, Fichte undertakes a synthetic approach to the two central and, at the time, contemporary positions on gender relations, namely, (1) the enlightenment notion of the equality of man and woman as rational beings, and (2) the principled acceptance of the naturally given differences between the sexes. In the following, my interest is in how Fichte attempts to carry out this intended synthesis as well as in the results to which his attempt leads.

1 Definition of Marriage

Fichte begins his discussion on the rights of marriage with the chapter entitled, "Deduction of Marriage" (FNR: 264). This deduction does not belong to the transcendental deduction of the concept of right because Fichte demonstrates marriage prior to every possible juridical process as a natural and moral relation. He underscores that "the following deduction is not juridical; but it is necessary in a doctrine of right" (ibid.). It is only on the condition that this deduction could in fact be executed that marriage could then be addressed from the point of view of right.

> Thus marriage is not an … arbitrary arrangement, but rather a relation in which the spouses' union is necessarily and completely determined by nature and reason. (FNR: 274)

This is the case because marriage – which is essentially a union of both genders in the satisfaction of the sexual drive and the realization of the end of nature – has a fully appropriate foundation in nature and reason. The consummation of marriage is not an institution and is not bound to an institution (Church, state), but takes place in sexual intercourse:

> Where intercourse has occurred, the couple is assumed to be married … Where no intercourse has occurred, the couple can have any other kind of relationship, but not true marriage. (FNR: 281)

For Fichte, marriage is, above all, a natural and moral relation, and only thereafter a juridical one. I will now analyze these three aspects – the natural, moral and juridical – in that order.

2 The Natural Relation of the Two Sexes

Fichte integrates marriage, as natural relation, into the whole of nature. Mankind can only survive through continual reproduction. For the sake of this end, two distinct sexes exist with an inherent sexual drive. One finds a natural drive in oneself "without exercising freedom" (FNR: 267). The natural is thus everything that occurs without reason.

> The drive is itself an end of our nature, but for nature in general it is only a means. (FNR: 264)

The satisfaction of the sexual drive in intercourse – which realizes the end of nature – has, according to Fichte, the structure of the male sex being "entirely active" and the female sex "entirely passive" (FNR: 266). Fichte justifies the dichotomy of activity and passivity with the metaphysical argument that such a distinction is the guiding principle of nature in general.[3]

Fichte draws fatal conclusions from this. In view of this so-called natural arrangement, the female sex exists "at a level below" the male sex (FNR: 268). "Man can acknowledge his sexual drive and seek to satisfy it " (ibid.), but woman *cannot*.[4]

> Man can court, woman cannot. If she did, it would constitute the most severe self-contempt. (ibid.)

Fichte continues and emphasizes rhetorically:

> Reasoning based on the concept of right is of no use here; and if some women are of the opinion that they must have the same right to seek a spouse as men do, one can ask them: who is contesting that right, and why don't they therefore avail themselves of it? It is as if one were to ask whether the human being might not have the same right to fly as the bird. Let us, rather, allow the question of right to rest until someone actually flies. (ibid.)

But these are the theoretical premises. In practise, woman *can* satisfy her sexual desires, but this would degrade her and make her "sink *below* her nature" (FNR: 267); or she *can* chose the first available husband – to have children, for example – but this would show no self-respect because she had not married him out of love.[5] The satisfaction of the natural drive fulfills the natural end of reproducing the human species, regardless of whether one knows this or not. As a cultural being, however, only men know the meaning of this drive and can refine their satisfaction morally (FNR: 265).

In the *Sittenlehre*, Fichte differentiates the natural drive in terms of whether human beings are conscious of it or not – as in hunger and digestion respectively (SW: IV, 126). In a conscious drive, human beings can be active, since they are in the position "to choose actively among several possible satisfactions of the same drive" (ibid.: 162). Between the unconscious possession of drives and the conscious processing of them "lies the transition of the rational being to independence, which is here the determinate, sharp boundary between necessity and freedom" (ibid.: 125–6). Now, the sexual drive is also a conscious drive; therefore, the human being has the possibility of free choice in relation to it. This possibility of choice is the presupposition for conceiving gender relations as also a moral relation.

3 The Moral Relation between the Sexes

Fichte defines marriage as "the *perfect union* of two persons of each sex grounded upon the sexual drive" (FNR: 273). Marriage is based upon the sexual drive and is a union of *persons*, that is, marriage is a moral relation, a relation between rational beings, who are both determined through freedom and self-activity. Correspondingly, according to his own concept of morality, marriage would have to be a relation between man and woman in which both could act freely. This can only be realized through mutual recognition, whereby the man and the woman recognize one another in their personality, dignity and freedom.

Such a conception of marriage as a natural *and* moral relation, according to Fichte, contradicts the initial premise about the passivity of the woman as a principle of nature. The connection between the sexual drive and reason with respect to the man represents no problem at all; for, his sexual drive is characterized through activity and also, by definition, reason. But the woman cannot make the satisfaction of her natural, sexual drive into a rational end of her activity insofar as she cannot wish for passivity. Thus, the female sexual drive must appear

> in order to be able to coexist with reason … even as a drive towards activity, indeed as a characteristic natural drive towards an activity unique to this sex. (FNR: 266)

The specific form of the female natural activity Fichte calls *Love*. For Fichte, love is "the noblest of all natural drives" and "innate only to woman" (FNR: 269). In the context of love, the sexual union is simply the means for the man to achieve sensual satisfaction, but, for the woman, it is the means to realize her own characteristic end, i.e. "satisfying her heart" (FNR: 270). So construed, the function of "love" is problematic in four points:

1) In Fichte's philosophical concept, reason is considered as independent of drive and drive as non-rational. But, on the other side, for Fichte, the woman's fundamental drive is:

   > a rational drive, and this is why her entire system of feelings is rational and geared toward reason. In contrast, a man must first, through effort and activity, subordinate all of his drives to reason. (FNR: 304)

   Her sexual drive acquires "the character of freedom and activity" (FNR: 270), i.e., a rational quality.

> In woman, the sexual drive took on a moral form … Love is … the only juncture where nature penetrates into reason. (FNR: 269)

But it remains totally unclear how a natural drive can obtain moral and rational dignity. Woman is "rational" by a natural drive; man is "rational" by reason. Her love is the result of a natural drive; his love is the result of a rational decision and a concept. Fichte does not even grant women, with reference to marriage, any morality on the basis of concepts, i.e. women do not need their own free will to decide because their nature, as it were, "decides." Thus Fichte's unusual concept of the woman's love states:

> love is self-sacrifice for the sake of another, not on the basis of a concept, but as a result of a natural drive. (FNR: 269)

The sexual drive is not only viewed as the leading activity for the reproduction of the species; but, for women, it also becomes a rational drive or, in other words, the woman's rationality is love.

2) Fichte describes love as the "woman's natural drive to satisfy a man" (FNR: 269). She thereby becomes a means for another. Her status as a person, however, requires that she can be viewed as an end in herself.[6] Fichte tries to solve this logical problem by considering love as the specifically female way of preserving the dignity of reason in two ways. First, the woman's love is to make herself *freely* "into a means" (ibid.), i.e., into a means to satisfy the man. Second:

> in sexual union, the woman is not in every sense a means for the man's end; she is the means for her own end, that of satisfying her heart; and she is the means for the man's end only to the extent that we are talking about sensual satisfaction. (FNR: 270)

Fichte therefore retains the active/passive dichotomy in the moral realm. The woman is the means of another's end; the man is his own end (FNR: 310).

3) Fichte himself would like to uphold the ideal of a harmony between husband and wife in which each tries to satisfy the needs of the other. To this end, he characterizes the love of the woman as "self-sacrifice, as the result of a natural drive" (FNR: 269); but the magnanimity of the man as a "conscious self-sacrifice in accordance with concepts" (FNR: 273). The hope of realizing mutual sacrifice on the basis of the

hierarchical premises of marriage is, in my opinion, illusory. The civil reality of marriage is, similarly, not a reciprocal sacrifice, but was and still is (in many cases) the power of the man and the exploitation of the woman. This is only ideologically romanticized as "love" and nothing else.

4) Historically, Fichte has been acknowledged for the characterization of marriage, not as a contract, but as a relation grounded in love. For this reason, interpreters have appreciated the modernity of his account;[7] for, whoever puts forth such an interpretation assumes an understanding of love in which mutual affection functions as the basis of marriage. Also, Fichte is thought to have conceived the ideal of marriage as a mutual relation of love (FNR: 272). However, his concept of love conceals a relation of subordination. For instance, the emergence of the marital relation is not characterized through mutual love, but through the

> boundless love on the part of the woman and the boundless magnanimity on the part of the man. (FNR: 291).

From the start, therefore, the marriage relation is not a love relation on both sides. In the first place, the woman is supposed to sacrifice and subordinate herself to the man – and do so unconditionally. Only as a reaction to this is the man himself softened into becoming tender and caring to his wife. The woman is thus doubly inferior. First, she is supposed to sacrifice herself by submitting to the man:

> The greater the sacrifice, the more complete is the satisfaction of her heart. (FNR: 272)

Second, the woman cannot expect the man to love her in return, but must, as it were, conquer him through continually new forms of submissiveness. The recognition of the woman through the man does not occur because she is a rational being, but only if and because she is submissive to the man.

> She has ceased to live the life of an individual. (FNR: 271)

Her husband overtakes her public life and the representation of all her rights. From here the question is how Fichte defines the juridical relation between husband and wife.

4 The Juridical Relation

Fichte understands marriage as a natural and moral institution, not as a contract. That is to say, women are not allowed to be married or be forced to marry by their families; for, they are supposed to marry out of love: "marriage must be entered into with absolute freedom" and the state has the duty "to keep watch over this freedom in marriages" (FNR: 278). If the relationship between spouses – i.e., love on part of the wife and magnanimity (perhaps sometimes later even: love) on part of the husband – is nullified, the marriage is thereby cancelled:

> Therefore – spouses divorce each other out of free will, just as they became united out of free will. (FNR: 291)

But what is the status of right in marriage? In contradiction to his own concept of right as "the concept of the necessary relation of free beings to one another" (FNR: 9), Fichte does not ground the right of marriage on mutual recognition, but on the active/passive dichotomy:

> The concept of marriage entails that the wife, who surrenders her personality, also gives her husband ownership of all her property and all the exclusive rights she has within the state. (FNR: 282)

Yet Fichte explains that the woman "regains her personality and all of her dignity only by having surrendered herself out of love for this one man" (FNR: 270). The problem of how it is possible for a woman "to give up" her own personality still remains. Personality is the characteristic of a rational being. It is impossible to give it up; for, there is just as little rationale for giving up your body or mind insofar as they are also constitutive for human beings.

The decree of the man over the woman is unrestricted because he is "the sole juridical person" (FNR: 282). The two sexes together do not constitute personhood, but only the man alone does. According to Fichte, "there is no need for a law of the state governing the relationship between spouses" (FNR: 283). The wife has no rights and therefore has no legal opportunity to defend herself against a despotic husband, danger within the marriage, spousal abuse or degradation. She can ask for a divorce, but only if her love has ceased. The state, then, only has a function when the divorce is desired by only one of the spouses or when there is a disagreement about the allocation of property. It is interesting, however, that a double standard is again applied here. If the husband files for a civil divorce because of his wife's adultery, the state's duty is to release the husband from his wife. The wife's adultery has shown that she does not love her husband (FNR: 293). If, on the other hand, the wife files for a juridical divorce due to her husband's adultery, she should be encouraged to wait. To forgive the husband is "honorable" (FNR: 294). If she insists on getting divorced, her love is destroyed and nobody should force a woman "to remain subject to her husband" (FNR: 295).

The wife's refusal of her so-called "conjugal duty," which proves that she does not love her husband, is a rightful ground for divorce.

> A wife's suit for divorce on account of her husband's failure to perform his conjugal duty is a dishonor to her sex and a sin against nature. (FNR: 295)

The state, however, cannot accept such a suit. This argument contradicts Fichte's preliminary thesis, namely, that the purpose of sexual union is to produce descendants. But a wife has no right to demand this from her husband.

Fichte does not deny the woman's capacity to have rights. Insofar as women are human beings, they are entitled to every human and civil right. But, as wives, they are not entitled to exercise their rights because they cannot will it (FNR: 298). "The husband represents her entirely" (FNR: 282). He becomes

> her legal guardian; in all things, he lives out her public life, and she retains only a domestic life. (ibid.)

Every wife gives up the exercise of her right to vote in public affairs to her husband. Fichte assumes that the husband, in an intact marriage, discusses all matters with his wife and "will express politically to the people only the result of their shared will" (FNR: 299). Yet, this concession is half-hearted, if not "chauvinistic"; for, from where should the woman, who is confined to the household domain, obtain the ability to judge public affairs? Besides, Fichte is of the opinion that women exercise their public right indirectly through the private influence they have on their husbands:

> This is also confirmed by the history of all great revolutions. Either they were instigated by women, or guided and significantly modified by women. (FNR: 299f.)

Fichte perverts the demand of political co-determination into a mere pretence or illusory demand, first, because it would, in any case, already be realized and, second, because it would conceal the pure vanity of the woman to want to validate something in the public domain. Women who are interested in public activity "seek glory" alone:

> Vanity and the thirst for glory are contemptible in a man, but in a woman they are corrupting; they destroy that modesty and that devoted spousal love on which her entire dignity depends. A rational and virtuous woman can be proud only of her husband and children, but not of herself, since she forgets herself in them. (FNR: 300)

Fichte formally concedes that widows, divorcees or women who have never been married, have a voice in the republic and may come before a judge to represent themselves (FNR: 301), knowing full well that the social climate of a patriarchal society makes such things difficult or impossible.

5 Intellectual Capacity of the Sexes and Education

Because the woman's destiny is to love and, if she loves, to marry, she cannot hold public office. If she is married, her husband is *ipso facto* the public person. If she is unmarried, the act of marrying will make her husband the public official. Since all unmarried women, according to their destiny, could marry at some point, they are viewed, in principle, as unfit for public office. This has an important consequence with respect to education:

> women, quite naturally, are not educated to administer what they never ought to administer, and they are not sent to schools and universities. (FNR: 303)

Fichte is aware of the objections against this view: it neglects the intellectual capacity of women, keeps them in a state of innocence and denies them access to the arts and sciences. How does Fichte answer these objections? His main point is that women are not inferior to men in intellectual talents, but that, nevertheless, there is an intellectual difference between woman and man by nature. The woman is rational on the basis of a natural drive: "her entire system of feelings is rational" (FNR: 304), she "has a natural feeling for determining what is true, proper, and good" (ibid.). The woman, therefore, does not need any education because her intellectual talent – which is limited to love – presumably comes naturally to her. On the other hand, the man must, "through effort and activity, subordinate all of his drives to reason" (ibid.). The man has to form and refine his rationality, which, in part, requires education. Fichte therefore does not include women, when he writes:

> the human being must *be educated* and must *educate* himself to the status of morality; for he is not moral by nature, but must make himself so through his own labor. (FNR: 132)

The "woman sees no further, and her nature extends no further, than love" (FNR: 270), but the man "is able to acknowledge everything" (ibid.). He has the rational capacity to reflect on his drives. Where the woman's rationality is "supremely practical" and only such, the man's rationality is also "speculative" (FNR: 304). Behind the veil of a positive characterization of what women ought to become – i.e., loving wives – Fichte actually tells us what they ought not and even cannot become: women cannot become public officials, scientists, teachers, physicians, sextons, innovators, philosophers, mathematicians and so on. Although women are supposedly "supremely practical," they are not actually free beings capable of deciding, determining or controlling their own futures. As girls, they have to do what their fathers tell them and, then, as wives, what their husbands decide and even demand.

6 Conclusion

Given Fichte's rather impressive deduction of the outside world, intersubjectivity, the body and the concept of right as constitutive conditions of individuals as rational beings, his account of marriage is disappointing. It seems to me that Fichte has difficulties in applying his own transcendental philosophy to concrete, empirical matters. Instead of using his own available theoretical repertoire with respect to equal rights, he reinforces a presupposed and, to him, morally desirable hierarchy of the sexes as something given by nature. Fichte's position contains blatant weaknesses, which I will summarize in five points:

1 Fichte bases his entire argument on a metaphysical assumption about how "nature" is to be constituted: "This one difference between the sexes is the basis of every other difference between them" (FNR: 268). On the basis of this, he comes to the fatal conclusion that, in accordance with nature, the female sex "exists at a level below" the male (FNR: 268). If, however, the first link in the chain of proof is untenable, then the entire course of the argument is untenable.[8]
2 The cultural relation between the sexes is determined by the natural constitution of the sexes. This has consequences for several cultural realms:

(a) *morally*: the subordination of the woman to the man and depersonalization of women in general;
(b) *economically*: the relinquishment of property by the woman;
(c) *legally*: the loss of rights for the woman in marriage and the transfer of political power to the man;
(d) *cognitively*: the depiction of the woman as rational by nature, which diminishes her intellectuality and denies her the right to higher education.

3 The concept of love is methodologically instrumentalized to hide the inconsistency of the argument as well as Fichte's inadmissible change of levels (from nature to morality).
4 Fichte dissociates the legal treatment of marriage from his own philosophical concept of right; i.e., right as the mutual recognition of persons considered as rational beings, on the one hand, and the subordination of the woman under the man (dedication of her personality, rights and property to the man), on the other.
5 Fichte does not provide any basis or any legitimate arguments for the assumption and even demand that marriage requires the woman, as a wife, to give up her personality, independence, public life and property.

The explanation for this unacceptable conception of women and marriage can only be that the conclusion of the demonstration, in fact, *pre-determines* the demonstration.[9] Fichte proceeds in this manner because he remains imprisoned by the "common sense" of the time with respect to concrete interests such as the position of woman. However, some of his contemporaries rebelled against this so-called "common sense." The romantic philosopher, Friedrich Schlegel, who was familiar with Fichte's work, brings this correctly and concisely to the point:

> Women must only remain prudish, so long as men are sentimental, dumb and bad enough to demand eternal innocence and lack of education.[10] (KA, II, 170: 31)

What he means – perhaps as a jab at Fichte – is that marriage could be understood in such a way that each person ought to be "an individual for itself" and not "an integrated part of the communal personality" (KA: II, 170, 34). Schlegel, for example, writes:

> Indeed, manhood and womanhood, such as they are taken and usually practiced, are the most dangerous obstacles for humanity.[11] (KA: VIII, 45)

The romantic biographies speak of the unconventional relation of marriage and, above all, of the rebellion of women against captivation in the domain of the household. The romantics abandon precisely the so-called natural, emotional, and spiritual differences between the sexes. In fact, they place great worth in the social and legal equality of women, i.e., in their personal sovereignty.

Fichte established, with his concepts of morality and right, a universal concept (universal demand of equality) of mutual recognition from the best possible theoretical premises. His postulate of biological difference, however, makes each form of equal partnership impossible because it extends into the spheres of morality and right. His *Foundations of Natural Right* breaks up into a right of reason and, in the case of marriage, a naturally conditioned right. These two kinds of right cannot be synthesized. Fichte undermines his own universal approach with naturalism – at least, with respect to the female half of humanity.

Notes

1 I am very grateful to Howard S. Ponzer (New School University, Graduate Faculty, New York) for his help in translating my paper and to Georg Mohr (Universität Bremen) for his critical remarks and to Elizabeth Millán-Zaibert (De Paul University, Chicago) for final proofreading.

2 See Marion Heinz/Friederike Kuster (1998) for a summarization of feminist orientated discussions of Fichte's gender-theory and for proof of the methodological foundations of feminist reception of Fichte.

3 David Archard (2001) writes: "Nothing in his [Fichte's] general argument shows that if there must be a division, it should be into an active and a passive sex, nor that each gender should be exclusively one or the other, nor that male and female are necessarily active and passive respectively" (190). Again: "Fichte's view conforms to a popular cultural metaphor of the seed and the field: paternity is represented as primary, dynamic, essential and creative; whereas maternity is seen as purely passive, receptive, inessential and empty" (ibid.).

4 I fully agree with Archard (2001): "Fichte's understanding of female sexuality is thoroughly traditional. A woman's impulse to sexual satisfaction can never be represented to herself as that; it can only take the form of an impulse to love him, whose impulse to sexual satisfaction through her can be represented as such. This echoes a familiar picture of woman as naturally chaste creatures, or at the least creatures who are best brought up to subdue their own sexual feelings, to conceal them behind a veil of modesty" (189).

5 See also Isabel H. Hull (1996): "The first reason is a restatement of the old association of the sexual drive with animalistic nature; the second is a weakly argued identification of a woman's honor with sexual monogamy and another attempt to establish monogamous marriage on putative female nature. Both are transparent; neither is at all peculiar to Fichte" (316).

6 I cannot agree with Daniel Morrison (1996), who argues that, for Fichte, "the individual is not an end in itself" and "individuals are to be overcome and subsumed into larger wholes" (189), for example, families. Morrison cannot see the unsolveable problems in Fichte's concept of marriage. His background is the critique of the individual as "solely private," who "has not had the experience of the self-restriction born of love, which characterizes the unitary famliy, and thus … enters the public domain as a wild beast, whose actions are kept in check … by fear of the state's punitive apparatus. This is why the dissolution of the family, as an aggregate of individuals joined in love and sharing a common will, results in the collapse of civil society and the state" (188). In my opinion, Morrison puts forth the common will of the harmonious family as the solution to the problems of modern societies and undermines the sovereignity of the persons who constitute a family.

7 For example, Archard (2001) writes: "Some of what Fichte has to say is traditional and outdated. This is especially true of his views on the division of gender roles; other comments of his are strikingly modern, such as his understanding of marriage as a relationship of love" (187).

8 See Archard (2001): "Nothing in Fichte's supposedly philosophical deduction of male sexual activity and female sexual passivity establishes its required conclusion. Nothing that is besides the traditional non-philosophical prejudices and the effort to rationalise them" (190).

9 Hull (1996) describes Fichte's argumentation historically: "He … expressed in sexual terms what most Enlightened advice and educational literature had been recommending for several decades, namely, that women should be raised to please men. All of the stages of Fichte's argument had been long prepared: the interpretation of women's sexual activity as a 'giving up,' the imperative to direct her actions to 'satisfy the man,' the appeal to her dignity (honor), the hope that her sacrifice would happen voluntarily (a critical consideration to which we shall return), the appellation 'love' as the shorthand for this process, and, finally, the assertion that the process was 'natural'" (317).

10 In German: "Die Frauen müssen wohl prüde bleiben, so lange Männer sentimental, dumm und schlecht genug sind, ewige Unschuld und Mangel an Bildung von ihnen zu fodern."

11 In German: "In der Tat sind die Männlichkeit und die Weiblichkeit, so wie sie gewöhnlich genommen und getrieben werden, die gefährlichsten Hindernisse der Menschlichkeit."

References

Archard, David, "Family Law (First Annex)," in Jean-Christophe Merle (ed.), *Johann Gottlieb Fichte. Grundlage des Naturrechts* (Berlin: Akademie Verlag, 2001): 187–96.

Breazeale, Daniel and Rockmore, Tom (eds), *New Perspectives on Fichte* (Amherst, NY: Humanity Books, 1996).

Heinz, Marion and Kuster, Friederike, "Vollkommene Vereinigung." Fichtes Eherecht in der Perspektive feministischer Philosophie," *Deutsche Zeitschrift für Philosophie*, 5, Berlin (1998): 823–39.

Horster, Detlef (ed.), *Weibliche Moral – Ein Mythos?* (Frankfurt am Main: Suhrkamp, 1998).

Hull, Isabel V., *Sexuality, State and Civil Society in Germany, 1700–1815* (Ithaca and London: Cornell University Press, 1996).

Merle, Jean-Christophe (ed.), *Johann Gottlieb Fichte. Grundlage des Naturrechts* (Berlin: Akademie Verlag, 2001).

Meyer, Ursula I., *Einführung in die feministische Philosophie* (Aachen: Ein-Fach-Verlag, 1994).

Meyer, Ursula I., *Das Bild der Frau in der Philosophie* (Aachen: Ein-Fach-Verlag, 1999).

Morrison, Daniel, "Women, Familiy, and State in Fichte's Philosophy of Freedom," in Daniel Breazeale and Tom Rockmore (eds) (1996), *New Perspectives on Fichte* (Amherst, NY: Humanity Books, 1996): 179–91.

Nagl-Docekal, Herta, *Feministische Philosophie. Ergebnisse, Probleme, Perspektiven* (Frankfurt am Main: Fischer Taschenbuch Verlag, 2000).

Schröder, Hannelore, *Die Rechtlosigkeit der Frau im Rechtsstaat. Dargestellt am Allgemeinen Preußischen Landrecht, am Bürgerlichen Gesetzbuch und an J.G. Fichtes Grundlage des Naturrecht*s (Frankfurt am Main and New York: Campus-Verlag, 1979).

Chapter 12

Political Obligation and the Imagination in Fichte's *Naturrecht*

Jeffrey Kinlaw

In his 1796 *Grundlage des Naturrechts*, Fichte refers to the imagination only on five separate occasions and in the context of several distinct lines of thought. And yet, as I will attempt to show, the function of the imagination provides a pivotal premise in Fichte's argument for political obligation, specifically an argument designed to convince a prudent rational agent that her self-interests would be secured by entering a commonwealth. The general task of the imagination, as Fichte develops that task with reference to theoretical reason in the 1794 *Grundlage des gesamten Wissenschaftslehre* and practical reason in the *Wissenschaftslehre Nova Methoda*, is to reconcile opposites which otherwise are irreconcilable by discursive thought. By oscillating between opposites or among mutually opposed elements, the imagination holds these opposed elements in tension while simultaneously fashioning a substrate or image within which the opposites can be represented as to some extent reconciled and thus to make possible the perception of a particular object or the projection of a specific goal for action. In its oscillation between the inability to unite opposites and the requirement to resolve their opposition, the imagination constructs a sphere within which unity within opposition can be represented.

Consider, for instance, an agent's ability freely to exploit objects and events in the world in order to reach a goal or complete a project. All purposeful action involves an initial projection and representation of a goal to be achieved, namely, a determinate way of shaping objects in the empirical world to serve her end. An agent's free efficacy indicates the successful translation of a projected goal into a perceptible event in the natural world. In short, she makes something happen which corresponds with her aim. As Fichte avers in the *Wissenschaftslehre Nova Methoda*, the agent must select a specific goal to accomplish from among a potentially infinite number of possible goals, and she cannot make that selection without being able to grasp in one image several relevant, prospective, and opposed actions. For this purpose, thinking operates as the imagination.

> … in just this way, the same power of the imagination, in an act of pure thinking, combines absolutely opposed possibilities of action in one determinable something. Therefore, one could certainly say that the imagination is the power to grasp what is determinable {as such}, which is something that thinking cannot do, since thinking is purely discursive: nevertheless, there is a specific power to grasp opposites: the power of imagination.[1]

The imagination therefore must project the initial extension or range of an agent's prospective action, much like – to use Fichte's analogy – a painter projects a shape onto the canvas before retracing the ideal outline with her brush.[2]

Additionally, the concept of an agent's free efficacy presupposes that the object(s) within her range of action can be manipulated in as many ways as her aims require. But since an object has a determinate nature, it limits the range of an agent's prospective action and to that extent resists her efforts to attain her goals (e.g., the eastern face of a mountain precludes an eastern ascent except for the most highly skilled climbers). Thereby an opposition arises: to achieve an end an agent must appropriate objects to facilitate the attainment of her objectives, while the nature of the same object might impede her objectives and thus negate the efficacy of her action (e.g., she prefers an eastern ascent but her skill level as a climber is far less than professional). The conflict, as Fichte explains, is mediated by the imagination. In the act of oscillating between the agent's determining the object and her action being determined by the object, the imagination fashions a substrate – here time itself – within which determining and being determined can be represented. The agent's free efficacy is portrayed as a successive determination or manipulation of the object through an interval of time and toward the final attainment of her goal.[3] The task of the imagination is therefore to make *visible* the temporal and spatial substrate within which an agent can execute free actions within the sensible world.[4]

The initial reference to the imagination in the *Grundlage des Naturrechts*, however, bears directly on the issue of natural right and the problem of reconciling the free efficacy of two or more potentially competing agents. As Fichte stipulates, the concept of *Recht* requires that an agent limit her freedom so that other agents can pursue some of their freely chosen ends. *Recht* is thus "the concept of the necessary relation of free beings to one another" (GNR: 8). A representation of this community of shared freedom – the projected sphere in which one's freedom can co-exist without irresolvable conflict with the freedom of another – requires the work of the imagination. Fichte writes: "I thus describe through my imagination a sphere for the freedom within which many individuals separate themselves" (GNR: 8). Again, the imagination makes this sphere visible and accordingly enables competing agents to see how their various projects can co-exist.

Fundamental to Fichte's project in the GNR is to establish and defend the most effective medium through which to resolve competing property claims and simultaneously protect one's property – the range of one's free activity – from violation. Fichte's initial move is to provide an alternative account of individuality, one that attempts to demonstrate that individuality is a communal concept and thus to reveal the inaccuracy of traditional atomistic conceptions of individuality inherited from seventeenth and eighteenth century political theorists. Fichte clearly was convinced that his view of individuality and the relation between free individuals in a political society marked a significant advance on previous theories, which, as he insisted, had failed to provide a theory of genuine community and thus at best had established only a mere aggregate of individuals arbitrarily collected into a group (GNR: 207–8). Central to Fichte's theory of political consent, however, is an argument designed to convince the standard self-interested agent to *act* on the basis of his (Fichte's) alternative account of individuality. That is, he aims to demonstrate to the prudent agent that her self-interests are protected – and that she can have certainty of their protection – by entering a political society or commonwealth. In short, Fichte argues that negative freedom – the freedom from intrusion and violation of others – can be secured with certainty only by positive freedom – the free decision to commit a portion of one's freedom and resources to a functionally interconnected communion of free beings within which one's self-development and thus one's freedom can be attained and preserved more effectively.

A sub-argument within Fichte's overall argument defends the claim that traditional contracts, that is, as conceived between two discrete parties, fail because they cannot provide a rationally compelling motive for a prudent agent to trust the efficacy of contracts. And – here is the key claim – the problem lies precisely with the nature of the traditional model for contracts, namely, that contracts attempt to solidify a relation between two otherwise isolated parties. Herein lies also the fragility of the original conception of *Recht* whose deduction is completed in GNR 1–4.[5] Fichte's solution, as already suggested, is to present an alternative conception of the contractual relation, wherein one forms a contract not with another discrete individual but rather with a functionally interconnected whole that becomes the common will of the parties and comes to exist in the very act of inaugurating the contract. My specific claim is that a vision of the alternative theory of an association of individuals provides precisely the rationally compelling motive Fichte thinks should convince a rationally self-interested agent to offer her political consent. And more important for my purpose, the imagination alone can make that alternative conception of political community visible for the prudent agent. Put differently, the prudent agent can be convinced to enter a commonwealth for the purpose of creating a genuine *volonté générale* because the *volonté générale* will ensure that her interests are protected. And the imagination makes this general will visible as a prospective and attainable goal for action.

I will construct an argument, which, although in its details not following the letter of Fichte's presentation, remains nonetheless consistent with his overall argument and which indicates clearly the centrality of the imagination in Fichte's defense of the rationality of political consent. In short, Fichte argues implicitly that the free decision to participate in the inauguration of a commonwealth is a secondary goal toward the ultimate end of preserving the certainty that the integrity of one's property will be protected. Attaining that penultimate goal requires that one form a conception of it, and the imagination alone can make that goal visible and thus provide assurance that attaining it likewise will assure the ultimate security of one's property. As we shall see, the imagination provides the pillar of Fichte's defense of the viability of the property contract (*Schützvertrag*) – properly conceived – and thereby the corrective for the fragility of contracts in general and the law of *Recht* underlying them.

My essay will proceed as follows. In section 1 I will reconstruct Fichte's argument for the weakness of natural right and contracts, a weakness that highlights the fragility of natural right based principally on the lack of entailment between establishing a rightful relation between two individuals and *perpetuating* that relation. The fragility of natural right undermines the viability of contracts by offering no more assurance than another's good will that contracts will be honored. In the second (and final) section, I will construct a Fichtean argument (again, an argument that is consistent with the logic of the text) for political consent and show how the imagination informs the pivotal premise in that argument.

1

In his deduction of the concept of natural right, Fichte argues that individuality is a communal or relational concept, meaning that being an individual entails being in relation to other free beings, which in turn requires that we recognize others as free agents and therefore uphold the law of right. Fichte demonstrates in GNR 1–4 that the law of right – namely, recognize other rational beings as free and independent if you desire for others to recognize you as a free and independent being, and treat them accordingly – receives robust justification by being deducible from self-consciousness. For our purposes, we can assume Fichte has successfully deduced the law of right by the end of section 4. However, as Fichte emphasizes, we can establish only a hypothetical justification for sustaining the law of right and consistently treating others accordingly. After all, making the law of right a necessary guideline for one's action is a matter of free choice, and indeed one might elect not to will the existence of a community of free beings. The merely hypothetical justification for the rule of right thus exposes a crack in the theory of right, even if one acknowledges that natural right has been successfully deduced in GNR 1–4. In sum, an agent enters a rightful relation of her own free will. But there is an initial twofold response to this alleged weakness. First, one could contend, as does Fichte, that understanding oneself as a free and independent being requires as its necessary condition that one recognize another agent as a free and independent being. Since recognition of another's freedom requires the limitation of one's own freedom, recognition is a short step from a full blown relation of right between oneself and another person. Second, one could make the case that everyone desires to some extent the existence of a community of free and independent beings, again as a necessary requirement for the efficaciousness of one's own freely chosen aspirations. On the other hand, there is a difference between recognizing another agent as free and thus as having legitimate property claims and perpetually treating that person as free and continuing to honor her property claims. The fissure in the application of the law of right, originally caused and exposed by natural right's mere hypothetical justification, remains unrepaired. My recognition of S as a free and independent being and my respect for her property today does not entail my recognition and respect tomorrow. Whether I extend my recognition and respect tomorrow is the result of my own free decision.[6]

Hypothetical justification of the rule of right therefore exposes the fragility of natural right and rightful relations Fichte readily acknowledges. And this fragility undermines the rule of right and the contractual relations, which are extensions of natural right and necessary for social relationships. Suppose agents A and B recognize each other as free rational agents, make the concept of right the law of their conduct in relation to one another, and enter some form of contract. A has no assurance, apart from B's free chosen good will, that B will continue to recognize her, act rightfully toward her, and maintain their contract. Accordingly, A, assuming that she is a typical, rationally self-interested agent, has no rationally compelling motive to trust the law of right or enter a contract with B. As Fichte stresses, no agent is rationally compelled to act simply on the unverifiable good faith of others (GNR: 199). If prudent agents therefore have no rational justification for trusting the integrity of contracts, they equally have no rational justification for trusting another's future recognition since contracts are based upon a relation of natural right.

We can sketch Fichte's argument as follows.

1) Being and individual means being in relation to others.
2) Being in relation to others requires that one recognize others as free and independent beings.
3) Recognition of others as free and independent beings requires that we abide by the law of right, assuming, of course, that we intend for our actions to be consistent with our thinking.
4) Recognition and the law of right, however, provide no non-question begging assurance that those whom we recognize as free and independent beings will continue to recognize us and treat us rightfully.
5) Without certainty that others will choose consistently and perpetually to recognize us as free and independent beings and to uphold the rule of right, we have no rational justification for trusting in the efficacy of the law of right and thus the fulfillment of contracts.
6) Unless we can trust the law of right and the honoring of contracts, we have no rationally compelling motive to abide by the law of right and/or enter contracts.

In a corollary to theorem three in the deduction of natural right, Fichte concludes that individuality is a reciprocal and communal concept (*Wechselbegriff*), a "*mein und sein; sein und mein*" (GNR: 47–8). Accordingly, agents are obligated to one another "by their very existence" and united with one another through their actions (GNR: 48). This conclusion follows, according to Fichte, from the conjunction of the *Aufforderung* and an agent's ostensible desire to be recognized as a free being. In oversimplified form, the argument goes like this: X cannot posit itself as a free, rational being except by responding to the *Aufforderung* to act freely. The *Aufforderung* entails the existence of another free, rational being Y who issues the *Aufforderung*. Issuing and responding to the *Aufforderung* requires that X and Y express knowledge of each other as free beings. But X and Y cannot know that each is a free being unless they limit their own freedom in relation to each other and thereby allow the other to respond as a free being. So, if X and/or Y desires to be treated as a free and independent being, she must recognize the other and treat her accordingly. Doing so thereby obligates the agent to revise her aspirations (the range of her free efficacy) when the goal of her action involves another rational being. In sum, any *Wirken* toward the other must become *Einwirken*; that is, rational influence must replace causal determination.[7]

Suppose my goal is to get my wife Pamela to attend a political rally and fund raiser for George W. Bush Jr (a very ambitious goal indeed!). I will not physically compel her to attend, nor will I use threats or trickery to entice her to do something that she would not normally choose to do. Rather, I will attempt to construct a convincing argument for her to attend, and in so doing, I will depend upon her to complete my goal by freely stating that, after considering my argument, she agrees to attend the fund raiser. My relation with her is communal; that is, it is a reciprocity of influence and dependence (GNR: 66, 73–4). In sum, my attempt to convince Pamela will be guided necessarily and consistently by my knowledge and recognition of her as a free and independent being.[8] My rightful relation to her demands that I treat her in conformity with Kant's second formulation of the categorical imperative.[9] My respect for Pamela as a free and independent being follows (in this case) solely from my free choice to treat her rightfully. Fichte assumes, moreover, that I am a rationally self-interested agent who may lack a compelling reason to treat Pamela consistently in a rightful way. For instance, my real motive for convincing Pamela to attend the Bush fund raiser could be an unbridled aspiration for public office and thus the need to convince West Texas folks that Pamela and I consider a God and country rally where Bush is the featured speaker to be the perfect way to spend a Saturday evening. In this case, I would resort to deception to convince Pamela (not altogether uncommon for a politician), precisely because my self-interest would override my otherwise consistently rightful treatment of her. After all, my consistent rightful relation to her is based upon my free decision to enter that relation and my free decision to sustain it.

Whereas one can construct a strong modus ponens argument for an agent's consistent faithfulness to the rule of right (in the above example, my treatment of Pamela), that argument turns on a fragile hypothetical premise, which would confer less certainty on the second premise than the argument would demand.[10] Hypothetical justification for the law of right is too weak to convince a rationally self-interested agent that the law will be upheld consistently by other agents. Therefore, an agent has no rationally compelling motive to trust the longevity of any rightful relation. She obviously has the right to demand consistency from anyone with whom she enters a rightful relation. Simply put, she expects, as Fichte maintains, that the other person subordinate all of his future ends to the absolute end that he treat her as a free and independent being (GNR: 52). The validity of the relationship and the confidence in its validity depends absolutely on the perpetual sustaining of the relation. However, the fact that Susie recognizes John as a free and independent and treats John rightfully up to time t2 does not entail, and thus does not guarantee, that she will continue to treat John rightfully at any time after t2. There is therefore no non-question begging route from rightfulness at t2 to rightfulness at t3, t4, or…tn and thus no non-question begging justification that a conjunction of the law of right and free rational beings will ensure the perpetual efficacy of the law of right. Fichte writes:

> But that, even after self-consciousness is posited, rational beings henceforth must influence in a rational manner the subject of self-consciousness is not thereby posited and cannot thereby be derived without requiring the conclusion to be proved as the ground of proof. (GNR: 87)

If we assume, as Fichte does, that all agents are basically self-interested, there is no rational justification and thus no assurance that Susie's demonstration of her willingness to respect the rights of others will be maintained consistently by her. Again, in another context but making the same point, Fichte writes:

> Therefore, what is to prove another's rightfulness and capacity for rightfulness, her subjection to law, only proves this to the extent that what is to be proven is already presupposed and thus has neither validity nor meaning if not presupposed. (GNR: 138)

The same problem of circularity would apply were two parties to attempt to restore a rightful relation that has been violated. Viable restoration of the relation would depend on the original violator's consistent rightful treatment of the victim on all future occasions, but sustaining the relation on all future occasions would presuppose the restoration of a rightful relationship (GNR: 100). Why then should a rationally self-interested agent cede a portion of her freedom (i.e. limit her own freedom in relation to the other) in exchange for the certainty that her freedom will be honored and protected when she has no rational assurance or expectation that her freedom will be respected.

The same difficulties obtain when Fichte turns to a discussion of contracts. As Fichte notes, a rightful relation among individuals is contractual, since a rightful relationship requires that the parties adjudicate property rights and carve out their respective spheres of their free activity (GNR: 195). There is no assurance that contracts will preserve the security of one's freedom and interests and thus no rationally compelling motive for entering contracts.

Suppose that Susie, John, Joe, and Jim enter a contract to respect each other's property claims. Fulfilling their respective contractual obligations is simple: each does not intrude upon the others' property claims. Susie, for instance, refrains from violating their property and expects an equal commitment from them. The strength of the contract is its simplicity and negativity.[11] And yet, Susie (nor the others) has no non-questioning begging justification for trusting that Joe's (for instance) respect for her property at t1 will continue after t1. Again, she is not expected to rely simply on Joe's (and others') good will as collateral for the contract. On the other hand, there is a more serious structural weakness in the property contract that applies directly to the motive for the contract in the first place, namely, the protection of one's property.

Suppose, that Jim decides that his best interest is served by misappropriating a portion of Susie's property and violates the contract. What can Susie expect from John or Joe? According to the specifications of the contract, nothing – each is merely required to honor Susie's property claims. Therefore, Fichte seeks to underwrite the property contract, the first subcontract within a general civil contract, by introducing a protection contract, which requires Susie, John, Joe, and Jim to protect each other's property from violation by each other or a party outside their association. In contrast to the property contract, the protection contract is positive: each party must make an affirmative commitment to the others' protection and come to her aid in the event of a violation. So construed, however, the protection contract is "empty and void" (GNR: 198), precisely because it is an impossible contract, impossible because there is no way for Susie (for instance) to demand legally a right of protection from the other parties. The association's contract requires Jim (for instance) to aid Joe, John, and Susie from incursion by each other or anyone else. The contractual obligation is reciprocal, however: Jim earns the right to be assisted by Joe (for instance) only insofar as he has actually protected Joe (*mutatis mutandus* for the others). But if Joe has never had his property violated, then he has no obligation to protect the others with whom he has formed the protection contract. Since Joe has never been assisted by the others, he is thus under no obligation to assist them.[12] In this form, the contract actually never gets off the ground, so to speak. Contractual obligations do not become operative until there is an improper incursion on someone's recognized property claims. But when the first violation occurs, none of the other parties have been injured, so no one has protected them, and therefore they are under no contractual obligation to protect anyone else (GNR: 199). As Fichte indicates, this type of contract is void from the start, since no contracting party initially earns the right to receive the benefits of the contractual agreement. And, again, if an agent cannot benefit from entering a contract, namely, if her primary self-interests (the security of her freedom and property) cannot be safeguarded, then she has no rational motive for entering contracts, except perhaps when doing so is prudent.

Even if we presuppose, however, that the protection contract is viable, Fichte remains convinced that we would fail to assure a rationally self-interested agent that others would fulfill their obligations and defend her property and freedom. Simply stated, we cannot persuade her that the contract provides more resources for safeguarding her property than she alone could contribute. The protection contract underwrites the property contract for any rationally self-interested agent only if the following expectations are met. First, her defense of another's property directly shields her own self-interests. Her protection of the other is thus simultaneously a protection of herself, and she must *see* the connection. She might infer from this connection, however, that all protection is simply self-protection and that her own resources are therefore sufficient to safeguard her interests (GNR: 199). If so, then she will have little motivation to enter the protection contract. When an agent construes her obligation in this manner, fulfilling the first expectation actually undermines the rationale for protection contracts in the first place. Second, her protection of others legally entails their protection of her. But this expectation cannot be met, because, as we have seen the entailment relation, while legally valid, is materially false. Reciprocated defense of an agent's interests remains a free choice, and one can never predict with absolute certainty that a party will elect consistently to discharge her obligations. Therefore, the protection contract, which is designed to remove the weaknesses in property contracts (and contracts in general), also fails either because the contract cannot be properly executed or because it cannot offer benefits exceeding an agent's own resources.

Fichte's solution to these problems, of course, is the existence of a state with sufficient power to enforce contracts and deter their violation. In fact, the foundation for the state and the justification for political consent is a protection contract. One could present what I have reconstructed as a rational justification for inaugurating and entering a commonwealth. It must be clear to the rationally self-interested agent, however, that entering the state will correct the deficiencies inherent in standard contracts (particularly protection contracts). She must be convinced that the protection contract will meet her legitimate expectation of assurance that her freedom *will* be secured – put differently, that violations of contracts will not occur. In short, the protection contract must be a different contractual relation and therefore must more effectively unite the contracting parties.

One finds an adumbration of Fichte's solution at the end of section eight of GNR, where Fichte initially refers to Rousseau's *volonté générale*. A synthesis of natural right and power, Fichte contends, can provide justification for an agent to believe that her freedom will never be violated. The general will, as Fichte appropriates it, is a will exercising power only when willing rightfully, and when willing rightfully doing so with infallible power. In short, the general will is a unity of multiple individuals whose sole point of connection is their mutual commitment to natural right (GNR: 105–7). This is precisely the bond or unity that is effected by a unification contract, which, once it is established and executed, creates a functional interconnection among all the participants in the contract, a functionally interconnected whole that is Fichte's vision of the state. Within this whole or state, every singular violation of an individual's rights ostensibly becomes a violation of everyone's rights (GNR: 109). The key is that the contractual relation created by the unification or social contract is the type of contractual relation that can successfully assuage the agent's concerns about the security of her freedom and property.

In section two, I will offer a descriptive analysis of the unification contract with an eye toward emphasizing the nature of the contractual bond that exists among individuals within the state and explain why Fichte is convinced that this model for the state would persuade a self-interested agent to enter the state. My own reconstruction of the internal logic of Fichte's argument – admitting that I do not follow the precise line of thought in the text – for political consent and obligation will disclose the way in which the imagination supplies a pivotal premise in that argument.

2

The unification contract, a type of protection contract inaugurating a political community or state, stipulates that upon entering the state an individual contributes a portion of her resources for the maintenance of the state. Entering the commonwealth itself constitutes fulfillment of the requirements of a protection contract. To paraphrase Fichte, the promise and fulfillment ostensibly embedded in the original property contract are synthesized (GNR: 201–2). In this way, the inauguration of the state coincides with each individual's commitment of resources for protection of everyone's interests. Fichte contends that this form of contract is self-justifying, precisely because the foundation for sustaining the contract is intrinsic to the contract itself. Fichte writes: "This contract guarantees itself. Within itself it has the sufficient ground that it will uphold, just as everything organic has within itself the complete ground of its being" (GNR: 207). The analogy with an organism is instructive, precisely because Fichte's organic model of the state establishes in his judgment the functional interconnectedness among individuals sufficient to sustain the organization and resources to persuade a self-interested individual that her freedom will be safeguarded in such a political association. Fichte illustrates his point in section seventeen of GNR by appropriating Rousseau's distinction between *volonté de tous* and *volonté générale* to which he had referred earlier in section eight.

The will of all (*volonté de tous*), following Rousseau, is simply an aggregate of individuals, along with each party's private interests collected into a group. But the whole that emerges from this aggregate has no intrinsic or – more importantly – necessary interconnection among its members. Each party is simply a discrete individual who has entered isolated contracts with separate members of the group. Fichte's point is that civil contracts (property and/or protection contracts), as normally construed among individuals forming a loose association (e.g., agreeing not to misappropriate or trespass upon each other's property), are reducible practically to a network of two party contracts. But the network as such is simply an enumeration of the individual contracts. As a result, any synthesis of the individuals into a collective whole is arbitrary and thereby contrived; in short, the alleged political community is not a genuine *synthetic* whole. Since the network of contracts is formed by simple aggregation of discrete contracts and thus without any guiding rule determining the way in which the contractual relations are gathered together, the unity among the contracting parties is arbitrary and thereby without any inherent bond among the members (GNR: 207). In sum, there is no authentic *Begriff* of a collective unity of individuals. In Kantian language, their unity has no objective validity.[13] By contrast, Fichte writes, "one cannot conceive a true unification until one has indicated a bond of unification *from the concept*" (GNR: 208, emphasis mine), namely, from a determinate rule prescribing the ground and manner of unification.

By contrast, the communal will (*volonté générale*) fulfills the above requirement, precisely because it refers not to individuals as such, but rather to the functional interconnectedness among them. And their interconnection – and herein lies what Fichte views as his original contribution to theories of the state – results directly from the type of social contract that they enter. The newly conceived unification contract or refined protection contract is not (cf. GNR: 195–6) a series of two party contracts between discrete individuals. The key lies in the inherent indeterminacy of the *specific* individuals to whom one has committed to protect against violations of their freedom. The second party to the contract is neither a single individual nor all individuals taken as an aggregate of discrete persons, but rather their collective commitment to the law of natural right expressed by their functional interconnection. The one to be protected could be anyone and everyone, though her or their specific identity remains purely indeterminate until an actual violation occurs.[14]

The inherent bond that the unification contract forges among individuals, when conjoined with the fact that each individual upon entering the state commits a portion of her resources to ensure that the contractual association of persons has sufficient deterrent and enforcement power, provides a strong basis, so Fichte maintains, for convincing a rationally self-interested agent that her freedom is best preserved within the body politic. In traditionally construed contracts, the rightful connection among partners depends inescapably upon something contingent and thus unreliable, namely, the free choice of another to uphold her contractual obligations. And, as Fichte reminds us repeatedly, no prudent agent is required to trust merely the good will of others. Accordingly, no rationally self-interested agent has a compelling motive to enter traditional contracts, since she has no adequate justification for believing that such contracts will protect her interests. The bond established by the contract is simply too fragile.

Entering a state, however, serves to mitigate what Fichte sees as the excesses of individualism and thus to forge a real and necessary cohesive unity among members of the state. Protection (and property) contracts become viable for the prudent agent precisely by reconfiguring the way in which contracting parties are related, that is, organically rather than atomistically. In this way, the deficiencies in the original protection contact – that it is impossible to execute and that if executed would rely upon contingent choices from individuals to sustain it – are eliminated in the very indeterminacy of who is to be protected by the contract. Fichte writes:

> That is, in the concept of who is to be protected all individuals merged into a unity resulting from the necessary indeterminacy as to which individual will need visible protection – and what is more – as to which individual(s) will come to benefit from the law's invisibly impeding evil wills before they erupt [into some action]. (GNR: 208)

The indeterminacy of the precise, concrete recipient of protection in the unification contract transforms protection contracts from an aggregate of discrete contracts collected into a general, abstract contract to one *among* interconnected persons who are bonded specifically by the indeterminacy of the potential target of their protection. The unification contract thereby creates a natural union among members of a polity, which (along with the resources each commits to the state) more adequately ensures that a member of the state will have her interests secured and thus giving her a rationally compelling reason for political consent.[15]

Justification for the existence of and one's commitment to the political community (the unification contract) must be sufficient to convince the prudent agent that her contribution of protection is simultaneously tantamount to her own self-protection. Fichte must demonstrate how the state can deliver the requisite security claimed in the protection contract. The agent must see how the unification contract inaugurates a type of state that can offer genuine security. As we shall see, the imagination is a pivotal premise in the argument for this justification.

Now we can reconstruct what I take to be Fichte's rational justification for the unification contract as follows:

1) a rationally self-interested agent enters a contractual relation in order to safeguard her property claims;
2) she can be certain that the goal will be attained, because the unification contract creates a functionally interconnected whole expressing and enforcing the communal will of the members of the state;
3) in order to maintain her ultimate goal of safeguarding her property claims, the rationally self-interested agent sets a secondary goal of entering the state and thus contributing to the formation of the state that will protect her rights;
4) entering the state can be a secondary goal for the agent if and only if she can form a clear conception of the nature of the state and thus *see* the way in which the nature of the state provides an adequate medium through which to protect her interests.

Premise (4) follows from Fichte's general account of willing. For an agent to will a particular end, she must first represent the end to be attained. In the context of the argument for political consent, the agent must represent the goal of assisting in the formation of the state to make that goal her end. She must do so precisely so she can see that this secondary goal becomes an effective means for attaining the primary goal of protecting her property and securing her freedom. How is she to represent a functional interconnection of persons, which does not exist prior to the formation of the state? The indeterminacy of the recipient of protection in the proposed unification contract – that is, the indeterminacy in the identity of the other parties to the contract (who is to be protected) – provides the catalyst.

Since the identity of the individuals to be protected is in oscillation and thus cannot be identified, the imagination oscillates within this indeterminacy and fashions an image of the organization of individuals as a functionally interconnected whole which mirrors that very oscillation. Fichte writes:

> Thus, the concept of the one to be protected is in oscillation. It is an indeterminate concept, and from it originates the concept not merely of an

> imagined (*eingebildeten*) whole but of a real (*reeles*) whole, which is united *through the thing itself* (*durch die Sache selbst*), not simply an [aggregated] all (*Aller*) but an [integrated] all (*Allheit*). (GNR: 202, emphasis mine)

Here Fichte contrasts the image of a whole formed arbitrarily by the imagination – taking the imagination in the traditional sense of a free-floating association of ideas – and a mode of representation that follows a rational guideline, that is, the imagination in the technical sense of intuition when it follows a rational rule. As Fichte states in section five of the GNR, reason in intuition is the productive imagination (GNR: 58). That Fichte has in mind this technical sense of the imagination is evident from the text:

> This indeterminacy, this uncertainty as to which individual will be attacked first, thus this oscillation of the imagination, is the bond of unity. It is that by means of which all merge into one, and united no longer in an abstract concept as a *compositum* but in the act as a *totum*. (GNR: 202)

The imagination, in its oscillation between attempting to identify, as required, the injured party and its inability to do so, fashions an image of an organic whole of all potential victims.

The role of the imagination is thus central to the vision of the way in which the state is to originate and the underwriting of the unification contract. The conjunction of the inability of a contracting party to identify the second party to the contract and the demand that the party be properly identified – again, the oscillation in the imagination between the inability to unite opposites and the demand to unite them – binds the contracting party to other members of the inaugurated state. And the image of that oscillation the imagination fashions arises from the *real* functional interconnection among members created by the imagination's oscillation.

It is now evident how the imagination provides the pivotal premise in Fichte's argument for political consent. The imagination provides the bond of unity among individuals in the state and by fashioning an image of their functional unity enables a self-interested agent to see how the unification contract corrects deficiencies in the protection contract (or contracts in general) and the fragility in the concept of right.

Now we can complete (what I take to be) Fichte's argument.

5) The imagination enables the agent to represent the structure of the state and to project as her goal the formation of the state and her entrance into the state.

6) Since the imagination enables her to represent the structure of the state, she can see that the state to be produced by the unification contract is a state within which she has the best prospects of securing her property and freedom.
7) Therefore, the rationally self-interested agent has a rationally compelling motive, as a prudent agent, to enter the unification contract and commit herself to the body politic.

I have attempted to demonstrate the pivotal role the imagination plays in Fichte's description of the nature of the state and his argument for the rationality of political consent. As I have tried to show, the imagination has a dual role in Fichte's argument. First, it provides the point of connection among individuals entering the unification contract and thereby becomes the organizing principle for their communal will and commitment to the rule of right. Equally important, the imagination provides the key premise in Fichte's argument for political consent. The imagination alone makes visible the unique dynamics of the unification contract and the functional interconnection of wills which *is* the foundation for the state. By making these dynamics visible, the imagination enables a prudent agent to see that her freedom and property can best be secured within the state. She thus has a rationally compelling reason for entering the state and contributing to its strength and perpetuation.

Notes

1 Fichte, *Wissenschaftslehre Nova Methodo (1796–1799)*, ed. and trans. Daniel Breazeale (Ithaca: Cornell University Press, 1992): 401.

2 Fichte, *Grundlage des Naturrechts nach Principien der Wissenschaftslehre*: *Fichtes Werke III*, ed. I.H. Fichte (Berlin: Walter de Gruyter, 1971): 58. English translation, *Foundations of Natural Right*, ed. Frederick Neuhouser, trans. Michael Baur (Cambridge: Cambridge University Press, 2000). Unless otherwise indicated, all translations are mine. Hereafter cited as GNR. The climber gradually acquires the climbing skill, experience, and knowledge of the mountain in question to attempt an eastern ascent. But, as an expert would counsel, that takes time.

3 GNR: 28–9.

4 The imagination represents one's sphere of operation much like the imagination in Fichte's epistemology fashions time and space as the perceptual field within which one represents objects.

5 In GNR 1–4 Fichte argues that a *rechtlich* relation to others, the mutual recognition of others as free rational beings and the treatment of others accordingly as recognition requires, is a necessary condition for self-consciousness and the understanding of oneself as a free agent. The *preservation* of the *rechtlich* relation, however, is not entailed by the initial recognition of the other person. For this (and other) reason(s), *Recht* has only a

hypothetical justification and imposes a conditional obligation. As we shall see, the fragility in the law of *Recht* carries over into contracts and thereby undermines the confidence that any prudent agent could have in contractual relations.

6 One point that Fichte does not address directly: even if my recognition of S as a free and independent being were guaranteed, I might choose to recognize her freedom and exploit her assumption of my recognition toward some devious end. That is, some forms of subterfuge might require a rather strong degree of recognition and respect for another's freedom and exercise of that freedom – for instance, in forms of some genuine confidence operations in which the deception is to be preserved indefinitely.

7 The argument outlined assumes full recognition, unlike the insidiously designed partial recognition described in note 6 above.

8 I acknowledge that my example is not consistent with Fichte's view of the marital relations. The problem, however, lies with the consistency of Fichte's view rather than my example. Rigidly construed, the law of right seems clearly to preclude the inferiority of women in the marriage relation (or any human relation).

9 This requires, of course, a strictly rightful construal of that formulation. Put differently, treating Pamela consistently in such a way that she is not placed by my treatment of her in a position in which she would not choose freely to be is a legal or rightful requirement independent, as Fichte maintains, from moral relations or obligations.

10 The argument would go something like this: if an agent S desires a community of free beings, then S consistently and perpetually recognizes other rational beings as free and independent and makes the rule of right an inalterable guide for his action. S desires that there be a community of free beings, QED.

11 Suppose that the property contract protected not only against the misappropriation of a party's property but also included a no trespass rider. The property contract would have the following provisions: 1) each party stays off the property of the other parties; 2) the contracting parties agree to a peaceful settlement of disputes concerning property boundaries and thereby form a common will; 3) the content of their common will amounts to mutual respect for the established property lines of the other parties (i.e. one limits one's own claims); and 4) this mutual respect or common will guides all future actions of all parties where the use of property is involved. Clearly, the contractual demand is simple and easily verifiable. Each person limits her appropriation and use of property, and the test is whether or not she has done so. See GNR: 193.

12 In Fichte's terms, it always remains problematic whether Joe or the others have fulfilled an obligation under the protection contract (GNR: 199).

13 The envisioned collective unity that emerges from a *volonté de tous* is a product of the productive imagination. Without following a determinate rule (= concept), the imagination simply gathers individuals or individual contracts into an aggregate representing simply the sum of all members or contracts. The way in which the individuals are collected is purely *willkührlich*, as Fichte indicates (GNR: 207–8).

14 That is, the actual bond among them emerges *when* violation occurs.

15 Hansjürgen Veweyen objects that the transition from a disconnected aggregate of rational egoists to an authentic, organic communal will (*Gemeinwille*) is a non-sequitur. Any grouping of rational egoists, Verweyen contends, can effectuate only a quantitative whole (cf. Rousseau's will of all) but not make the qualitative leap to an organization that is more than an aggregate of isolated egoists. Verweyen writes: "That is, if the will holds in view exclusively its own welfare, then a positive, mutual recognition can arise accidentally and becomes absurd in light of the sameness of right and duty. This 'communal will' is always still not a qualitative or organic whole: quality never comes to be from quantity."

See *Recht und Sittlichkeit in J.G. Fichtes Gesellschaftslehre* (Freiberg: Karl Alber, 1975): 112. The problem, as Verweyen sees it, lies initially in the theory of natural right itself, where one finds a tension between limitation, which presupposes two discrete individuals without any determinate mode of uniting them and the *Aufforderung*, which by contrast presupposes that individuals are "always already" in unity. Verweyen writes: "How can individuals, if their perfect communal organization were possible, be transposed into an interpersonal relationship constitutive of actual freedom on the basis of an understanding of freedom in which each *primarily* limits his own sphere of freedom and *first*, though *secondarily* (perhaps for the sake of maintaining his own sphere or from an ethical impulse), recognizes the another's freedom – and in each case only as a sketched out quantity" (93–4, emphasis mine)? In sum, Veweyen makes out an inconsistency between self-limitation and the *Aufforderung*. But the root problem, according to Verweyen, is Fichte's separation of *Recht* and *Sittlichkeit*, namely, Fichte's contention that an organic community can be forged from a quantity of rational egoists without presupposing the moral transformation of these purely prudent agents. Although I cannot pursue this issue in this space (or this paper), I do not find this criticism convincing. And I am less inclined to believe that the indeterminacy intrinsic to the unification contract cannot do the job.

Chapter 13

The Universality of Human Rights and the Sovereignty of the State in Fichte's *Doctrine of Right*

Hans Georg von Manz

Introduction

The relationship between the protection of human rights and state sovereignty is not unambiguous. Human rights can be endangered by the power of the sovereign; human rights can be protected through the sovereignty of a legal state.

In this chapter the quite controversial issue of the concept of sovereignty in the history of political ideas cannot be discussed; as an introduction only a rough sketch for a possible classification of problems will be given. Sovereignty understood as ultimate authority can be distinguished in two aspects: internal sovereignty and external sovereignty. "Internal sovereignty" refers to the sovereign's capability to maintain law and order within the state. "External sovereignty" refers to the sovereign of a state as being capable to act independently towards other states and the state's independency being recognized by other states.

Using this distinction between internal and external sovereignty and the consideration that the relation between protection of human rights and sovereignty can be of positive or negative quality, I wish to outline four possible models of the relation between sovereignty and human rights, which shall serve as guideline for the discussion of Fichte's relevant concepts.[1]

1) Human, that is, civil rights as opposed to the power of the sovereign.
   The first formulations of human and civil rights referred primarily to liberal rights; they expressed the claim for protection of the individual from unjust despotic rule, like freedom from arbitrary arrest or detention, the right to a fair and public trial, freedom of opinion and expression

etc. This concept of human rights aims at limiting and justifiying the power of the sovereign. In this context the fundamental question arises if there is a right to revolution, i.e., a right for the people to overthrow the current government in order to establish a new constitution. Also relevant for this concept of human rights is the question of the right to civil disobedience.[2]

2) The sovereignty of the state as guarantee for the protection of human rights.

   In this model the sovereign guarantees by constitution and by its power human and civil rights. Here these rights are understood not only in their limiting function against the power of the sovereign, but rather the sovereignty as enabling power to grant positive rights from the basic right to such social rights as the right to work, to housing, to health care, etc.[3]

3) The infringement of human rights through foreign nations.

   It is obvious that human and civil rights are endangered in cases where a foreign power attacks a nation and tries to subjugate it.[4]

4) The protection or restoration of human rights through foreign nations.

   This model encompasses the following questions: Do foreign nations have the right to judge the situation of human rights in other nations? Do they have the right to influence other nations in order to have them restore human rights in their territory? Is there is the right (or maybe even the obligation) to other nations to intervene on humanitarian reasons?[5]

Fichte dealt with all four subject areas from his earliest writings in 1793 until his last ones in 1813 (*Doctrine of the State/Staatslehre*). In this chapter, I want to limit myself to Fichte's Doctrine of Right as it is presented in his *Foundations of Natural Right (Law)* of the year 1796.

1 The Universality of Human Rights in Fichte

The reasons for the universal validity of human rights can be found in Fichte's transcendental deduction of the concept of right. The deduction of the concept of right, which is the foundation for his Doctrine of Right, places this concept into the framework of the Science of Knowledge (*Wissenschaftslehre*). In the Science of Knowledge Fichte analyzes the necessary conditions of knowledge and consciousness. If the Doctrine of Right ought to have a fundamental unquestionable basis and justification – and Fichte does intend this as it is indicated in the title of his work: *Foundations of Natural Right/*

Law according to the principles of the Science of Knowledge – the concept of right has to be revealed as a constitutive part of the conditions of knowledge and consciousness.

In other words: the concept of right is a constitutive part of subjectivity.[6] How does Fichte achieve this assertion? The core argument is found in his theory of interpersonality. The central characteristic of subjectivity is freedom. The original experience of freedom cannot be initiated by the subject himself; for this the subject is dependent on an impulse from outside. This impulse must not be a physical restraint – otherwise the subject would find himself within deterministic, mechanical structures that exclude experience of freedom. The impulse rather must be of such kind that it initiates a free action. Fichte finds this type of non-coercive impulse in the summons [or asking/appealing] (*Aufforderung*). The summons requests a free answer, either to comply or not to comply.

Experience of freedom and consciousness of oneself, and thus subjectivity, can only be enabled within the correlation – or dialogue – of free subjects. Fichte sums up his deduction:

> The human being (like all finite beings in general) becomes a human being only among human beings; and since the human being can be nothing other than a human being and would not exist at all if it were not this – it follows that, *if there are to be human beings at all, there must be more than one.*[7]

For the existence of subjectivity it is not only necessary that there is a plurality of other beings, but that the free interaction (in the framework of asking and answering) between the human beings does really take place. This implies that the free rational beings mutually recognize each other as free rational beings. Fichte defines the specific structure of the community in which the coexistence of free rational beings is possible through their mutual recognition as the relation of right (*das Rechtsverhältnis*)[8]. Recognition of the other as a free rational being implies the concession of a sphere of action to him. Insofar as one subject A concedes a sphere of action to subject B or C, subject A relinquishes these spheres of action for himself, i.e., subject A limits its sphere of action in order to enable other subjects their spheres of action.

> The relation between free beings that we have deduced (i.e., that each is to limit his freedom through the concept of the possibility of the other's freedom, under the condition that the latter likewise limit his freedom through the freedom of the former) is called the relation of right.[9]

As an intermediate result it can be said that human existence is only possible on the basis of the relation of right. The only alternative would be a community in absolute morality, i.e., a community of beings whose will always fulfills the moral ideal. Insofar as the relation of right is irreversibly connected to human existence the right to recognizing[10] human beings as free rational beings can be called *universal.*

There is one question left: Fichte's concept of right is developed under the hypothesis: "*if there are to be human beings at all* ...." The Doctrine of Right does not answer the question if there shall be human beings or not. The justification that *there shall be* human beings has to be found elsewhere.

2 The Protection of Human Rights and the State

The transcendental deduction of the concept of right cannot be taken directly as the legal and political framework for the coexistence of real persons. To install the concept of right in a real world one has first to determine the preconditions of its application. According to Fichte the realization of the concept of right is only possible within a commonwealth (*Gemeinwesen*).

> Accordingly, there is no *natural right* at all in the sense often given to that term, i.e., there can be no rightful relation between human beings except within a commonwealth and under positive laws.[11]

Only in a commonwealth are there political rights, only in this context can one speak of a person having "a right to ...." In other words: the guarantee of fundamental rights can – according to Fichte – only be given within a commonwealth. The crucial point is how this commonwealth has to be structured in order to fulfill the following task: "how to bring about a power that can enforce right (or what all persons necessarily will) amongst persons who live together."[12]

Fichte solves this problem with a construction of three types of contracts that are interconnected with each other; all three types of contract are finally summed up in the civil contract (*Staatsbürgervertrag*). This is also the point where the fundamental rights of the individual are connected to the power of the state, its sovereignty. The first type of contract lays down the limits of the spheres of action of the individuals. It puts the relation of right into effect.

> There can be no rightful relation among persons without a positive determination of the extent to which each individual's use of is freedom ought to be limited;

> or, what amounts to the same thing: without some determination of property in the broadest sense of the word (i.e. insofar as it denotes not just the possession of real estate or the like, but a person's rights to free action in the sensible world in general).[13]

Fichte calls the fundamental sphere of action "property." "Property" is not a concept denoting (owning) objects, but possibilities of action. Thus the fundamental rights are summed up – in Fichte's terminology – as right to property. The right to property reflects the "original right (*Urrecht*)" which Fichte has deduced as the primary element in the systematic application of the concept of right. "[T]he concept of original right … is … that right that should belong absolutely to every person as such."[14] In a formal sense it is the quintessence of human rights and thus by definition universal. Fichte defines the original right: "Original right is thus the absolute right of a person to be only (a) cause in the sensible world (and purely and simply never something caused)."[15] The original right covers the rights to life, against arbitrary bodily injury, and the rights to resources that are necessary to maintain the person's life.[16] "To be able to live is the absolute, inalienable property of all human beings. We have seen that a certain sphere of objects is granted to the individual solely for a certain use. But the final end of this use is to be able to live."[17]

The agreement of the individuals concerning the demarcation of their respective spheres of action is laid down in the property contract. It is a contract of all individuals with all individuals, in which each individual grants all other individuals their sphere of action and vice versa.[18] The property contract on its part has to be guaranteed – in order that violations are prevented respectively that they can be redressed. This is done in two steps.

1) All individuals promise each other mutual protection of their property. Fichte calls this a protection contract, a contract in which "each individual would promise to all the other individuals … that he will use his own power to help them protect the property that is recognized as theirs, on condition that they, for their part, will likewise help to defend his property against violation"[19].
2) As this protection contract is initially only based on individual intentions, nobody can determine which individual actually needs the protection first. Thus this contract cannot be brought into effectiveness and remains hypothetical. The basis for its effectiveness is that all individuals unite their intentions and power into a higher unity, i.e., that they constitute a whole (*totum*), an organized commonwealth. This is the state.

The state is the medium where the individual intentions to protect the property of each are united as well as the individual power is bundled. As all individuals form a homogeneous whole by constituting the state by what Fichte calls the unification contract, this unity represents the will to right of all and has at the same time the power to coerce violators of right. Insofar as each individual contributes his part in the form of his vote and taxes, he is part of the sovereign. The individuals constitute the sovereign, and the state in his sovereignty grants the protection of the rights of the individuals.

Fichte's construction of the ideal state is of republic constitution: its characteristic is the identity of the individuals, the people, and the sovereign. The fundamental rights are after all granted by the individuals themselves, mediated through the state of republican constitution.

There are some crucial implications in Fichte's conception:

1) It is remarkable that Fichte does not mention defensive rights against the state in the Doctrine of Right. The origins of the concept of human rights in the beginning of modern times were the formulations of negative rights, i.e., liberal rights limiting the power of the sovereign towards the individual like freedom from arbitrary arrest, detention, or exile; the right to a fair and public trial; freedom of thought, conscience, and religion; freedom of opinion and expression; freedom of peaceful assembly and association. All these rights require abstention rather than the intervention of government. Fichte seems to be so convinced of his model of an ideal state and its function to promote freedom and to protect positive rights, above all the right to property, that he does not include considerations of liberal rights including the right of civil disobedience. Even the chapter on the constitution deals with measures of how the state ought to control its citizens rather than naming fundamental human and political rights.

   Fichte discussed the question of a legitimate transformation of a constitution in his work on the legitimacy of the French Revolution (*Beitrag zur Berichtigung der Urteile des Publikums über die französische Revolution*, 1793). In his Doctrine of Right, Fichte does nevertheless outline structures of control of the state and government, as uppermost structure the institution of the ephorate endowed with absolutely negative power and its ultimate remedy against misuse of governmental power in form of the state interdict.[20]
2) The relation of right (*Rechtsverhältnis*) is only being effected in and through the state. Since any communication between individuals necessarily requires the relation of right, any individual – according to Fichte – can be forced to enter into a state.

> [E]very individual has the right to force any other individual he encounters either to enter into a state with him or to stay out of the sphere of his efficacy. If one of them already lives in a state and the other one not, then the first will coerce the other to join him in his state. If neither already lives in a state, the two will unite to form at least the beginning of one. From this follows the proposition: someone who does not live in a state can rightfully be coerced by the first state that encounters him either to subject himself to it, or to stay away from it.[21]

Turned into the sphere of the law of nations, Fichte consequently takes the view that a community or a nation that is not a state can be forced into a state:

> If a nation has no government – and thus is not a state – then an adjoining state has the right either to subjugate it, or to force it to establish a constitution, or to drive it away from its vicinity. The reason for this is the following: whoever cannot guarantee the security of the other's rights has no rights of his own. Hence, such a nation would be an outlaw, devoid of all rights.[22]

These statements seem rather problematic in view of our historical experience.[23] However, this is one rare point where one gets some explicit information of how Fichte would justify humanitarian interventions. It is Fichte's opinion that there is a right to intervene in the case that a community or nation is not able to guarantee the rights of its individuals. This is however only valid for nations that are not states. Concerning the relationship between *states*, a state has no right to judge the inner constitution of another state. According to Fichte there is no interference into the internal affairs of other states.[24]

3 The Plurality of States

As shown above, the protection of fundamental rights is effective only within a state of republican constitution. Actually, it would be sufficient if there were only one single state for all human beings. According to his proposition that each individual can be coerced to enter into a state Fichte presumes that "all human beings living on the earth's surface would gradually become united in a single state."[25]

The fact that there is a plurality of states is a mere result of accidental circumstances such as geographical and historical conditions. As long as human beings living in different states do not know of each other and do not encounter each other, there is no relation of right between them. If however human beings of different states encounter each other the problem arises how their fundamental rights are protected respectively and how violations are compensated or punished.

Fichte suggests that the states mutually "guarantee the security of the other's citizens, just as each guarantees the security of its own."[26] In order to achieve this, states enter into contracts with each other. The protection against violations of rights by citizens of another state seems to be the main reason for Fichte for international agreements.

The condition for international contracts is the mutual recognition of the states. This recognition however is only possible if the contracting states are mutually assured that they are able to be responsible for their own citizens, and that they have legal constitutions.[27] Concerning the judgment of the legality of the other state, the criterion consists only in the fact that the other state is a capable agent in an external legal relationship. "It is none of its business to inquire about the other state's inner constitution, and it has no right to pass judgment on that. This is what is meant by the reciprocal *independence* of states."[28]

Fichte thus holds on to the well-known principle of international law that nations do not interfere into the internal affairs of other nations. Violations of human rights in one state are none of the business of the other state. The sovereignty of the other state must not be infringed on any such reasons.

The violation of fundamental rights of the citizens of a state through foreign powers is legitimate reason to wage war against the offending state. Fichte considers three cases:

1 the direct assault on the rights of the citizens of a state through an attempt of subjugation by another state. Each nation has the right to pursue its own development of freedom and thus it is even an obligation to defend itself against attacking powers;[29]
2 the breach of the contract between two states by one of them;
3 the denial of recognition of a state by another state.

In both latter cases, the violating state shows "that it is incapable of entering into a legal relation and therefore has absolutely no rights."[30]

To secure the rights of the citizens in different independent states, Fichte – as mentioned above – recommends a contract of reciprocal guarantee. However, it is not sufficient that states contract with each other individually. To reinsure these individual contracts, it is necessary that an assaulted state has the power to repulse the unjust attack.[31] This can be achieved if the states assure themselves mutually support against attacks of third parties and unite for this purpose in an alliance. Since the alliance is formed voluntarily, Fichte suggests calling it a *confederation of nations*.[32] The benefit of this confederation which incorporates supranational power and justice leads to its expansion and finally to the guarantee of the world peace.[33]

4 Conclusion

In the Doctrine of Right Fichte stresses the strong connection between the fundamental rights of the individuals and the sovereignty of the state. Prerequisite is the structure of the commonwealth as a republic state, i.e., the sovereign is constituted by the individual members of the commonwealth. As Fichte has depicted the *ideal* of the state, he has no motive to explicitly postulate liberal rights.

Each nation has its right to pursue its way towards the realm of reason (*Freiheitsentwicklung*). Thus any intrusion from outside that infringes the rights of its citizens must be rejected. The preservation of the sovereignty of a nation is inviolable right. As the judgment of the inner constitution of a state is none of the business of other states, interventions to protect basic rights are illegitimate according to Fichte. The only function of a confederation of nations is to safeguard nations against external threats. Considering Fichte's explicit writings on state sovereignty and international law, it is hard to find new solutions from his considerations to today's problems like the question of humanitarian intervention.

Another approach would be to adopt Fichte's fundamental principles and apply them to problems of today. An example would be the application of his theory of recognition in international relations in a broader sense as Fichte did himself. The states would recognize each other not only on the basis of external legal relations, but would include as condition for recognition that they grant their citizens equal fundamental rights. This form of recognition is comparable to the interpersonal recognition that is not only founded on reciprocity but includes as well an appeal to the moral law. If the confederation of nations were not restricted to legal and security relations, but also were based on moral as well as on cultural and economic grounds, there would grow a community of nations which would promote the establishment of fundamental rights gradually all over the world.

Notes

1 There are only few papers which deal with Fichte and the right of nations respecting international relations, e.g.: Richard Schottky, "Internationale Beziehungen als ethisches und juridisches Problem bei Fichte," in Klaus Hammacher (ed.), *Der Transzendentale Gedanke. Die gegenwärtige Darstellung der Philosophie Fichtes* (Hamburg: F. Meiner, 1981): 250–77; Richard Schottky, "Selbstbehauptung und Anerkennung als Prinzipien der internationalen Politik," in Helmut Girndt (ed.), *Selbstbehauptung und Anerkennung. Spinoza – Kant – Fichte – Hegel*, in collaboration with Karl Hahn and Manfred Walther, with a Foreword by Richard Schottky (St Augustin: Academia, 1990): 119–27; Ives Radrizzani, "Ist Fichtes Modell des Kosmopolitismus pluralistisch?," in Klaus Hammacher, Richard Schottky and Wolfgang H. Schrader (eds), *Kosmopolitismus und Nationalidee. Fichte-Studien*, 2 (1990): 7–19.

2 Fichte dealt with this problem in his 1793 work *Reclamation of the Freedom of Thought from the Princes of Europe (Zurückforderung der Denkfreiheit von den Fürsten Europens, die sie bisher unterdrückten)* and *Contribution toward Correcting the Public's Judgments of the French Revolution (Beitrag zur Berichtigung der Urteile des Publikums über die französische Revolution).*

3 These are crucial points in Fichte's *Foundations of Right* and *The Closed Commercial State (Der Geschlossene Handelsstaat).*

4 Fichte dealt with this question in his considerations of the Napoleonic invasion.

5 Cf. my article "Menschenrechtsschutz und Achtung staatlicher Souveränität – eine Pflichtenkollision internationaler Politik? Ethische Überlegungen zu Bedingungen, Rechtfertigung und Notwendigkeit humanitärer Intervention," in G. Orsi et al. (eds), *Prinzipien des Rechts, Rechtsphilosophische*, Hefte Bd VI (Frankfurt am Main u.a.: Lang, 1996): 71–98; reprinted in Kurt Seelmann (ed.), *Aktuelle Fragen der Rechtsphilosophie* (Frankfurt am Main u. a.: Lang, 2000): 105–30.

6 Cf. my book, *Fairneß und Vernunftrecht. Rawls' Versuch der prozeduralen Begründung einer gerechten Gesellschaftsordnung im Gegensatz zu ihrer Vernunftbestimmung bei Fichte* (Hildesheim: Olms-Verlag, 1992): 93ff.

7 FNR: 37; SW, III: 39.

8 SW, III: 41; FNR I, §4.

9 FNR 49; SW, III, 52.

10 *Recht auf Anerkennung.*

11 FNR: 123; SW, III: 148.

12 FNR: 133; SW, III: 150.

13 FNR: 168, SW, III: 195.

14 FNR: 102; SW, III: 122/113.

15 FNR: 103; SW, III: 113.

16 "A principle of all rational state constitutions is that everyone ought to be able to live from his labor" (FNR: 185; SW, III: 212).

17 FNR: 185; SW, III: 212.

18 "Each individual has said to all of them: I will to possess this, and I demand of you that you give up your claim to have any right to it. And all of them have responded: we shall relinquish our claim on the condition that you relinquish your claim to everything else" (FNR: 169, SW, III: 195).

19 FNR: 171; SW, III: 197.

20 Cf. FNR: 151; SW, III: 172.

21 FNR: 320; SW, III: 369.
22 FNR: 323; SW, III: 373.
23 Fichte immediately qualifies these propositions: "Let no one fear that powers thirsting for conquest have anything to gain from this proposition. A nation of the kind described is unlikely to exist at all; this proposition has been introduced, not so much to be applied, but to make our argumentation complete. Any nation, provided only that it has someone to lead it in war, undoubtedly has a government" (FNR: 323/4; SW, III: 373).
24 FNR: 323; SW, III: 372 (II: App., §5).
25 FNR: 320; SW, III: 369.
26 FNR: 322; SW, III: 371.
27 Fichte refuses to combine the judgment of the external legal constitution of a state with the internal one (FNR, Law of Nations, §5). The separate consideration of internal and external legal consitution leads to a discrepancy: How can it be demanded of a state to guarantee for citizens of a foreign state, if it itself is not able to guarantee the fundamental rights to its own citizens? And vice versa: How can a state demand from other states to guarantee the fundamental rights to its citizens, if the state does not guarantee these rights to its own citizens?
28 FNR: 323; SW, III: 372.
29 Cf. Fichtes remarks in the *Staatslehre*, SW, IV: 412.
30 FNR: 327; SW, III: 377.
31 "But now war is the only means by which a state can be coerced: and so the only problem would be how to arrange things so that the just cause in a war is always the stronger and victorious one. Strength arises out of sheer multitude; thus several states would have to *confederate* for the purpose of maintaining rightful relations among themselves and using their unified strength to attack the unjust state" (FNR: 329; SW, III: 379).
32 Fichte denotes here a difference in the relation of right among individual persons and among nations. While the relation of right among persons can only be effected within a state (and thus individuals can be forced to enter into a state) the legal relation between states is not dependent on state-like structures (just on the mutual recognition). That's why Fichte chooses the concept of confederation instead of a state of nations (*Völkerstaat*), which ultimately would imply a world-state.
33 "As this confederation expands and gradually encompasses the entire earth, the result will be perpetual peace, which is the only rightful relation among states. For war – if it is waged by states who are judges in their own cases – can just as easily cause injustice, as justice, to be victorious. Or – even if it is waged under the direction of a just confederation of nations – it is still only a means to the final end, the preservation of peace; but it is certainly not the final end itself" (FNR: 329f.; SW, III: 382). Richard Schottky points to the contradiction between the assertion that international peace would be granted through an alliance of nations and the essential principles of Fichte's rational doctrine of right (Schottky, 1981: 252; Schottky, 1990: 124).

Chapter 14

Schelling's Aphorisms on Natural Right (1796/97): A Comparison with Fichte's *Grundlage des Naturrechts*

Michael G. Vater

It is commonly assumed that Schelling's early essays are Fichtean, perhaps imitations and popularizations of Fichte's formidable arguments, or, more charitably, fledgling attempts to occupy the standpoint of transcendental idealism. A look at the historical record surrounding the writing of *The Possibility of a Form for All Philosophy* and *The I as Principle of Philosophy* shows that the young Schelling was indeed following Fichte's lead, but without having a full text of his exact writings. A philosophical look at these essays shows that the young writer tended to substantialize or solidify the transcendental agency that Fichte more delicately tried to indicate with phrases such as "self-reverting activity" and "self-consciousness." Where Fichte tries to transcendentally, i.e., hypothetically, think through the noumenal spontaneity that Kant claimed is responsible for but not apparent within phenomena, Schelling habitually reifies this self-reverting activity and readily refers to it in quasi-objective fashion as "the absolute" or "the unconditioned." At the beginning of his career, then, Schelling wrote *as* a transcendental idealist, but one who did not fully "get" the position, reading Kant's and Fichte's hypothetical, constructivist accounts of cognition or self-consciousness through Platonic or Spinozistic spectacles.

After he had offended Fichte by suggesting in *Philosophical Letters on Dogmatism and Criticism* that the old metaphysics which Reinhold had dubbed "dogmatism" was a live philosophical option, not merely a symptom of moral failure, it is not surprising to see Schelling take a dogmatic approach in the *New Deduction of Natural Rights.*[1] This short work, consisting of 163 aphorisms, was written while Fichte was at work on the *Foundations of Natural Right* in 1796, though not fully published until 1797.[2] Schelling had no model from the master available this time, but, working from the same basic sources – Kant's moral philosophy and Rousseau's political philosophy – he fashioned an account of natural right (but not of politics) that contrasts interestingly with Fichte's longer, more elaborately argued treatise.[3]

A reading of the two texts, side by side, shows off their contrasting features: Fichte's contribution is more communitarian or social-theoretical, though he defends the private moments of "body" and "personal property"; Schelling's contribution is more libertarian, linking individual agency directly to the raw freedom which is the theory's basis. Both writers work with the vocabulary of "freedom" established by Enlightenment moral and political thinkers, but made problematic by the episodes of mob rule and totalitarian control within the recently stabilized French Revolution. Both thinkers subscribe to the paradoxical political axiom: no freedom without limitation of freedom.[4]

Fichte makes a novel contribution to the well-established social contract tradition of social-political philosophy in his phenomenological description of empirical freedom or agency, locating it by stages in the *body* as the arena of action, in the public space of *shared visibility* as the platform of interpersonal interaction, and in the shared sociality of living under common laws which actualizes the *reciprocity* implicit in the concept of right. Among the German idealist philosophers, Fichte's chief strengths are that he argues for his claims, though oftentimes at immoderate length, and that he notices and theoretically accounts for most of the empirical details – in this case, of social organization, law, and basic political structures. Schelling's contribution – more on the order of a Romantic "fragment" than a ponderous system[5] – is a vigorous defense of individual liberty, both against state power and against majoritarian morality. But his typical lucid style is lacking, and the text breaks off before it can elaborate a theoretical foundation for politics. I suggest that the essay is a suitable candidate for Straussian interpretation: Schelling's aphorisms employ the opaque terminology of the will's "form" and "matter," on both individual and general levels, to mask the fact that he is actually weighing the competing claims of *individual freedom* and *public morality*, and that he defends the right of the individual to free conduct – even if its content is immoral or antisocial. Whether this near "libertarian" individualism prevented the young philosopher from going on to elaborate a version of social contract pacification is an interesting question, though it cannot be pursued here.

What is clear is that when one compares the social-political theories of Fichte and Schelling, the former offers a pervasively social account of human action, law, and politics, while the latter offers a stark individualism based on the Spinozistic concept of action as power. Fichte asserts that right is self-limitation of free action for the sake of the possible free action of another; in Schelling's language, this is a restriction of the "matter" of willing. Schelling himself contends that in its "form," free action is illimitable, and that all restriction, if any, of the content of action must embody, or at least not attack, the freedom of agency that is the individual's alone. Both thinkers come at the central paradox of modern social philosophy: how to adjust the free conduct of diverse individuals through the imposition of a legal and political structure which can be justified only by appeal to that very freedom. How is self-limiting freedom *not* an oxymoronic notion, even if masked in the "nicer" language of a synthesis of freedom and law, or an ideal overlap of legality and morality?

In this chapter, I will first orient the two treatments within the tradition of social contract legal and political theory and broadly characterize their common structural approach. Then I will offer, without much comment, a brief summary of each author's account. A third section will discuss the points where Fichte and Schelling agree and where they disagree.

1

Fichte and Schelling place themselves within the natural rights-natural law tradition of modern political theorists. Since Hobbes, it had become axiomatic that existing cooperative arrangements – social-economic, legal, and political – can be plausibly justified only through appeal to "natural right," which, when stripped of social fictions, rests upon two psychological and biological ultimates: security and self-preservation.[6] The social contract tradition, as it evolved through Spinoza, Locke, Rousseau and Kant, became increasingly aware that stories of *surrender of rights in order to secure rights socially* were just that, narrative devices joining ultimate antithetic human states, the utter violence of lawless interludes and civil war and the settled disposition of all to minimally cooperate with all. As existing states became increasingly secular, national, and operated by, if not for, bourgeois individuals, philosophers became more reluctant to offer justifications of social cohesion and state power premised on theological or moral ideas, or even on traditions of jurisprudence. The social contract story was still attractive, because it is at least a secular or purely anthropological story. Unlike the early writers on political economy, however, the German Idealists could not accept at face value the thin psychology of the contract tradition, with its limiting emphasis on fear, greed, and competition. So with the wild French "experiment" of revolution losing steam, though still without settled purpose or structure, Kant and his followers turned again to the question of foundations: What is right or legality? What is its origin and justification in the order of human action? What are the standards of legitimacy for institutions that claim to embody it or manage it?

Fichte and Schelling approach the task in a common way: first, a deep-structural or ontological account of the springs of rational action, second, an account of original rights, their transformation under the stress of violence or coercion, coupled with a contractarian explanation of the transition from pre-political to political societies, and finally, a description of ideal political institutions suited to the deep structure of rights. Schelling does not complete the whole agenda, claiming that at the transition from rights of coercion to an order that re-establishes and secures original right, the threshold of a new science is reached. That the transition would be mediated by some sort of social contract, one limiting the matter of free action, but not abrogating its formal freedom, is clear. Fichte's deep-structural account is more detailed and far more compelling, since it makes appeal to the theoretical foundations of *Wissenschaftslehre* in a simple and direct way and since it unfolds through a convincingly detailed phenomenology of social interaction. His three-stage model is simple too: a statics of rights in the sections describing their essence and their original form, a dynamics of rights (a dash of Hobbesian violence) in the treatment of the right of coercion, and a static politics to cap things off. A thoroughly social model of practical activity, and a thoroughly practical-social model of human self-consciousness pervade the work. Doubtless today's reader, suckled on notions of interactive communication and the social construction of reality, feels at home in this text. It is fairly safe to say that few of its original readers quite understood the impact of its axiom: no self-consciousness without practical interaction with the other.[7] Schelling's treatment gives the impression of romantic formlessness in its aphoristic style, and in the wandering style of its initial theoretical appeals, utilizing concepts lifted now from Spinoza, now from Kant, now from Rousseau. Once he finds his themes, however – the independence of right from morality, and of the free individual both from other individuals and from the collective (general will) – organization and logic appear. He then argues his way rather lucidly to a triple-stack of rights: the *individual's* right of *moral freedom* over against the general will or social pressure, the right of *formal equality* among multiple individual wills, and the *right* that pertains to will as such *over nature*, in whole or part.[8]

2

Fichte begins with an introduction discussing philosophical method and historical precedents. He aligns himself with Kant's treatment of rights, especially in its theoretical independence from morality, and tries to distinguish his philosophical work from the formalism of Reinhold's treatment of consciousness and its conditions. The initial description of right is offered in language that is quite plain: "right" means the possibility of community among free beings; the very conditions of self-consciousness–conscience and cognition, knowledge and action–compel me to live with others in society.[9] The first chapter is dedicated to the elaboration and justification (Fichte's term is "deduction") of the concept of right. There are three phases to this account, the first a description drawn from *Wissenschaftslehre* itself, of how the rational being must be efficacious, purpose-proposing, or *will* in order to be self-conscious. This involves positing itself as active or intervening in a sense world. A second phase describes the social condition of self-consciousness: to be active in a world I have to be among other rational agents and interact with them: "The human being (like all finite beings in general) becomes a human being only among human beings."[10] A third phase describes the logic of that social interaction, *reciprocal recognition.* I call myself a rational being in distinction from others and claim to have "the inner track" on human reality, while the others remain external, serving as incitements to my acts and limitations upon their scope. Fichte's point here is that internal-external denominations are a boundary put up from both sides; *each* self-conscious or rational being is so because she is both incited (or "called") to act and limited by others. This duplication of consciousness and reciprocity in the recognition of self-consciousness in the outside "other" is what cements the structure of right. If in one situation, with one other rational being, I must go through this process of recognition, I must arrange things into the future, and into a horizon of interacting with many rational persons. This is to set up the structure of right or "social permission," whereby in all situations, I find myself obliged to acknowledge the free entity outside me. "I must limit my freedom by the possibility of the freedom of the other."[11] A second chapter is devoted to showing the applicability of the concept thus explained, a methodological nicety that escapes Schelling. Whereas the "formalist," argues Fichte, drags objects into his philosophy merely because he *can* think them, the real philosopher describes the activity whereby his object takes origin, proves that this is the sole, hence necessary concept, and finally shows its applicability.[12] The first part of the application proof is fairly straightforward: to be self-conscious is to have efficacy, and to be active and effective, I must posit myself permanently in space in an articulated material body. The body, then, is the material condition of action.[13] But, secondly, there is also an intersubjective condition: I must be in and among, but separate from other rational beings. Fichte grounds this intersubjectivity in the very capacities of the body to serve as the tool of intelligence; the "higher" sensitivity involved in sight lets beings interact with one another while not overtly acting upon one another. The public visibility, then, of bodies occupying spaces near each other is the medium through which social interaction happens. If, that is, one can philosophically explain how one takes a perceived "human body" and recognizes it as a rational being like oneself. One may take the free movement of the animal body as the sign of a high degree of organization, but it takes a leap of recognition to see the indeterminate purposiveness of a free agent within the articulated human body. Not being quite able to explain that intuitive leap, Fichte proposes that one treat all those of human shape as rational beings.[14] A third step is even more problematic: even if one recognizes other humans in the sense world as rational agents, what impels me and them to recognize one another and to conduct our affairs under the limiting condition of right? If it was (more or less) by deductive logic that we worked our way from isolated self-consciousness to a world of embodied humans acting upon one another, at this point it is only the hypothetical logic of reciprocity that can *suggest* and invite rational beings into community. What is established, then, is only that *if* there is to be a social-political order, I must limit my freedom in view of the other, and vice versa. The conclusion is problematic, its scope limited to those desiring to participate; one cannot coerce a human to be a free being, or a social one.[15] Though Fichte uses the language of syllogistic deduction in all this, it is obvious that some of the connections are fairly soft or intuitive. He does not think everything can or ought to be proved, or that every assumption can be supported. He is more impressive as a philosopher in that he is willing to present an argument with warts, when he could cover over the lack with rhetoric.

The third chapter of Fichte's treatment of right is the actual science of right, divided up into original right, right of coercion, and right as law of the state. Only the first two divisions concern us, since only those sections are comparable to Schelling's aphorisms. The section on original right begins with an explicit disavowal of social contract theory as history. All thinking on rights starts from a *possible* human community and the restrictions that must be placed on freedom of action if that is to occur. To advance the argument, philosophy introduces stories of social contract, talk of "original rights" and "rights of man," but these are assumption, explanatory fictions, and not realities.[16] As for these fictional "original rights," since the free being is to be efficacious, it requires permanence or persistence. For that, the instrument of its agency is required, namely, the body. And for the body to effect the will's agenda, not only (relative) permanence of body is required, but the persistence of its influence upon the sensible world.[17] The basic assumption these right-claims make is that I require that empirical reality (I and the world) stay structurally the same, and that practically *things stay as I have put them*. The latter claim is the basis of property, argues Fichte, which is therefore not a social-political right, but a pre-political or natural right: the result of subjecting something to my will and wanting it to stay that way.[18]

With original right secured, we move into the territory of interaction among right-bearers, and thus into potential conflict, the realm of coercion. No problem arises for an isolated individual; her right is infinite. As soon as there is a plurality of agents, however, restrictions upon my freedom arise. Free beings signify their rationality among themselves through refraining from acting upon the bodies of others and through the designation of individual property.[19] Property results from the subjection of a thing to my will. Though the object designated as property is arbitrary, in subjecting it to my will I signify that I am a being with free rationality: I wish to act in the world in such a way that my perceptions match the purposes I project. Since this subjection to rational will happens in a world of many rational beings, somehow it must be public and known into the indefinite future. The will's staking itself in this object as its social representation, then, must be socially signified. Otherwise, various agents may claim the same objects, either at the same or at different times. However we agree and announce our claims to one another, the right of property rests on this very agreement and announcement, that is, upon reciprocal recognition of our claims. All property, reasons Fichte, is grounded in the merging into one will of many wills. And in such agreement, property indeed becomes private, but I am excluded from use of the other's objects not by the will of the other, but by my own free will, given in agreement.[20] Private property, then, is a natural or original right, but since it depends on the publicity of the announcement and agreement over which objects signify my rationality and which are your works of freedom, it requires the political order to sustain and perpetuate the agreement.

If we have property, theft cannot be far behind, so we are on the threshold of the right of coercion. A right of coercion is a social arrangement that uses force to produce rightful mutual security, where suspicion and falsity have undermined the good will and trust that support original right.[21] Fichte begins his treatment of it by calling attention to the logical shoddiness of his previous reasonings. The deduction was circular; it assumed what it wanted to prove. It showed that right obtains *if* the agreeing parties are as good as their word, but it fails to show any necessary mechanism (consistent with freedom) that would compel a free person to live up to her word. We have not seen reasons why a free person should subject her will, now and into the indefinite future, to the rule of law–for the envisaged security may not materialize.There is good reason, on the contrary, to think that a person will not live up to her word, and hence for fear for one's life, property, and security. Conflict (the Hobbesian state of war) hovers about as a perpetual possibility. In short, concludes Fichte, we have deduced the necessity of *trust* in an area where it is not wise to trust.[22] What is needed is an arrangement to force a would-be wrongdoer into desiring only what is lawful. Such coercion–social engineering would be a kinder name–is justified against a free agent because without it, he would contradict his will in pursuing short-range ends inconsistent with its ultimate end: preservation of body, efficacy, property and ultimately freedom itself.[23] Coercion works by mechanically attaching subsidiary purposes to my main goals; I am constrained, for instance, to pay close attention to conditions that promote *mutual security* if I hope to secure *my* continued existence into the future. If such a system of coercion or body of socializing constraints works, I am automatically forced to pay attention to the security of others at least as much as I am moved to look after my own.[24] Only a political community, a common entity erected on the basis of the will of many, can institutionalize such a system; when realized, these constraints are the content of positive law. With this, we are at the threshold of Fichte's detailed treatment of political organization and institutions, an exercise of ideal politics for which there is no parallel in Schelling's aphorisms.

Structurally, there are two parts to Schelling's *Neue Deduction des Naturrechts*, a "deduction" of the science of right and its principles, which is followed by an application of these to original right, natural right in its pre-political shape. Schelling begins in a frankly metaphysical vein, asserting that what theoretical philosophy cannot reach, the unconditional or the absolute, the individual rational agent must realize practically. In so doing, the unconditional must disappear as object and reappear in the place of the subject; accordingly, I must identify the ultimate ground of being with what is ultimate in me, my freedom. The demand of practical philosophy is thus: stop being an appearance, strive to be in-itself! This command and what it commands, even the striving to realize it, are all unconditional, asserts Schelling, so they cannot be determined by any outside object or effort. Being free means I am self-determining, or that my striving is unrestricted. I rule the phenomenal world; my autonomy shows up even physically in the way I remake the world according to my will.[25] This claim, initially, seems a strange mixture of ideas, some borrowed from Spinoza, some from Kant, but it is a precise use of

Spinoza's idea of *conatus* or "endeavor to exist" which is here displayed in the practical subject. Schelling characterizes the absolute or unconditioned in one of two ways usually, as subject-object or as "absolute subject"; in either case, it is totally nonobjective.

Coming closer to the empirical world, Schelling argues that noumenal striving expresses itself in phenomenal causality, my will endeavoring to impress its form on phenomena in realizing purposes. If there is resistance to my purposive willing, there is *nature*, but where there is moral resistance to my will, that is *humanity* and I must stop and respect its integrity. Many similar experiences convince me I am a member of a moral world, each of whose members has unlimited freedom. The other – to whom I am bound in the world of right yet to be developed – announces herself by resistance to my will, i.e., moral resistance.[26] Schelling does not plainly state as yet that he uses "moral" in a peculiarly Spinozistic sense, connoting only a free being's will to assert itself; the "ethical" designates relations *among* free beings. A "moral world," therefore, is a world of self-asserting individuals, more like Hobbes' state of nature than a community ruled by ethical standards.

The will emerges as *mine,* as individual, in this context of "moral" striving and counter-striving. The will's causality, though its goal is realizing the unconditional in an infinite act, finds itself expressed in time as empirical striving. Since the others are in the same situation, absolute freedom or will as such gets expressed in the contentious empirical striving and resistance of persons, or as the *opposition* of my freedom to that of all others. This is what makes will mine, and sanctions my individual will. Since every person is an "I" thus privileged, antagonism of the will results, which can be abated only if every person renounce unlimited empirical freedom as the way of obeying the absolute practical command.[27] Schelling's line of thought is not much different from Fichte's in this matter: freedom of will can be sustained only by willing self-limitation. Schelling's formulation makes clear the paradoxical nature of the situation: *one can fully actualize one's will only by not actualizing it.* Since he will not introduce any fundamental social axiom into this line of reflection, it will remain paradoxical. But if, with Fichte, to be will is to be alongside and among other rational beings, the paradox is lessened; there can be social realization of individual freedom only where individuals restrict themselves.

Schelling now embarks on a series of remarks that move us from "morals" to "ethics" (in his sense of the terms), or from individual will to the will of all individuals, Rousseau's *general will.* If the moral, i.e., self-asserting, being must surrender unlimited empirical freedom in order to save her freedom as such, she must stop regarding herself as *individual* in her striving in order to simply assert herself in it at all. Since all practical beings assert their individuality, striving for individuality *as such* must limit the empirical striving of each. Willing as such, then, or the "will of all" must limit the empirical individual and allow for the coexistence of this *general will* with personal will. When willing as such or *überhaupt* limits individual self-assertion, we are at the boundary between morals and ethics; morality concerns the isolated individual and make one sole demand: the absolute selfhood of the individual. Ethics (presuming a realm of "moral" beings) secures the selfhood of all individuals by the demand it addresses to the individual.[28] The command of ethics expresses *general will*, not the "moral" will of the individual, but it is grounded in and conditioned by individual will, and ultimately serves the interest of individual will. It is *not* the case that I lay claim to individuality because I am impelled by the universal will. Rather, *because I lay claim to individuality*, I submit to universal law.[29] The reader might wish for explanation and argument at this point. Schelling seems to accomplish the slide from individual will to will as such, and from the will of all individuals to "general will" by playing with words. It is not evident how willing as such can constrain individual willing. Or perhaps, this is a conclusion the author hopes the reader will come to. Ultimately in this philosophy of right, all collective entities show themselves to be fictive, and the general will to be effective only insofar as it represents individual will, even while it restricts it.

Schelling earnestly works at this problem of how general and individual will interact for the next few pages. The problem of ethics, he announces, is to maintain individual freedom through universal freedom, to sustain individual will through universal will. This is equivalent to harmonizing the empirical will of the single individual with that of all others. The harmonization means a coalescence of the will of all and individual will, not the subjection of one to the other. The mutual restriction or harmonization of individual wills, then, correlates to the absoluteness of will as such; there is will *überhaupt* if and only if my will and that of all others condition each other. Therefore, concludes Schelling, "there is absolute will only insofar as there is socially restricted individual will, and vice versa."[30] Here again, the limitations of the chosen form of aphorism let Schelling announce a solution rather than argue for it. Assume the hardened egoist listens to this. "Right, mate! Restriction of will: what's in it for me?" So far, Schelling has done nothing to silence this voice.

Next Schelling considers the domain of ethics more carefully and finds that its apparent shortcoming, viz., sacrifice of individual will to the collective, is really the preservation of individuality. The command of ethics, well-formulated by Kant, is expressed in these ways: Act in such a way that your will could be absolute will, or so the entire moral world could will your action, or so that your action treats the other rational being not as object, but as cooperating subject. If I follow this command, in any of its forms, I renounce my individuality, i.e., I cease to oppose my freedom to that of others. But I do so only on the condition that the cessation is reciprocated. If reciprocal de-individualization of willing is achieved, I then have submitted to the general will in order to sustain and preserve individual will. This can happen only insofar as general will is grounded in and conditioned by individual will, that it translates and conveys its essential form, freedom. As this complicated relation is developed, there are further twists and turns. I assert my will against the individual will of others by taking on the general will. But since I do so in order *not* to be subject to the will of others, I really do it in order to *make my will the will of others.* [31] Here is the answer we sought above. What is "in it" for the individual in taking on the restrictions of the general will is the preservation of its essential freedom, this not by submitting to the individual will of other persons, but making them submit to mine. The ethical world preserves the moral world in its restrictions; it does not supplant it.

Schelling finally moves toward a definition of right, the domain of the permissible, by contrasting permission with ethical command. He does this by contrasting the possibility of willing as such with the actuality of will that is commanded by ethics. Freedom or individuality is absolute, and aptly expressed by the identity formula, I = I. Were will not restricted materially by the command of ethics, it would be an absolute theoretical axiom. But under this restriction, it can be asserted only as a *practical possibility.* Now if one analyzes the modal distinction of possibility and actuality, the strange fact emerges that possibility is unconditioned because not actual, while what is actual is conditioned, due to the very fact that it exists as thing alongside things. The practical possibility of my freedom, therefore, is unconditioned and this is the concern of a problematic science that is different from ethics. Such a *science of the practically possible*, of uses of freedom which are permitted rather than commanded, is *rights.* Ethics and rights, then, are independent of one another and form contrasting domains, ethics attempting to harmonize universal and individual will by imposing the former on the latter, rights attempting the harmonization by infusing individual will, in its form at least, into the general will. The two domains may in fact treat the same forms of conduct, ethics expressing its commands categorically but negatively, rights expressing its permissions in terms of possibility.[32] Schelling will later make much of the interesting contrast that rights may allow kinds of conduct that ethics forbids, insofar as the freedom of the individual, upon which ethics rests, is sustained and secured. Though Schelling's line of reason is highly complicated, it is capable of shedding light on some of the interesting paradoxes of democratic societies (other than Singapore) that find themselves constrained to legally permit conduct that is morally repugnant.

Having accomplished the definition of rights in its distinction from both "morals" and ethics, Schelling turns to the topic of original right in various forms. Crucial to this discussion is a distinction he constantly utilizes between the *matter* and the *form* of willing, the former signifying the object or contents of action, the latter its style of execution, freedom. Freedom is to predominate, or to determine matter, and where it does not, it turns out that the form of willing has a subversive function; it re-individualizes the collective.

In the domain of right or permissive action, therefore, I am permitted to do everything that is a matter of right. Whatever takes place through the sheer form of individual willing, I can assert. Now the freedom of my will is unconditional; the only way it can be suspended is if the matter of my will is determined by another's freedom, if my action is dictated by another. The problem of right is to maintain freedom of individual will, despite the possibility of many claimants contesting its matter. Therefore rights assert that you can do anything that asserts the matter of your will, insofar as it is conditioned by its form. All the problems of rights, then, center on the relationships possible between *my will,* the *will of other individuals*, and the *general will.* While other individuals and society at large may attempt to impose the content of my action upon me, I am entitled to resist in the name of freedom, will's very form.[33] From the standpoint of rights, it is not appropriate that actions, virtuous or not, legal or criminal, be imposed upon or forbidden for a free being. Schelling seems to relish these islands of paradox that emerge in societies that take freedom seriously.

Over against the general will, I as individual will have no right; as formally the author of the general will and the purpose of its legislation, I can make no valid claim against it, unless it works against the very freedom – my individual will – that is its basis. The general will can have only an imperfect right over me; if it suspends my freedom, it destroys its own basis. It even restricts my freedom if it attempts to alter the matter of my act. There is a general principle appropriate here: I have the right to selfhood of will against the general will, even materially, provided I thereby assert my right to selfhood of will, formally regarded. In passing, Schelling argues that powerful though the general will is, no individual is allowed to usurp it and serve as its executor, aligning its legislation with an individual will opposed to mine.[34]

Schelling treats Fichte's right of coercion under the title of "conflict of individual rights." He considers two cases, the first where both parties make equally unlawful claims against the other, the second, where one of the claimants has right on her side. A general principle is laid out: I have a right to the matter of my will, in opposition to every other individual. This is then applied to a matrix of four cases, which distinguish whether one supports or opposes the matter of a lawful action (morality) or its form (freedom). In Schelling's eyes, all encroachments upon freedom of individual will, all attacks on form then, deserve resistance, even if one's own will is unlawful. Assaults on the matter of my willing are resisted too, because of the conditioning linkage between matter and form. Where both wills are materially unlawful, therefore, I have a right to assert my materially unlawful (i.e., immoral) will against the formally unlawful (despotic) will of another. I also have a right to my materially lawful will against every formally unlawful will. This right of resistance holds only vis-à-vis individual will, not general will.[35]

A final, somewhat quixotic section, elaborates the claims of individual will against will as such. This turns into a universal claim for dominion over nature on the part of the free being. The relevant principle here is: against every will I have the right to assert the selfhood of my freedom through unlimited domination of nature. Hardly a principle a contemporary environmentalist would embrace, this seems a vast inflation of the symbolic claim to property that Fichte advances. Objects are viewed as lacking being unless referred to a human will, hence having a value of zero.[36] Schelling concludes with a list of the rights he has considered – right to moral freedom against the encroachments of the general will, to equal freedom vis-à-vis other individuals, and an unlimited right over nature or the phenomenal world insofar as my individual will represents will as such.[37] That Schelling breaks off the discussion at the border of the political realm leaves the contrasts and tensions among these claims unresolved. The political stabilization of the realm of rights, however, would seem to require some sacrifice of the vigorous claims for individual freedom that he advanced.

3

Finally, I offer a brief recitation of the commonalities and differences between these two treatments of right. I have argued above that the strength of Fichte's philosophy of right is the thoroughly social view he introduced of both the foundation and the edifice itself of rights. This is correct and illuminating, insofar as rights are an institutionalized reflection of human social relations and serve to stabilize them. I have also praised the resilient individualism of Schelling's account, because, at least when transferred to some vaguely appropriate political arrangement, rights function to protect the individual both from others and from abstract collectives. The political problem of balancing the social dimension of human reality against the individual is formidable enough to tolerate the existence of a plurality of cogent accounts of right.

Let me list the areas of convergence between Fichte and Schelling. Both accounts follow a common narrative structure, seen in genetic accounts of social and legal orders since Plato. One moves from an initial but abstract theoretical basis, the original conditions of consciousness as described by *Wissenschaftslehre* or the nature of will as striving for absoluteness, to a consideration of original right. Then comes an account of potential or actual unlawfulness and the coercive power needed to restore it. Finally, one moves to the political order in order to stabilize and perpetuate the regime of socially surrendered freedom that has opened up the common space. One could argue that social contract argumentation is implicit in the initial appearance of right in both theories – in the very concept of the auto-limitation of freedom for the sake of the other's freedom in Fichte, in the subjection of individual will to general will in Schelling – and thus is at its very foundation. Equally one could argue that contract thinking is a discrete step in the march from original right to politically stabilized right. Strangely enough, the contractarian idea becomes more powerful the more it is taken as metaphor rather than history.

Both thinkers agree, also, that rights and morality (in the conventional, not Schelling's peculiar sense) are separate, if overlapping domains. Fichte puts it concisely: *morals forbid, rights permit*. He agrees with Kant too that moral causality does not show up in the phenomenal world, while the effects of rights claims can make an appearance.[38] Schelling gives a more elaborate account with much the same content: *ethics legislates in the negative* and categorically, while *rights allow positive action*, but only problematically.

The thinkers agree in a third point: the culmination of natural rights in their basic or pre-political form is the designation of the individual's freedom in *individual property* or (Schelling's grandiose equivalent) total *dominion over nature*. For both thinkers, then, the political order is not what grants either freedom or its symbolic equivalent, though it can preserve it or secure it through limitation or redistribution. Fichte sees things plainly and correctly: property is a social token of freedom. Its significance is not that an object is owned or altered, but that it exhibits the "I" and "mine" through a system of social signification.

There are significant differences between the thinkers, of course. Schelling and Fichte have different basic or deep-structural starting points, Fichte's the account of self-reverting, self-affecting and self-conscious activity that *Wissenschaftslehre* furnishes, Schelling's the power ontology borrowed from Spinoza and dressed out in Kantian language. Since Fichte had already accomplished a comprehensive appropriation of transcendental idealism that freed its central insights – like the "primacy of the practical" – from Kant's language, his contribution is original and fresh. The Spinozism of this piece from Schelling is an anticipation, at best, of his thorough appropriation of it in the 1801 *Exhibition of My System.*

The thinkers also adopt different expository or narrative strategies. Schelling's highly abstract, logical terminology and his borrowings from other writers make it difficult to grasp his meaning. Perhaps it is not stretching things too far to suggest another interpretation, that he wanted to mask the subversive, even antisocial intensity of his libertarianism or individualism to avoid controversy. Fichte's approach, by contrast, is to quickly leave the realm of abstract theoretical foundations and move, with phenomenological accuracy, toward a plausible account of the empirical realm of intersubjectivity. There is something fresh and exciting in his descriptions of the conditions of action, of embodiment of will, or communication via visibility, and of the structure of recognition itself.

Finally, there are different points of emphasis in social and political theory. Fichte gives a thorough social or intersubjective account, founded on the phenomenon of mutual recognition between free beings. Schelling offers, instead, a highly individualistic account. Fichte seems sanguine about the sacrifice of freedom involved in the self-limitation of the rights stance; a highly stable and secure political order is at the pinnacle of his theory. Schelling's account is jealous of individual freedom; doubtless a political philosophy, had he fully elaborated it, would have laid great emphasis on the protection of the individual from the power of the collective. I suspect, also, that at the time of writing, his politics were a bit more Jacobin than those of Fichte, though no German writer on political philosophy exactly wanted to bring the French experiment home. Whatever their differences, however, in style or substance, both thinkers manifest in an intellectual way the exhilaration of their time and their cultural place. To be working in such a robust intellectual culture, with a vast political experiment underway just across the border that was overturning centuries of settled assumptions, and to be fired with enthusiasm for contributing to the realization of a free society under law was to be in a very fortunate situation.

Notes

1 *Neue Deduktion des Naturrechts*, ed. Wilhelm G. Jacobs, in Friedrich Wilhelm Joseph Schelling, *Historisch-kritische Ausgabe,* Werke, ed.. Hartmut Buchner, Wilhelm Jacobs, and Annmarie Pieper, Vol. 3 (Stuttgart: Fromann-Holzboog, 1982). Hereafter cited as W 3.

2 Johann Gottlieb Fichte, *Grundlage des Naturrechts nach Principien des Wissenschaftslehre, in J.G. Fichte-Gesamtausgabe*, ed. Reinhard Lauth, Hans Jacob and Richard Schottky, I (Werke), Vol. 3 (Stuttgard-Bad Carnstatt: Friedrich Frommann Verlag [Günther Holzboog], 1966). Hereafter cited as GA, I, 3. English translation: Fichte, *Foundations of Natural Right*, ed. Frederick Neuhouser, trans. Michael Baur (Cambridge and New York: Cambridge University Press, 2000). Hereafter cited as ET.

3 Wilhelm Jacobs suggests a rich mix of contemporary ideas in social-legal philosophy that Schelling may be reacting to in the *New Deduction.* He had heard Johann Friedrich Flatt's criticisms of Moses Mendelssohn's *Jerusalem oder über religiöse Macht und Judenten.* He knew of Kant's *Perpetual Peace* through a review by Fichte, and was aware as well of the latter's early essays on freedom of thought in Europe and the French Revolution. It is surmised that he knew, through Hölderlin, of Fichte's intention to lecture on natural right in the winter semester of 1795–96. "Editorische Bericht" to *Neue Deduktion des Naturrechts*, W, 3: 120–24.

4 An early formulation of the axiom can be found in Moses Maimonides. Speaking of how to secure the welfare of the body, Maimonides outlines two requirements: "One of them is the abolition of their wronging each other. This is tantamount to every individual among the people not being permitted to act according to his will and up to the limits of his power, but being forced to do that which is useful to the whole." The other is the acquisition of moral qualities. *Guide of the Perplexed*, trans. Schlomo Pines, Vol. II (Chicago: Chicago University Press, 1963): 510.

5 Friedrich Schlegel writes in 1798: "A fragment should be, like a miniature, completely separate from the surrounding world and complete unto itself like a hedgehog" (*Athenäum Fragments*, 206 in *Theory as Practice: A Critical Anthology of Early German Romantic Writings,* ed. and trans. Jochen Schulte-Sasse et al. (Minneapolis and London: University of Minnesota Press, 1997): 322). My suggestion is anachronistic, of course, and one might question to what extent any work on the foundation of politics can have the hedgehog's self-containment.

6 Hobbes argues that one is "by nature" in a situation of personal insecurity because of human intra-species aggression; the necessity of self-preservation endorses a "right to all," that is, a right to anything useful for defense under the conditions of warfare in the state of nature. But the exercise of this right can be secured only by association, the combination of several wills into one will. One can therefore exercise right only by the surrender of individual wills to one common will, the Sovereign power. *On the Citizen*, ed. and trans. Richard Tuck and Michael Silverthorne, Ch: V, 1–9 (Cambridge and New York: Cambridge University Press, 1998): 69–73.

7 *Grundlage des Naturrechts*, GA, I, 3: 347–8; ET: 37–8.

8 *Neue Deduktion,* §§2–7; W, 3: 139–40.

9 *Grundlage des Naturrechts*, GA, I, 3: 320, 321–2; ET: 10–11.

10 GA, I, 3: 347; ET: 37.

11 GA, I, 3: 358; ET: 49.

12 GA, I, 3: 316n, 319; ET: 7n, 9.

13 GA, I, 3: 361–5; ET: 53–8.
14 GA, I, 3: 365–79; ET: 59–74.
15 GA, I, 3: 388; ET: 84.
16 GA, I, 3: 403–4; ET: 101–2.
17 GA, I, 3: 407–9; ET: 106–8.
18 GA, I, 3: 406–8; ET: 104–6.
19 GA, I, 3: 412–13; ET: 111–12.
20 GA, I, 3: 417; ET: 116–17.
21 GA, I, 3: 427; ET: 127.
22 GA, I, 3: 423–5 ; ET: 123–5.
23 GA, I, 3: 426–7; ET: 126–7.
24 GA, I, 3: 428–30; ET: 128–30.
25 *Neue Deduktion,* §§2–7, W, 3: 139–40.
26 §§10–13; W, 3: 141–2.
27 §§19–27; W, 3: 143–4.
28 §§28–33; W, 3: 144–5.
29 §§29–30; W, 3,144–5.
30 §§36–44; W, 3,146–8.
31 §§46–51; W, 3, 148–9.
32 §§54–75; W, 3, 150–54.
33 §§78–139; W, 3, 155–69.
34 §§96–109,W, 3, 160–63.
35 §§110–28; W, 3: 163–7.
36 §§129–53; W, 3: 167–8
37 §140; W, 3: 169–70.
38 *Grundlage des Naturrechts*, GA, I, 3. 357–60; ET: 48–51.

Chapter 15

Transcendental Conditions and the Transcendence of Conditions: Fichte and Schelling on the Foundations of Natural Right

Steven Hoeltzel

At some point in 1795, evidently while tutoring a pair of young barons bound for law school at Leipzig, Schelling drafted a series of aphorisms on the subject of natural right. By the spring of 1796, he had resolved to publish it. In Jena, meanwhile, during the winter semester of 1795–96, Fichte lectured on the same subject. Knowledge of Fichte's activities seems to have encouraged Schelling to publicize his own work without undue delay: as he indicated in a March, 1796 letter to Niethammer, he was loath to let "another" publish on the topic first, as the public might then judge that Schelling was simply following that other author's lead, rather than philosophically finding his own way.[1]

Schelling need not have worried much about such potential misunderstandings – not in this instance, at least. Of course, it seems fair to say that his prior publications had been received in a way that occasionally overemphasized affinities with Fichte and underestimated the originality of his own ideas. And as it turned out, Fichte did publish on *Naturrecht* before Schelling's treatment of the topic appeared in print.[2] Still, the differences between their respective renderings of right are textually evident (albeit conceptually complicated) and philosophically far-reaching. Indeed, and as one would expect, these divergences refer back to, and unfold out of, the very foundations of each man's philosophy – and in a way that makes vivid the radical differences between them even as early as 1795 or 1796. In Fichte's *Foundations of Natural Right*, right is grounded as a co-enabler, in the manner of a transcendental condition, of the *a priori* articulation of empirically individuated selfhood. In Schelling's *New Deduction of Natural Right*, by contrast, right is grounded as an enabler of an ideally-envisioned *a posteriori* escape from individuated status, by way of an unceasing endeavor to transcend the conditions definitive of finite selfhood.

The difference just denoted pertains primarily to the course taken by the philosophical derivation and legitimation of right by each author. Despite diverging in that dimension, Fichte and Schelling do not deeply disagree concerning what right should amount to in relation to our practical possibilities as finite, free intelligences. Both regard right as a principle that sets up and secures a sphere of self-sovereignty, a circumscribed space wherein the individual will should operate independently of any externally-originating compulsion. Right thus guarantees, ideally if not actually, that the spontaneity ontologically essential to selfhood (*Ichheit*) may obtain practical purchase in the world of appearances. As such, right protects and promotes the actualization, in experience, of every subject's essential potential as a finite, free intelligence.

Of course, the fact that Fichte and Schelling agree upon some such practically pertinent points (and on related matters noted below) does not mean that the differences between their respective deductions of *Recht* are merely methodological variations that lack any more substantive philosophical import. Because both authors are so strongly committed to systematicity in philosophy, these differences in derivation inflect the idea of *Recht* with a different systematic significance in each case. That and how this is so can be made clearer, first by sharpening the already-indicated contrast, and then by briefly attending to some of its most important antecedents.

1 Transcendental Conditions vs the Transcendence of Conditions

In the context of Fichte's Jena *Wissenschaftslehre*, right is derived and legitimated roughly as follows. An *a priori* act whereby a subject freely circumscribes its own essential impetus to unlimited efficacy – an act necessarily accompanied, Fichte argues, by the same subject's positing of another rational being who, likewise, spontaneously sets limits to its own freedom – is shown to play an indispensable transcendental role within the structural self-articulation of world-related, empirically individuated selfhood.[3] Right, thus understood, originally unfolds out of the *transcendental, concretizing contraction* whereby an originally-pure potency for intelligent agency (an "absolute I"), intuiting and elaborating in various ways upon the unsurpassable boundedness of its being, *a priori* acknowledges and elementally understands its status as an individual finite self. The subject, for Fichte, can grasp itself as an empirically determinate individual only on the basis of the transcendental acts that *a priori* originate *Recht*.

For Schelling, by contrast, *Recht* originates only subsequently to the subject's having discovered itself as an empirically determinate individual. And not only that. Right, for Schelling, originally operates as an underwriter of an *absolutizing ontological expansion*, by an already-empirically-individuated self, toward a no-longer-conditioned condition, an ideal status wherein all finitizing limitations have been transcended and sheer being reposes in the beatitude of "absolute unconditionality." Right receives its derivation and legitimation thus: not as a *transcendental ground* of our *empirically manifest condition* as finite, free intelligences sharing a world; but, instead, as a *practical enabler* of the individual's empirically-specified striving for the *achievement of an ideal of unconditionality* – a striving which every finite self finds itself essentially impelled to undertake.

According to the *New Deduction of Natural Right*, right obtains because and insofar as it subserves the "highest demand of all practical philosophy," which is simply this: "*Be*! in the highest sense of the word; cease to be appearance *yourself*; strive to become a being in itself!"[4] Schelling presents this supreme demand as a challenge.[5] This provocation, addressed to a living spontaneity that finds itself enmeshed in its own phenomenality, calls upon that being not to limit itself but to actively unmake its every limitation and, in so doing, to win ever-more-unlimited expression for its pure potentiality as active intelligence. In relation to this supreme practical demand, the principle of right is derived and legitimated as a subordinate principle that secures for the self an ideally-inviolable sphere of self-determination, whence it can strive to "outdo" the empirical impediments to its essential potential.

Schelling's deduction of right, therefore, cannot be understood "from the ground up" until one understands his basis for maintaining that "Strive for unconditionality!"[6] is the supreme principle of practical philosophy. The *New Deduction of Natural Right* addresses this issue in an abbreviated and essentially unargued way.[7] The idea emerges much more clearly from Schelling's contemporaneous writings, especially *On the I as Principle of Philosophy* (1795) and *Philosophical Letters on Dogmatism and Criticism* (1795/96). Accordingly, I proceed, with reference to these and related writings, to outline the ideas that ground Schelling's understanding of practical philosophy's "supreme demand." Thereafter I turn to the *New Deduction of Natural Right*, sketching the pivotal steps in Schelling's deduction of right and further sharpening various points of comparison and contrast between his position and Fichte's.

2 Inexplicable Egress, Practical Progress

Like Fichte (and likewise following Reinhold), Schelling began his philosophical project with a metaphilosophical commitment to a very strict standard of foundationalist systematicity.[8] Again like Fichte, he aspired to anchor his system in the disclosure of an absolutely original ground (*Urgrund*): "an ultimate point of reality on which everything depends, from which all firmness and all form of our knowledge springs;"[9] and he conceptualized that ground in a manner that is ontologically more appropriate to the living essence of active intelligence than to the lifeless opacity of the objective. Nevertheless, Schelling operated from the first with a very different conception of the specific nature – it may be better to say: the unspecific non-nature – of the foundation of all philosophy.

Fichte's Jena writings endeavor to found a philosophical system in and upon "the absolute I:" an integrated, self-articulating complex of intrinsically interrelated intellectual acts, one and all simultaneously spontaneous and subject to ineluctable limitations.[10] These manifold *a priori* activities and limitations are theoretically countenanced insofar as their postulation contributes to a transcendental account of the basic organizing structures of experience. By contrast, Schelling's earliest attempts at system-building focus first and foremost upon "absolute unconditionality" (*schlechthin Unbedingtheit*)[11] as the definitive mark of the properly ultimate. This seems to push Schelling's system well beyond the methodological and metaphysical boundaries of a transcendental theory of finite selfhood such as Fichte's – a fact that Fichte himself was quick to note.[12] Still, Schelling transgressed those limits not out of carelessness, but on the basis of conviction: that only by grounding everything in an absolutely unconditioned *Urgrund* could philosophy hope to understand life and subjectivity in an ontologically appropriate way: by rendering intelligible their origination out of metaphysically more primordial elements, but without thereby reducing life and subjectivity to mechanically-engendered, meaningless modifications of a spiritually inert objectivity.[13]

Early on, inspired by the idea that any object's existence must be a conditioned existence (that there could be, as he was wont to say, no "*unbedingtes Ding*"—no unconditioned thing),[14] Schelling understood the unconditioned ultimate as something specifically similar to spontaneously self-positing subjectivity, figured on the early Fichtean model. But Schelling's early *Urgrund*, as distinct from Fichte's, was, in effect, a self-positing subjectivity systematically stripped of all forms of finitude: a perfectly independent and unlimited, seamlessly self-reverting and self-realizing activity.[15] Perhaps unsurprisingly, then, Schelling's earliest efforts seem to have foundered upon the apparent impossibility of understanding why there should (or how there could) arise a world of finite minds and conditioned things, given the supposition that what originally exists is a radically non-objective, entirely unconditioned absolute. On such an assumption (at least given the way in which Schelling first conceptualized it), our conditioned experience of a world of determinate things seems to be separated from its absolutely unconditioned ground by an ontological divide which the finite intellect can find no way back across. We have undergone an "egress [*Heraustreten*] from the absolute."[16] Out of the initially seamless self-identity of the unconditioned absolute, there has unfolded "the original opposition in the human mind:" the articulated epistemological structure of subject–object differentiation-relation; the invisible ontological seam between the pure potency of active intelligence and its empirically conditioned instantiation.[17] But to inquire about the reasons for this development is, on Schelling's view, to pose the theoretically insoluble "riddle of the world, the question of how the absolute could come out of itself and oppose to itself a world."[18]

Still, finite subjectivity finds itself impelled to relate to the unconditioned not only by endeavoring (unsuccessfully) to acquire knowledge about the unconditioned, *qua* ultimate explanatory ground of all conditioned existence. Finite subjectivity also (and more fundamentally) relates to the unconditioned by being impelled to *achieve* unconditionality, *qua* utterly unrestricted actualization of the pure potential for intelligent agency that every finite self essentially *is*.[19] Coming into being as a finite subject (as Schelling seems to conceptualize this in the mid-1790s) means finding oneself existing as a pure potency for active intelligence, but one that has become bound by manifold limitations: constraining conditions that have inexplicably accreted to one's ideally-unconstrained essential potential, limitations which one is impelled to strive to surpass. (Of course, these claims are to be understood not as bits of empirical-psychological description, but as ontological characterizations of the transcendental core of finite selfhood, all of which in one way or another index the finite subject's inherently "energetic" way of being.)[20] As Schelling would have it, "Everything not explicable from our pure being, from our absolute essence, is determined through a passivity."[21] But owing to our essential potential for ever-more-excellent intelligent agency – an ontological echo of our (un)condition prior to our "egress" from the absolute – "it is demanded that we become more and more reasonable, independent, free."[22]

3 Striving, Strife, and Self-supervision

"What I cannot realize theoretically, I ought to realize practically." So begins the text comprising Schelling's deduction of the "science of right" as such, and of the supreme principle (*Grundsatz*) of that science. "Now, the unconditioned toward which reason strives is beyond theoretical reason's reach, for it can never become *object* for me. As I try to capture it as object, it steps back within the limits of conditionality."[23] The unconditioned, *qua* unconditioned, must have a radically non-objective kind of being. Accordingly, if I am to represent such being in a way that is at least approximately appropriate, "I must think the ultimate that grounds all existence, the absolute being that reveals itself in every being [*das absolute Sein, das in jedem Dasein sich offenbart*], as *identical with myself*, with the ultimate, unalterable in me."[24]

Of course, the particular properties that constitute my empirically apparent persona are neither ultimate nor unalterable. They arise and alter as indices of my conditioned status as a finite being; and I can acquire quite distinct concrete qualities over time (or could have had such from the beginning), without *essentially* altering the spontaneous intelligence that, ultimately, I am. Ergo, if I am impelled to identify myself with "the ultimate, unalterable in me," and if that identification is to express itself in a striving (not encode itself in a cognizing), then I am inspired to "*Be*! in the highest sense of the word; cease to be appearance [*Erscheinung*] *yourself*; strive to become a being in itself! [*Wesen an sich*] This is the highest demand of all practical philosophy."[25]

As initially, most abstractly understood, practical reason's paramount imperative can sound outright immoderate. "If you are a being in itself," Schelling goes on to say, "no opposing power [*entgegenstrebende Macht*] can alter your status, none can limit your freedom. Therefore, in order to become a being in itself, *to be absolutely free* ... strive [*strebe*] by freedom to extend your freedom into absolute, illimitable power."[26] *Qua* ceaseless striver, one challenges oneself to become "a being that determines everything resistant [*alles Widerstrebende*] but is itself determined by nothing."[27]

This tone of ontological and ethical extremism is quickly moderated, however. In the preceding passages, which comprise the very first steps of the *New Deduction*, Schelling has abstracted from all of the definitive conditions of finite selfhood save one: the subject's positing itself as an intelligent agency opposed by a world of objectivity that the subject is impelled to understand and to improve.[28] The subsequent sections of Schelling's argument cite additional conditions of ineluctable limitation, and consideration of those limitations and their consequences makes it plain that the unconditionality toward which we are impelled to strive remains an infinitely distant ideal, so long as such conditions obtain.[29] Of course, that does not preclude the possibility of progressing past whatever particular point we might actually occupy at a given time, advancing in the direction of unconditionality. Moreover, what is directly demanded is simply that we *strive for* unconditionality – not necessarily that we actually attain it. It should suffice, therefore, simply to endeavor always to secure ever-more-unrestricted actualization of the pure potential for intelligent action that inwardly animates us.[30] In light of the concrete conditions that actually constrain us, to succeed on that score just *is* to achieve an increment of precisely the sort of "absolutizing ontological expansion" spoken of above. (So long as we remain finite, of course, such success would not signal the completion of the absolutizing project.) Understood in context, aiming for unconditionality by no means requires that we endeavor to conquer the cosmos by explicitly undertaking to expand our egos and our efficacy *ad infinitum*. As Schelling remarks in the Ninth of the *Philosophical Letters*:

> I should be absolute. But criticism would deteriorate into an excess of enthusiasm [*Schwärmerei*] if it should represent this ultimate goal as *attainable* at all (even though not as *attained*). It therefore employs this idea only practically, for the determination [*Bestimmung*] of the moral being.[31]

Of course, that is "only natural," given the sorts of limitations to which we find our spontaneity subjected. Under conditions of finitude, spontaneous striving "must *reveal* itself [*sich offenbaren*]" empirically as life (*Leben*): "autonomy in appearance," the "schema of freedom," the revelation *through* physical causality *of* the causality of freedom.[32] But life, despite being autonomous in its principle,[33] has limitations of which the living learn almost immediately. For one thing, "Where my *physical* power finds resistance, there is *nature* [*Natur*]. I recognize nature's superior power over my physical strength: I bow before it as a being of sense [*als Sinnenwesen*]; I *can* do no more."[34]

Worth noting is Schelling's implied distinction between *Erscheinung* (appearance), as the empirically evident reality we are impelled to improve, and *Natur*, as that in appearance which no amount of *physical* effort can do anything to alter. But nature, thus understood, does not offer up the only resistance that life encounters in striving for unconditionality. Also, and much more importantly, there is *humanity*, from which there can originate an opposition that engages one's willing as such (as distinguished from the physical manifestations of one's volition). "Where my *moral* power finds resistance, there can no longer be nature. Shuddering, I stop. Here is *humanity*!, it calls out to me [*ruft es mir entgegen*]; I *may* do no more."[35] As a peculiarly moral species of opposition, the resistance in question is attributed to a non-physical causality expressing an autonomy of its own.[36] Accordingly, "When I feel my freedom limited, I recognize that I am not alone in the moral world, and manifold experiences of limited freedom teach me that I am in a realm of moral beings, all of whom are entitled to unlimited freedom themselves,"[37] and all of whom, as such, strive for unconditionality.[38]

Were all of us ever to achieve such status, the transcendence of the conditions of individuation would cancel all possible conflict (indeed, all numerical distinction) between us.[39] But so long as conditions of finitude obtain, spontaneity is split up and strewn about in space and time. My striving is not your striving, even supposing their ultimate identity of aim.[40] And both of us strive for unconditionality not "once and for all," but through temporally manifold, innumerable instances of agency.[41] Given only so much space and time within which to work, and with outright unconditionality as everyone's ultimate aim, it seems that subjective striving cannot fail to occasion intersubjective strife (at least in theory, even if not in practice). *Quoth* Schelling, "[T]he unconditional causality of moral beings becomes conflicting in the *empirical* striving, and I begin *to oppose my freedom to the freedom of all others*."[42] Any two finite subjects striving for unlimited efficacy, empirically understood, have wills that must come into conflict at some point in the conceivable future; and to recognize this is to see that striving for unconditionality is, in essence, an irreducibly individual affair. In Schelling's words, "[A]s I think of my freedom as conflicting with the causality of others who are like me, it becomes *my* causality, that is, a causality that is not the causality of the moral being in general (of the entire moral world). I become a moral *individual*."[43]

This ontologically inflected notion of moral individuality incorporates all the elements that jointly propel Schelling's subsequent deduction of both the "commandment [*Gebot*] of ethics" and the "first principle [*Grundsatz*] of all philosophy of right." So long as we remain our *finite* selves, our being is a striving, circumscribed by spatial, temporal, and nomic conditions, in a world that we share with other spontaneous subjects. And so long as we remain our finite *selves*, as Schelling understands the latter notion, there smolders in each of us an ember of unconditionality that impels us to set ourselves against any conditions that in any way limit the pure potential for intelligent activity that animates us.

> I *cannot* cease to assert my freedom as long as the challenge [*Forderung*] "Strive for unconditionality!" is not fulfilled. Yet I cannot assert my freedom

> without at the same time absolutely opposing it to the freedom of others, insofar as theirs conflicts with mine in empirical striving. Therefore, *the individuality of my will itself is sanctioned by the highest demand* [*Forderung*] *of practical reason*.[44]

Before turning to a brief outline of Schelling's derivation and legitimation of right, we should note two things concerning the relation between this notion of moral individuality and Schelling's overall argument.

First, the steps by which Schelling's argument proceeds from its initial occupation with world-related subjectivity (§7) to its subsequent specification of moral individuality (§22), do not comprise a transcendental argument on the model of Fichte's procedure in §§1–3 of the *Foundations of Natural Right*.[45] To put it rather crudely, moral individuality in Schelling's *New Deduction* equals: generically world-related subjectivity, specifically manifest as life, and marked by the more specific modes of limitation indicated and occasioned by nature (§12) and humanity (§13), both of which are originally encountered as sources of resistance to the subject's spontaneity. By all appearances in the text, Schelling proceeds from generic structure to specific limitations, not by offering (as Fichte does) a regressive argument that figures the latter limitations as transcendental conditions of the already-evident generic structure; but instead, by way of simply reporting that as living subjectivity actively engages with worldly conditions, it simply *finds* its spontaneity being limited in further, more determinate ways.

(In the salient passages from §13 and §14, quoted above, Schelling uses "*finden*" to denote the subject's discovery of a specific sort of resistance by which its *Macht* is met as it endeavors to outstrip the objective. Of course, there is a sense in which for Fichte, too, subjectivity simply "finds" itself to be finite in various ways: its impulse to intelligent agency is always "checked" by an *Anstoß* or *Aufforderung*: a proto-experiential episode of "feeling" that occasions further subjective self-elaboration, but whose actual occurrence is inexplicable in the context of a transcendental theory of finite selfhood.[46] The important point for present purposes, however, is that in the *New Deduction*, Schelling nowhere seems to commit himself to the claim that the *a priori* "discovery" of any *specific* sorts of limitation is a transcendental precondition for the positing of the basic structure of subject–object opposition. If anything, he seems to figure the latter structure as a fundamental opposition-schema transcendentally presupposed by the subject's encounter with the more specific sources of limitation in question. And this is as one should expect, given Schelling's views (at the time) concerning the inexplicability of the original opening-up of the structure of subject–object opposition.)

Second, and much more straightforwardly. As already indicated, the manifold conceptual ingredients of Schelling's ontologically inflected notion of moral individuality comprise the bases for his deduction of right. But here again, the argument does not proceed by deriving right as a *transcendental condition* of any of the *structures of differentiation, relation, or conation* that inform moral individuality thus understood. Instead, right is derived as a principle that provides a *partial practical specification* of the *content of the superordinate demand*, addressed to every existing moral individual, to strive for unconditionality. Now, to the derivation itself.

The moral individual, *qua* moral, is impelled to strive for unconditionality. *Qua* moral *individual*, he or she is constrained to do so within a circumscribed segment of space and time shared with other selves, all of whom are understood to be striving for unconditionality, too – that is to say, all of whom are understood to be impelled by *one and the same* demand. "[T]his very demand is addressed to *all* beings"[47] – and understanding how best to meet the challenge posed by that demand, depends in part upon acknowledging that the same sort of striving is demanded of all of us.

Could it really be that "Strive for unconditionality!" demands of each of us an endeavor to become absolute as an empirical individual, such that, notwithstanding the unsurpassable limits established by nature, *no* empirical conditions could alter one's status or limit one's spontaneity? Clearly that cannot be what the demand demands. Given that we share a single slice of space and time, no one of us can attain the empirical equivalent of unconditionality without first shutting down the spontaneity of all others.[48] (So long as another's spontaneity exists, it can exert moral resistance even if its physical efficacy is obstructed.[49]) Now, if each and every one of us were called upon to snuff out the spontaneity of all others, then the call in question could just as well say, "Strive to impose conditions!" That is precisely what an endeavor for empirically absolute status ultimately amounts to. But that is precisely the opposite of that which the supreme challenge of practical reason demands. Thus, when properly understood, to strive for unconditionality under conditions of finitude, cannot be to endeavor to outstrip one's own limitations in a way that would obstruct the positive potential of others. Striving for unconditionality, therefore, must mean: aiming always to actualize one's own positive potential in a way that never impedes anyone else's endeavor to do the same.

> [E]very moral being must assert his freedom *as such*. And that is possible only insofar as every moral being renounces unlimited *empirical* freedom. For unlimited *empirical* freedom leads to endless antagonism in the moral world.

> ... Therefore, every moral being must yield his unlimited freedom in order to save his freedom *as such*.[50]

> We must think that all moral beings are striving to maintain their individuality. Therefore this universal striving of moral beings for individuality *as such* must restrict the striving of each for *empirical* individuality in such a way that the empirical striving of all others can coexist with the striving of each.[51]

Several sections later, Schelling remarks that the will can be considered absolute (*qua* finite will) only if every individual freely resolves never to impede the striving of another. Thus, what might superficially seem to be a restriction imposed upon striving proves to be precisely the change in orientation that first makes truly unrestricted striving practically possible.[52]

By this point, on Schelling's view, we have moved from the domain of morality into that of ethics – not to be confused with that of right.[53] Morality as such concerns only the individual, and it demands of the individual nothing more nor less than "absolute selfhood."[54] Ethics, on the other hand, presupposes the existence of a plurality of moral individuals and, by working out how striving for unconditionality is properly possible under such conditions, ethics "safeguards the selfhood of *all* individuals through the demand that it makes upon the individual."[55] But ethics is not the only safeguard for selfhood required under conditions of finitude. "[E]thics, being that part of morality which *demands* the *generality* [*Allgemeinheit*] of the will with regard to its *matter*, must be confronted with another science which *asserts* the *individuality* of the will with regard to its *form*."[56] Thus we arrive at the deduction of right, strictly so called.

Line by line, this deduction is quite detailed, but the argument's basic thrust is surprisingly straightforward. By "matter" of the will, Schelling is referring to the will's chosen end; "form" of the will denotes the freedom of willing as such. The highest ethical commandment demands that the matter of the moral individual's will be determined in a certain way, namely, via the adoption of unconditionality-for-everyone as an overriding general aim informing the formation of all of one's specific volitions. This ethical commandment (*Gebot*) subserves the higher moral demand (*Forderung*) to strive for unconditionality.[57] Strictly speaking, however, the determination of the individual will in accordance with the ethical command is not by itself a sufficient condition (although it is a necessary one) for the satisfaction of morality's supreme demand.

It is also necessary that the aforementioned ethical determination of the will involve no shutdown or surrender of spontaneous self-supervision by the individual whose will becomes determined in that way. The determination of the individual will in accordance with the ethical commandment must originate and occur within the spontaneity of that will itself – that is, it must be a matter of *self*-determination. Otherwise, ethical volition is not spontaneous striving for unconditionality, but the conditioned transmission of an impetus that originated elsewhere. A condition wherein all individuals are somehow brought to behave ethically would certainly be a great thing. But an existence wherein every individual freely brings itself into such behavior, by spontaneously willing spontaneity for all, would be a greater thing still: an existence more fraught with freedom, and thus more nearly approaching the ideal of unconditionality.

The moral individual therefore has a *right* to totally spontaneous self-determination. (As Schelling puts it, "[T]he supreme principle [*Grundsatz*] of all philosophy would be this: I have a right to everything by means of which I assert the individuality of my will as to its form."[58]) This right is irrevocable so long as one must strive for unconditionality – that is, so long as one remains a finite individual. At the same time, it is a right that one always *ought* to exercise in accord with the ethical commandment, so long as one remains a single individual amidst a plurality of persons who share one world. Finite freedom, for Schelling, can find its fulfillment in no other way.[59]

Notes

1 See Schelling's letter to Niethammer of 23 March 1796, in Horst Fuhrmans (ed.), *F.W.J. Schelling. Briefe* (Bonn: Bouvier, 1962).

2 Easter 1796 saw the publication of Part I of Fichte's, *Grundlage des Naturrechts nach Principien der Wissenschaftslehre.* (SW, III: 1–385; FNR). Schelling's aphorisms on natural right were not published until later that year, under the title *Neue Deduktion des Naturrechts*, in the (belated) April 1796 issue of Niethammer's *Philosophischen Journal.* (W, I: 247–80; UHK, 221–47).

3 See §§1–3 of the *Grundlage des Naturrechts* (SW, III: 17–40; FNR: 18–39).

4 NDN §3 (W, I: 247; UHK: 221). While references to UHK are provided throughout, the translations of Schelling in this essay are for the most part my own.

5 The operative term here, *Forderung*, can carry the connotation of a challenge, in addition to its more literal meaning as a demand.

6 "*Strebe nach Unbedingtheit!,*" NDN, §23 (W, I: 251; UHK: 224).

7 NDN, §§1–2 (W, I: 247; UHK: 221). Cf. section 3 of this chapter.

8 In Fichte, see *Über den Begriff der Wissenschaftslehre* (esp. SW, I: 49f.; EPW: 109f). In Schelling, compare *Über die Möglichkeit einer Form der Philosophie überhaupt* (W, I: 45–72; UHK: 38–55). Both texts were published in 1794. For analysis of Reinhold's influence, see Daniel Breazeale, "Between Kant and Fichte: Karl Leonhard Reinhold's 'Elementary Philosophy'," *Review of Metaphysics*, 35 (1982): 785–821. See also Frederick Beiser, *The Fate of Reason: German Philosophy from Kant to Fichte* (Cambridge, Harvard University Press, 1987): 226–65.

9 From §1 of 1795's *Vom Ich als Prinzip der Philosophie oder über das Unbedingte im menschlichen Wissen* (W, I: 162; UHK: 71).

10 Most salient in this connection is GWL (SW, I: 83–328); compare FTP. GWL is available in English translation: *Foundation of the Entire Science of Knowledge*, in Johann Gottlieb Fichte, *The Science of Knowledge*, trans. and ed. Peter Heath and John Lachs (Cambridge: Cambridge University Press, 1982). For analysis, see Günter Zöller, *Fichte's Transcendental Philosophy: The Original Duplicity of Intelligence and Will* (Cambridge: Cambridge University Press, 1998).

11 See §8 of *Vom Ich als Prinzip der Philosophie* especially (W, I: 179–82; UHK: 83–5). The quotation is from *Über die Möglichkeit* (W, I: 96; UHK: 44).

12 The *[Erste] Einleitung* to Fichte's *Versuch einer neuen Darstellung der Wissenschaftslehre* contains many implicit criticisms of Schelling's early publications (SW, I: 417–49; IWL: 7–35). For analysis, see Steven Hoeltzel, "Idealism and the Ground of Explanation: Fichte and Schelling, 1794–1797," in Daniel Breazeale and Tom Rockmore (eds), *New Essays on Fichte's Later Jena Wissenschaftslehre* (Evanston, IL: Northwestern University Press, 2002); Daniel Breazeale, "Editor's Introduction" to IWL; Reinhard Lauth, *Die Enstehung von Schellings Identitätsphilosophie in der Auseinandersetzung mit Fichtes Wissenschaftslehre 1795 bis 1801* (Freiburg/Munich: Verlag Karl Alber, 1975).

13 In this connection, Jacobi's influence on Schelling's early efforts is worthy of note. See Rolf-Peter Horstmann, "The Early Philosophy of Fichte and Schelling," in Karl Ameriks (ed.), *The Cambridge Companion to German Idealism* (Cambridge University Press, 2000), 117–40. Concerning Jacobi's galvanizing criticisms of (a certain sort of) systematicity in philosophy, see Paul Franks, "All or Nothing: Systematicity and Nihilism in Jacobi, Reinhold, and Maimon," in the aforementioned *Cambridge Companion*, 95–116; cf. Frederick Beiser, *The Fate of Reason: German Philosophy from Kant to Fichte* (Harvard University Press, 1987): 44–91.

14 W, I: 170f.; UHK: 77f.

15 See especially *Vom Ich als Prinzip der Philosophie*. For analysis and discussion, see Steven Hoeltzel, "Idealism and the Ground of Explanation: Fichte and Schelling, 1794–1797," in Daniel Breazeale and Tom Rockmore (eds), *New Essays on Fichte's Later Jena Wissenschaftslehre* (Evanston, IL: Northwestern University Press, 2002); compare Michael Vater, "Schelling's *Vom Ich als Prinzip der Philosophie* as a Reading of Fichte's *Grundlage der gesamten Wissenschaftslehre*," in Daniel Breazeale and Tom Rockmore (eds), *New Essays in Fichte's Foundation of the Entire Doctrine of Scientific Knowledge* (Amherst, NY: Humanity Books, 2001): 183–96.

16 From the Third of the *Philosophische Briefe über Dogmatismus und Kritizismus*, published in installments in 1795 and 1796 (W, I: 294; UHK: 163).

17 Ibid. Hölderlin is an important influence on the way in which Schelling formulates this basic problem and treats some of its implications throughout the *Briefe*. For concise discussion of Hölderlin's influence in this connection, see Andrew Bowie, *Schelling and Modern European Philosophy* (New York and London: Routledge, 1993): 25–9. For more detailed documentation, see Schelling, *Materialen zu Schellings philosophischen Anfängen* (Frankfurt: Suhrkamp, 1975).

18 From the Sixth of the *Philosophische Briefe* (W, I: 308–13; UHK: 173–6). Not much later, in 1796, while working on the *Abhandlungen zur Erläuterung des Idealismus der Wissenschaftslehre*, Schelling began working out new ways of understanding the relation between the finite and the infinite, such that the difficulties just mentioned became considerably less acute. (This text is available in translation as *Treatise Explicatory of the Idealism of the Science of Knowledge*, in *Idealism and the Endgame of Theory: Three Early*

Essays by F.W.J. Schelling, trans. and ed. Thomas Pfau (New York: State University of New York Press, 1994): 61–138.) In any event, the difficulties in question importantly inform Schelling's practical philosophy as articulated in the *Neue Deduktion des Naturrechts*.

19 In addition to material quoted in section 3 of this chapter, see the Fourth of the *Philosophische Briefe* (esp. W, I: 299; UHK: 167).

20 In this connection, the following passage from Fichte's 1794 *Recension des Aenesidemus* is worthy of note: "If, in intellectual intuition, the I *is because* it is and *is what* it is, then it is, to that extent, *self-positing*, absolutely independent and autonomous. The I in empirical consciousness, however, the I as intellect, *is* only in relation to something intelligible, and is, to that extent, dependent ... Since, however, the I cannot relinquish its absolute independence, a striving is engendered: the I strives to make what is intelligible dependent upon itself, in order thereby to bring that I which entertains representations of what is intelligible into unity with the self-positing I. This is what it means to say that *reason is practical*" (SW, I: 22; EPW: 75). Compare Schelling's remarks concerning theoretical reason and practical philosophy in the Fourth of the *Philosophische Briefe* (W, I: 299; UHK: 167).

21 From the Eighth of the *Philosophische Briefe* (W, I: 324; UHK: 184).

22 From the Eighth of the *Philosophische Briefe* (W, I: 323; UHK: 184).

23 NDN §1 (W, I: 247; UHK: 221).

24 NDN §2 (W, I: 247; UHK: 221). Cf. the Eighth of the *Briefe* (W, I: 317f.; UHK: 179f.).

25 NDN §3 (W, I: 247; UHK: 221). The Ninth of the *Briefe* closes with the following lines. "[M]y vocation is to strive for immutable selfhood, unconditional freedom, unlimited activity. Be! is the highest demand of criticism" (W, I: 335; UHK: 192).

26 NDN §4 (W, I: 248; UHK: 221–2).

27 NDN §6 (W, I: 248; UHK: 222).

28 This is clear from NDN §7, especially (W, I: 248; UHK: 222). The sentence with which Schelling closes that paragraph: "The entire world is my moral property [*moralisches Eigenthum*]," should, accordingly, be understood to characterize only self-positing subjectivity described in such an artificially abstracted way. Subsequent sections make it clear that this is not Schelling's considered position concerning the relation between spontaneous selfhood and its experienced world.

29 Concerning infinity, see NDN §17, for example (W, I: 250; UHK: 224).

30 This point seems to be made, albeit somewhat indirectly, by §§10–12 of NDN (W, I: 249; UHK: 223).

31 W, I: 335; UHK: 192.

32 NDN, §8 and §9 (W, I: 248–9; UHK: 222). Significantly, Schelling openly adverts to these invocations of revelation: "The proper expression that belongs here! ... To one who has understood Jacobi, it cannot seem strange" (fn. to NDN §8 [W, I: 248; UHK: 222]).

33 NDN, §8 (W, I: 249; UHK: 222).

34 NDN, §12 (W, I: 249; UHK: 223).

35 NDN, §13 (W, I: 249; UHK: 223).

36 NDN, §14 (W, I: 249; UHK: 223).

37 NDN, §15 (W, I: 250; UHK: 223).

38 NDN, §16 (W, I: 250; UHK: 223).

39 NDN, §19 (W, I: 250; UHK: 224).

40 NDN, §18 (W, I: 250; UHK: 224).

41 NDN, §20 (W, I: 250; UHK: 224).

42 NDN, §21 (W, I: 251; UHK: 224).

43 NDN, §22 (W, I: 251; UHK: 224).

44 NDN, §23 (W, I: 251; UHK: 224).

45 Strictly speaking, I do not mean to assert that Schelling could not have had any such thing in mind. The text, aphoristic in format, is sufficiently abstract in content that it might admit of interpretation along such lines. Still, I expect that, in that case, the interpretation offered in the present essay would much more naturally align with the text.

46 I take *Aufforderung* to be a species of *Anstoß*. See §3 of the *Grundlage des Naturrechts* (SW, III: 33–4; FNR: 32–3). Note that a regressive derivation of the occurrence of an *Anstoß* or *Aufforderung qua* transcendental precondition of experience, is not the same thing as an explanation of why an *Anstoß* or *Aufforderung* actually occurs in the first place. On the inexplicability of the latter within the context of the *Wissenschaftslehre*, see §6 of the *Zweite Einleitung* to Fichte's *Versuch einer neuen Darstellung der Wissenschaftslehre*: SW, I: 242–4; IWL: 74–6. On Fichte's doctrine of the *Anstoß* in general, see Daniel Breazeale, "Check or Checkmate? On the Finitude of the Fichtean Self," in Karl Ameriks and Dieter Sturma (eds), *The Modern Subject: Conceptions of the Self in Classical German Philosophy* (New York: State University of New York Press: 1995): 87–114.

47 NDN, §24 (W, I: 251; UHK: 224).

48 NDN, §26 (W, I: 251; UHK: 225).

49 NDN, §13 (W, I: 249; UHK: 223).

50 NDN, §§26–7 (W, I: 251–2; UHK: 225). The ellipsis indicates a break between paragraphs; no other text is omitted.

51 NDN, §29 (W, I: 252; UHK: 225).

52 NDN, §§43–4 (W, I: 255; UHK: 227).

53 NDN, §§52–3 (W, I: 257; UHK 229); cf. NDN, §§68–9 (W, I: 260; UHK 231–2). Fichte observes a parallel distinction between the "rule of right" and the "moral law" (the "commandment of ethics," in Schelling's parlance). See, for example, SW, III: 10–11; FNR: 10–11.

54 NDN, §31 (W, I: 252; UHK: 225).

55 NDN, §31; cf. §§32–3 (W, I: 252; UHK: 225–6).

56 NDN, §52 (W, I: 257; UHK: 229).

57 NDN, §33 (W, I: 252; UHK: 226).

58 NDN, §68 (W, I: 260; UHK: 231); cf. §74 (W, I: 261; UHK: 232). While I am unable to further develop this point here, it is worth noting the way in which Schelling's triad of practical principles (demand of morality, commandment of ethics, principle of right) instantiates the abstract structure that both he and Fichte (early on) insist must inhere among the principles of any systematic science. See the texts cited in note 9, above.

59 I wish to gratefully acknowledge the receipt of a James Madison University College of Arts and Letters Summer Research Grant in support of the ongoing project of which this chapter is a part.

Chaper 16

Fichte, Heidegger and the Nazis

Tom Rockmore

The political dimension of philosophy concerns not only specific political theories but also the political influence of specific positions. The initial reception of Fichte's political philosophy, roughly up to the First World War, was from a broadly socialist perspective.[1] After the First World War, Fichte was increasingly read from a nationalist perspective as anticipating German salvation (*die nationale deutsche Errettung*).[2] The latter approach leads seamlessly to a view of Fichte as a right-wing thinker. The more extreme view of Fichte as a kind of proto-Nazi derives from his influence on Nazi politics. Hans Sluga has recently extended this view in suggesting that Fichte also influenced Heidegger's Nazi politics. I think there is much to object to in Fichte's political philosophy, but no good reason to think he was a Nazi *avant la lettre*. I will be arguing that Fichte's political views are very different from what the Nazis, including Martin Heidegger, made of them. I will further be casting doubt on Fichte's influence on Heidegger's political views, which depend indirectly on *Volksideologie* and directly on his own revisionary reading of Nazism.

1 Philosophy and Politics

The complex relation between philosophy and politics cannot be adequately described in any simple way. The venerable distinction between theory and practice suggests philosophy is merely limited to carrying on a theoretical debate. Yet philosophical ideas sometimes transcend the narrow limits of academic discussion. The founding documents of the United States are influenced by Locke. At Stalingrad Hegel's left-wing and right-wing students met on the field of battle.[3] In our time Georg Lukács and Martin Heidegger[4] sought on the basis of their political theories to intervene directly in the political process.

Fichte, of course, would have been pleased by the opportunity to influence the world outside the university. His political engagement in favor of the

French Revolution was older than his philosophical position which, following his view of the events in France, he conceived as the first system of freedom.[5] He belongs among those philosophers who since Socrates have not only had formulated political theories but also acted on them. His reaction against the French occupation of the Germany in a period of need is well known.[6] Fichte thought, as many since Socrates have also believed, and as Plato explicitly claimed, that philosophy is specifically relevant to life in society.

With the possible exception of Hegel,[7] Fichte was the German philosopher of his time most concerned with political themes. Although he wrote extensively on political philosophy, and although he directly intervened in the political debate, his political theories have mainly been forgotten. Yet theories need not be consciously held or even directly discussed to be effective. Important philosophers like Fichte are precisely important since their ideas continue to exert their influence in ways which often cannot been foreseen.

Though a resolutely left-wing political thinker, paradoxically Fichte has influenced many right-wing thinkers and politicians. Hans Sluga has recently suggested that Fichte is a forerunner of what happened under the Nazis.[8] According to Sluga, Fichte's political theories were doubly influential in the Nazi period: in providing a kind of general political template which appealed to the Nazis, and in providing a source on which Heidegger relied in solving (or resolving) an existential crisis.

Sluga's view of Fichte raises several issues loosely grouped around the relation between philosophical theory and political practice. Is Fichte responsible for Heidegger's Nazism? Is he responsable for Nazism? In discussing these and other issues, I will mainly be interested in Fichte's relation to later political events and philosophical theories as illustrating one aspect of the complex question of the relation of philosophy to the good life.

2 Fichte and Nazism

Sluga's claim raises the familiar question of influence. Important philosophers influence the later discussion in ways that neither they nor others can foresee and that may not accord with their intentions. As befits an important philosopher, Fichte influenced a wide variety of important thinkers. These include post-Kantian German idealism (Schelling and Hegel), the left-wing Hegelian reaction to Hegel after the latter's death, especially Ludwig Feuerbach and Karl Marx, left-wing socialists like Jean Jaurès, right-wing thinkers like Max Stirner, Marxists like Lukács, historians of philosophy like Richard Kroner, neo-Kantians like Emil Lask, and so on.

In our time, Fichte's effort to intervene in the political process has been arguably more influential than his theories of political philosophy. Philosophers since Socrates have often been reticent to act on their convictions. Like Marx, Heidegger, Lukács and a few others, Fichte's position seamlessly unites political theory with political action.

Fichte's theoretical views of politics have mainly been forgotten, but his efforts to intervene politically continued to attract attention well into the twentieth century. His appeal to thinkers during the Nazi period as well as to specifically Nazi thinkers is often mentioned in accounts of the history of German philosophy in the 1930s and 1940s. Here as elsewhere a strict demarcation between *Weltanschauung* and philosophy simply cannot be drawn. Fichte's endeavor in promoting the French Revolution to bring about human freedom, if necessary by authoritarian means, was seen by conservative thinkers as anticipating their ideas.

Sluga draws an implicit, but questionable distinction between Fichte's attraction for Nazis and for someone like Heidegger. According to Sluga, the Nazis were attracted to Fichte because of "his nationalism, his elevation of Germanness to a metaphysical essence, and then his concern with the well-being of the whole nation ...."[9] Since the latter point in no way distinguishes Fichte from other political thinkers, the case for Fichte's specific appeal to the Nazis rests on his nationalism and his concern with Germanness (or Germanity).

These problematic notions suggest either that an apriori approach to political philosophy is extremely dangerous or that Fichte was not very good about differentiating between his personal proclivities, such as his own version of the usual German academic anti-Semitism, whose roots are already apparent in Luther,[10] and a theory constructed on reason alone. It is likely that right-wing thinkers were attracted by Fichte's strong version of academic anti-semitism.[11] In the same essay on which he announced his support for the universal rights which emerged from the French Revolution, Fichte suggested that Jews form a nation apart at war with all the other nations, and based on hate.[12] He further suggested that Jews should be tolerated but not be accorded the rights of citizens.[13]

Once it began, right-wing interest in Fichte seems to be fairly continuous. There is no demonstrable break between the right-wing philosophical interest in Fichte after the First World War and the specifically Nazi concern with his theories. Sluga points to Fichte's influence on the founding of the Fichte Society during the First World War whose purpose was to promote folkish ideas, later promoted through the German Philosophical Society founded by the Kant scholar and anti-Semite Bruno Bauch.

The first article in the first issue of the new journal, *Periodical for German Philosophy* (*Blätter für Deutsche Philosophie*), founded in 1927, was devoted to "Fichte as a Beacon in Our Spiritual Distress." Here are some other examples: Karl Larenz, who became a member of the SS in 1933, published a book on *The Idea Of An Essentially German Philosophy in J. G. Fichte* in 1929.[14] Felix Krueger, who was Chairman (*Vorsitzender*) of the German Philosopohical Society (*Deutsche Philosophische Gesellschaft*) from 1927–34, co-founded the Fichte Society (*Fichte-Gesellschaft*) in 1915, which after the war opposed the red *Volkshochschule*.[15] Arnold Gehlen,[16] who became known for his conception of philosophical anthropology, was, like Heidegger, among the first wave of German faculty to become Nazis. He wrote a book on *Germanness and Christianity in Fichte*[17] which further developed the pre-1933 conception of the education of the people (*Volksbildungsarbeit*) that was a theme of the Fichte School. This general line continues in Wolfram Steinbeck, who collaborated with the notorious Amt Rosenberg, and published books on Fichte in 1939 and 1941.[18] These and others adhered to the view, expressed by Alfred Baeumler in an article on the occasion of Hitler's fiftieth birthday, that we owe to Fichte "the beginning of the people [ein nationaler Aufbruch unseres Volkes] …."[19]

3 Fichte and Heidegger

Sluga claims that Heidegger's interest in Fichte was political, based on the need to solve (or resolve) an existential crisis. This suggests a distinction between the interest of one philosopher in another's writings in normal and abnormal times. If Sluga were correct, then Heidegger would not normally have been interested in Fichte, to whom he would only have turned in an abnormal situation. In fact, Heidegger's concern with Fichte pre-dated his turn to Nazism.

According to Sluga, who may be right, we owe to Fichte's *Addresses to the German Nation* the first effort to forge an explicit link between the four themes of crisis, nation, leadership and order.[20] But there is a distinction between philosophy as a guide to life and the appeal to this discipline in times of crisis. It is because philosophy is held to function as a guide to life in ordinary situations that it is regarded as useful for crisis situations.

The conviction that intellectuals have a special role to play arises early in Western philosophy. We are all familiar with the Platonic doctrine, to which Plato may not have subscribed, that some among us, call them men of gold, on grounds of nature and nurture, can literally "see" reality. If only intellectuals can know in the full sense, and if philosophy is the highest form of knowledge, then intellectuals, particularly philosophers, have a special social role, which is only increased in difficult times. As part of the self-assigned role of intellectual responsibility, there seems for a very long time to have been a perceived link between philosophy and existential crisis. Various versions of this view seems to have been widely held by philosophers, and are apparently still held.[21]

If one looks at the rare occasions when philosophers actually became involved in the political process, the view that philosophers in particular have superior political acumen seems doubtful. In attempting to protect Heidegger, Hans-Georg Gadamer makes the general but implausible claim that philosophers are intrinsically unable to understand politics.[22] Yet even as the reputation of philosophy as relevant to the world in which we live steadly declines, the conviction that philosophers have a unique political role to play, particularly in times of crisis, has not declined. Among recent philosophers, Edmund Husserl exemplifies this conviction in his famous call to resist Nazism by defending the ancient distinction between *doxa* and *episteme*.[23] Husserl, who thinks of philosophers as functionaries of mankind, believes that philosophy can indeed be the guide to the good life.

4 Heidegger, Fichte and Crisis

As I read Sluga, he is making three claims: first, Fichte is the first to thematize a number of concepts, including social crisis. Second, Fichte's view of crisis and how to combat it were influential on right-wing thinkers, including Nazis in the 1930s. Third, Fichte's conception of crisis, the same conception that influenced right-wing thinkers, also influenced Heidegger's Nazi turning.

Any suggestion that Fichte's thematization of crisis led Heidegger to appropriate his ideas seems dubious. We need here to distinguish between Heidegger's complex view of the crisis with which inauthentic individuals are perpetually confronted and for which authenticity, or the authentic form of life is his proposed solution, and his view of an existential crisis that arose in the 1930s toward the end of the Weimar Republic. One plausible scenario might be that Heidegger turns to Fichte to resolve the permanent, or constitutive crisis affecting human beings through the solution of the contingent crisis that arose in Germany as the Weimar Republic declined. Yet Heidegger does not rely on Fichte for his approach to either form of crisis. His idea of the permanent crisis affecting Dasein is already in place in *Being and Time* before he read Fichte. And his reading of the events of the 1930s seems unrelated to his grasp of Fichte.

Heidegger only became a member of the NSDAP in 1933. But according to Petzet, who knew him well, Heidegger already rallied to Nazism as early as 1931.[24] Yet he gave lectures on Fichte even earlier, in 1929. [25] Heidegger's way to Fichte was paved by his interest in Husserl. The latter lectured on Fichte, whose position he considered as one of the few adequate anticipations of his own conception of philosophy as rigorous science. It has been suggested that in his own thought Husserl completes Fichte's supposed turn to an ego from which the entire world emerges.[26] To make the same claim in other words, Fichte's *Grundlage der gesamten Wissenschaftslehre* (1794), which Heidegger only read for the first time in 1928, although he lectured on it in 1929, is important for Heidegger's understanding of philosophy as system.[27]

The suggested link between Heidegger and Fichte's concept of crisis is also unclear. In the wake of the German defeat in the First World War there was an existential crisis in Germany, which lasted at least until the end of the Weimar Republic. The widespread perception of the crisis, which the Weimar Republic failed to solve, helped the Nazis come to power. As Sluga points out, Spengler, on whom Heidegger lectured in 1920, articulated the idea of crisis in a way which was later taken up by Nazi ideologists like Alfred Rosenberg. But Sluga cannot show that Heidegger turned to Fichte in order to overcome an existential crisis since he was already interested in Fichte before he became interested in Nazism. At most he later returned to Fichte.

He also cannot show that Heidegger relied on Fichte when confronted with the Nazi rise to power. Sluga is specifically concerned with Heidegger's infamous *Rektoratsrede*, a speech delivered on his assuming the rectorate of the University of Freiburg in May 1933 as Hitler's *Führer* in the German university.[28] Sluga might mean that Heidegger specifically appealed to Fichte because of the existential crisis in 1933. But that also seems incorrect. Heidegger was aware of and worried by the financial crisis which swept the world in 1929.[29] He was also probably worried about the political crisis in Germany brought about through the collapse of the Weimar Republic, which had been put in place as an experiment in democracy. The failure of this experiment resulted in the National Socialists coming to power in early 1933. But in 1933, after the NSDAP had come to power, Heidegger did not sense a crisis but an opportunity, as he later said, to realize what is German.[30] This is consistent with the idea that he thought that a resolution of the contingent crisis through turning to National Socialism would also bring about a resolution of the deeper, constitutive crisis affecting all human beings. Heidegger significantly made this same claim again independently in an infamous passage in *An Introduction to Metaphysics* where he again suggests that National Socialism represents an unexploited opportunity.[31]

I believe that Sluga simply does not make his case that in the *Rektoratsrede* Heidegger relies on Fichte. In his later discussion of his period as rector, Heidegger does not speak of Fichte but of Nietzsche and Jünger. If we assume, against Heidegger, that Sluga is right, it remains to be seen what kind of interest Fichte held for him then. In the *Rektoratsrede* he apparently turned not to Fichte but to Plato in order to found National Socialist ideology on fundamental ontology, politics on philosophy. Like a few others, especially Carl Schmitt, Ernst Krieck and Alfred Bauemler, Heidegger seems to have seen the Nazi takeover of German institutions as a genuine opportunity. He was interested at the time in taking power in the German university system as Nazism came to power and even, as Jaspers later said, in leading the leaders.[32] And later, when he did sense the crisis brewing as Germany embarked on the path that led to the Second World War, he did not return to Fichte. As part of the mysterious turning in his position, he rather turned against philosophy in favor of thought (*Denken*) while turning toward Hölderlin and poetry in general.[33]

5 Fichte on the German Metaphysical Essence

According to Sluga, on slightly different grounds Fichte was interesting to the Nazis and to Heidegger. I think, however, that the implicit distinction, say between philosophy and politics, if it can be drawn at all, is overstated. Fichte's appeal to the Nazis and at least in principle to Heidegger as he joined the Nazi party lies in the vexed notion of Germanness, so awkward in English, underlying the related conception of German nationalism. Germanness resonates throughout Heidegger's writings in the 1930s. Thus, on the first page of the *Rektoratsrede*, he raises the question of the essence of the German people[34] he will continue to pursue in his writings on Hölderlin, metaphysics, Nietzsche, and so on. The main text for Fichte's conception of Germanness is the famous *Addresses*. Here we need to distinguish between what Fichte says and what others later made of it.

According to G.A. Kelly, who claims that Fichte is misunderstood as a prophet of folkish German nationalism,[35] the twin themes of the *Addresses* are education to reach Germanness and the idea of the German mission in world history.[36] In the *Rektoratsrede*, Heidegger links the realization of the essence of Germanness to the ancient Greek philosophical tradition. Fichte's view of language changed over time.[37] The fundamental insight in the *Addresses* seems to be that the German race, by which he means those who speak German, a language supposedly more alive than alternatives, has a vital interest in banding together to resist the French occupants in order to realize a divine plan based on reason.

Important philosophers are often understood in ways at variance with or even directly contrary to their thought. Fichte has long enjoyed an unsavory reputation as a kind of proto-Nazi, precisely the view which Sluga develops. There is an enormous difference between what Fichte is saying and what the German Nazis later made of it. One point is the important, but fragile difference between patriotism and nationalism. All patriots are not nationalists, although some are. Nationalism has an exclusivist character lacking in patriotism.

It is easier to draw the distinction than to apply it. Fichte is arguably a patriot and not a nationalist, or at least more patriotic than nationalist. In the midst of the French occupation, Fichte called, sensibly enough, for resistance against the invading forces in order for the Germans to realize their potential for further development. His view of the German nation as a potentially organic unity insists on the need to be self-motivating, self-enclosed and independent from other countries. Germanness is not defined on racial or biological criteria, but through the possession of a common language as culturally important as Greek. He attributes to philosophy the role of showing the Germans who they are and how, if they adopt the correct pedagogical methods, they can help themselves to become what they are capable of becoming.[38] The aim, he claims, is not only to rid Germany of foreign troops but to produce a new self and a new age by recovering what has been lost by holding up to the present a picture of a possible future.[39]

Like every social reformer, like Marx on the left and Heidegger on the right, in the *Addresses* Fichte insists on the prospect of moving from the present period to a better period, in his case the reign of reason. Unlike Kant, Fichte did not foresee anything like the community of nations, much less the European Common Market or what is now called globalization. Fichte can perhaps be faulted for failing to take an international perspective, for failing to realize that no nation can hope to realize its potentials on its own, outside the community of nations. In this limited sense, his view ressembles Carl Schmitt's idea that politics must be based on the distinction between friend and foe.[40] He can also be faulted for the ethnocentric idea that one natural language is more alive than another, more closely in touch with reality, closer to the God, or similar convictions. Yet such ideas, which should be rejected, do not provide license to conflate Fichte's call to resist an invader through a dubious view of German nationalism and the Nazi call to realize the essence of Germanness understood in a biological sense.

The Nazi political program was based on a biological conception of race, which included physically eliminating the Jews, gypsies and others while exalting the so-called Aryans. In *The Myth of the Twentieth Century*, Alfred Rosenberg, the chief Nazi ideologist, developed the idea of soul as the interior form of race and the racial soul as the effective motor of history.[41] Like many in the university, Heidegger was opposed to biologism.[42] But he apparently held other views of the ordinary Nazi. In particular, he regarded the Nazi accession to power as an opportunity for himself, for Germany, even for human beings in general.

In his metaphysical reworking of the concept of Germanness, which Sluga erroneously attributes to Fichte, but which is a common theme in *Volksideologie*, Heidegger follows *Volksideologie*[43] rather than Fichte. The concept of the *Volk* is difficult to define. It is associated with an irrational conception of action, which can be illustrated through Joseph de Maistre, an early forerunner of fascism, who speaks of "the fulfillment of an unfathomable divine purpose which men cannot, and should not try to, fathom – and which they deny at their peril."[44] The conception of the German *Volk*, which Heidegger stressed, means different things from different perspectives. What for the Nazis was a step to world domination was for the average German a way to restore self esteem, a means to correct the perceived injustices of the First World War, even a way to win back what was lost in the war. For Heidegger it is mainly a means for the authentic thought of being in general.

This idea is on display in a large number of writings from the 1930s, including the *Rektoratsrede*, the Hölderlin lectures, *An Introduction to Metaphysics*, *Contributions to Philosophy (From Enowning)*, which some see as Heidegger's masterpiece, and so on. For present purposes, it is not necessary to follow this concept throughout Heidegger's writings. It will be sufficient to identify Heidegger's metaphysical view of Germanness in the former text.

The commitment to the *Volk* resonates throughout the *Rektoratsrede*. Beginning in the first sentence, Heidegger links the spiritual leadership of the university to a so-called unyielding spiritual mission concerning the fate of the Germans. This arises from the beginning (*Aufbruch*) of its spiritual-historical being (*Dasein*) that belongs to Western philosophy. The aim is once again to capture the greatness of the beginning. In a world without God, Heidegger is suggesting that the way forward is the way back into the past in order only then to realize the mystical essence of Germanness, the Germans as a historical-spiritual *Volk*.

6 Germanness again: Fichte, Heidegger and the Nazis

Despite the similar vocabulary, the differences between Fichte's and Heidegger's conceptions of Germanness are clear and important. It is one thing to say with Fichte that Germans should band together to protect themselves against the invading forces. It is quite another thing like Heidegger to subscribe to a totalitarian movement publicly committed to killing citizens, restricting civil rights, creating concentration camps and other related practices. Ever since Plato, a number of philosophers, including Fichte, have thought that philosophy should help in bringing about a politics based on reason in order to help us to realize our capacities. But Heidegger thought that through fundamental ontology philosophy can replace political science, ground National Socialism, and realize the mission and fate of the German people.

In part, the problem is verbal. Fichte, Heidegger and the Nazis use the same word "Volk" in entirely different, unrelated ways. Fichte is a child of Enlightenment reason that reaches a peak in Kant's philosophy. Heidegger is a child of the anti-Enlightenment revolt against reason. In reference to the *Volk*, Fichte has in mind what he unwisely, since the word "race" has no biological meaning,[45] calls the German race. He has in mind a people united by their usage of the German language that, like Greek, is said to be living in that it retains the capacity to influence life, for instance through education. His point, which is surely correct, is that German is one of the great cultural languages.

The Nazi conception of *Volk* continues and develops nineteenth century conceptions of Germanness. This amorphous view includes such typical characteristics as love of the fatherland, Germanic racial unity (*germanische Bluteinheit*), shared folk-consciousness (*völkisches Bewusstsein*), and so on. Heidegger develops the Romantic revolt against reason that in National Socialist philosophies favors irrationalist myth.[46] He shared the folkish idea of the mythical destiny of the German people. But since he was not a racist, he was uninterested in resolving the question of the identity of the Germans in terms of racial biology. He solved this question in inventing the myth of the Germans as the legitimate heirs to the Greeks, understood not as the original Nazis, but rather as the founders of the *polis*.[47] In talking about the Germans, Heidegger has in mind that philosophy is to become a *Volksphilosophie* through which the people can freely submit to its historical fate.[48] In our time of need, only what is specifically German (*das Deutsche*) can save us.[49]

In the politically charged atmosphere of the German academy, over hundreds of years philosophers have been concerned to reform higher education, if necessary through authoritarian means. But an authoritarian attitude, which Fichte certainly displayed, and which I am not endorsing, is very different from endorsing totalitarian politics.[50] The political distinction between Fichte and Heidegger can be stated in a single sentence. Fichte is concerned to bring people to reason to realize their capacities whereas Heidegger is concerned to use philosophy to turn them against reason. Though Fichte influenced the Nazis, including Heidegger, he was misunderstood by the Nazis as anticipating their own metaphysical concept of Germanness, on which Heidegger draws in his own political thinking. Yet it is farfetched to think that Fichte is responsible either for Nazism or for the ways his left-wing views were transformed into a right-wing ideology. Anyone's ideas can be adopted in any form whatsoever by anyone else. Fichte is not responsible for what others have incorrectly made of his position. Whatever else he is, Fichte is not a forerunner of Nazi thought.

Notes

1 See, for instance, Marianne Weber, *Fichte's Sozialismus und sein Verhältnis zur Marx'schen Doktrin* (Tübingen: Mohr, 1900).

2 According to Stadler, the most important representatives of the nationalist reinterpretation are H. Freyer, F. Meinecke, R. Strecker, F. Medicus, G.A. Walz and H. Schulz. See C.M. Stadler, *Freiheit in Gemeinschaft. Zum transzendentalphilosophischen Rechtsbegriff Johann Gottlieb Fichtes* (Cuxhaven-Dartford: Traude Junghans Verlag, 2000): 13n23.

3 See Herbert Marcuse, *Reason and Revolution: Hegel and the Rise of Social Theory* (Boston: Beacon Press, 1969).

4 For discussion of Heidegger, see Tom Rockmore, *On Heidegger's Nazism and Philosophy* (Berkeley: University of California Press, 1995).

5 See Alexis Philonenko, *Théorie et praxis dans la pensée morale et pratique de Kant et Fichte en 1793* (Paris: Vrin, 1968).

6 See J.G. Fichte, *Addresses To The German Nation*, ed. G.A. Kelly (New York: Harper, 1968).

7 Hegel's interest in politics has been extensively discussed. See, e. g., Joachim Ritter, *Hegel and the French Revolution: Essays on The Philosophy of Right*, trans. Richard D. Winfield (Cambridge. MA: MIT Press, 1982).

8 See Hans Sluga, *Heidegger's Crisis: Philosophy and Politics in Nazi Germany* (Cambridge: Harvard University Press, 1993): 40–41.

9 Sluga, *Heidegger's Crisis: Philosophy and Politics in Nazi Germany*: 30.

10 See Martin Luther, *Von den Juden und Iren Luegen*, in *Luthers Kampfschriften gegen das Judentum*, ed. Walther Linden (Berlin: Klinkhadt und Biermann, 1936).

11 Kant, the apostle of pure reason, held that Judaism was simply false. See *Der Streit der Fakultäten* (1798), in Immanuel Kant, *Kant-Werke*, ed. Wilhelm Weischedel (Darmstadt: Wissenschaftliche Buchgesellschaft, 1975), IX: 302, 305–6.

12 See "Beiträge zur Berichtigung der Urtheile über die französische Revolution" (1793), in *Fichtes Werke*, ed. I.H. Fichte (Berlin: Walter de Gruyter, 1917), VI: 149.

13 See *Fichtes Werke*, VI: 150n.

14 *Die Idee einer wesenhaft deutschen Philosophie bei J.G. Fichte*. See George Leaman, *Heidegger im Kontext. Gesamtüberblick zum NS-Engagement der Universitätsphilosophen*, trans. Rainer Alisch and Thomas Laugstien (Hamburg: Argument, 1993): 92.

15 See J.Z. Müller, *The Other God that Failed: Hans Freyer and the Deradicalization of German Conservatism* (Princeton: Princeton University Press, 1987): 76f. Cited in Thomas Laugstien, *Philosophieverhältnisse im deutschen Faschismus* (Hamburg: Argument, 1990,): 92. Sluga says that the Society was only founded in 1917. See Sluga, *Heidegger's Crisis*: 265n20.

16 See Laugstien, *Philosophieverhältnisse im deutschen Faschismus*: 109.

17 Arnold Gehlen, *Deutschtum und Christentum bei Fichte* (Berlin: Junker und Dünnhaupt, 1935).

18 See Wolfram Steinbeck. *Das Bild des Menschen in der Philosophie Johann Gottlieb Fichtes; Untersuchungen über Persönlichkeit und Nation* (Munich: Hoheneichen Verlag, 1939); and Johann Gottlieb Fichte, *Politik und Weltanschauung, Sein Kampf um die Freiheit in einer Auswahl aus seinen Schriften*, ed. Wolfram Steinbeck (Stuttgart: A. Kröner, 1941). See also Leaman, *Heidegger im Kontext*: 81.

19 Alfred Bauemler, "Philosophie," in *Deutsche Wissenschaft. Arbeit und Aufgabe. Zum 50. Geburtstag Adolf Hitlers* (Leipzig, 1939): 32. Cited in Leske, *Philosophen im "Dritten Reich"*: 301n90.

20 See Sluga, *Heidegger's Crisis: Philosophy and Politics in Nazi Germany*: 31.

21 See Richard Rorty, *Philosophy and Social Hope* (London: Penguin, 1999).

22 See Hans-Georg Gadamer, "The Political Incompetence of Philosophy," in Tom Rockmore and Joseph Margolis (eds), *The Heidegger Case: On Philosophy and Politics* (Philadelphia: Temple University Press, 1992): 364–9.

23 See Edmund Husserl, *The Crisis of European Sciences and Transcendental Phenomenology*, trans. David Carr (Evanston, IL: Northwestern University Press, 1970): 6, 12.

24 H.W. Petzet, *Auf einen Stern zugehen: Begegnungen und Gespräche mit Martin Heidegger, 1929–1976* (Frankfurt am Main: Societäts-Verlag, 1983): 37.

25 See Martin Heidegger, *Der Deutsche Idealismus (Fichte, Schelling, Hegel) und die philosophische Problemlage der Gegenwart*, Freiburger Vorlesung SS 1929, ed. Claudius Strube (Frankfurt a. M.: Vittorio Klostermann, 1997).

26 See Rüdiger Safranski, *Ein Meister aus Deutschland. Heidegger und seine Zeit* (Munich: Carl Hansa Verlag, 1994): 103.

27 See Claudius Strube, "Heidegger's Turn to German Idealism: The Interpretation of the *Wissenschaftslehre* of 1794," in Tom Rockmore (ed.), *Heidegger, German Idealism and Neo-Kantianism* (Amherst: Humanity Books): 123–39.

28 This speech has been extensively discussed. See Rockmore, *On Heidegger's Nazism and Philosophy*: 54–72.

29 See Martin Heidegger, *Die Grundbegriffe der Metaphysik. Welt – Endlichkeit – Einsamkeit* (WS 1929/30), ed. F.-W. von Hermann (Frankfurt a. M.: Vittorio Klostermann, 1985).

30 "The rectorate was an attempt to see in the 'movement' that had come to power, beyond all its failings and crudities, something that reached much farther and that might some day bring about a gathering of what is German unto the historical essence of the West. In no way shall it be denied that at the time I believed in such possibilities ...." Martin Heidegger, "The Rectorate 1933/34: Facts and Thoughts," trans. Karsten Harries, *Review of Metaphysics*, 38 (March 1985): 498.

31 See Martin Heidegger, *An Introduction to Metaphysics*, trans. Ralph Manheim (New Haven: Yale, 1977): 199.

32 See "Den Führer führen? Heidegger und kein Ende," in Otto Pöggeler, *Neue Wege mit Heidegger* (Munich: alber, 1992),: 203–54.
33 See, e.g., Martin Heidegger, *Hölderlins Hymnen "Germanien" und "Der Rhein"* (WS 1934/35), ed. Susanne Ziegler (Frankfurt a. M.: Vittorio Klostermann, 1980).
34 See Martin Heidegger, "The Self-Assertion of the German University: Address Delivered on the Solemn Assumption of the Rectorate of the University Preiburg," trans. Karsten Harries, in *Review of Metaphysics*, 38 (March 1985): 470.
35 See Fichte, *Addresses To The German Nation*: xxxii.
36 See Fichte, *Addresses To The German Nation*: xxviii.
37 For a more developed account of Fichte's views in the context of German idealism, see Jere Surber, *Language and German Idealism* (Atlantic Highlands: Humanities Press, 1996).
38 See Fichte, *Addresses To The German Nation*: 107–8.
39 See Fichte, *Addresses To The German Nation*: 2.
40 See Carl Schmitt, *The Concept of the Political*, trans. George Schwab (Chicago: University of Chicago, 1996).
41 See Alfred Rosenberg, *Der Mythus des zwanzigsten Jahrhunderts, Eine Wertung der seelisch-geistigen Gestaltenkämpfe unserer Zeit* (Munich: Hoheneichen, 1930).
42 See "Letter on Humanism," in Martin Heidegger, *Basic Writings*, trans. David Krell (New York: Harper and Row, 1977): 231.
43 For discussion, see Georg Mosse, *The Crisis of German Ideology: Intellectual Origins of the Third Reich* (New York: Grosset and Dunlap, 1964).
44 Cited in Isaiah Berlin, "Joseph de Maistre and the Origins of Fascism," *The New York Review of Books*, 37:14 (27 September 1990): 64.
45 See Luigi Luca Cavalli-Sforza, *Genes, Peoples, and Languages*, trans. Mark Seielstad (New York: North Point Press, 2000).
46 For discussion of the genesis of this approach, see Georg Lukács, *The Destruction of Reason*, trans. Peter Palmer (Atlantic Highlands: Humanities Press, 1981).
47 See Martin Heidegger, *Hölderlins Hymne "Der Ister,"* Freiburger Vorlesung SS 1942, ed. Walter Biemel (Frankfurt a. M.: Vittorio Klostermann, 1984): 106.
48 See Heidegger, *Beiträge*, §15 "Die Philosophie als 'Philosophie eines Volkes'": 42–3.
49 See Martin Heidegger, *Heraklit*, Freiburger Vorlesung SS 1943/SS 1944: 107–8, 123.
50 Hans Sluga has kindly pointed to a passage where Petzet, who knew Heidegger well, calls attention to Heidegger's interest in a Fichtean attitude toward the University: "Der Nationalsozialismus sollte in den Dienst einer Universität Fichte'scher Prägung gestellt werdern – nicht umgekehrt. Welche Utopie! Fichte wird hier nicht ohne Absicht genannt. Denn was Heidegger vorschwebte, hing auf das engste mit seinem Nationalgefühl zusammen." Petzet, *Auf einen Stern zugehen*: 37.

Chapter 17

Rights, Recognition, and Regulative Ideas: On the Relationship Between Fichte's Theory of Rights and Contemporary Liberation Philosophies

Arnold Farr

1 Introduction

In recent years philosophy has experienced a bit of a paradigm shift due to the development of what I shall call liberation philosophies. Developments in feminist philosophy, Africana or African-American philosophy, subaltern studies, Native-American philosophy and to some degree postmodernism have introduced new questions into philosophy and have emphasized new methods of philosophical inquiry. In short, philosophy, which has traditionally understood itself as occupying a view from nowhere, has been shown to be a socially situated exercise. The above-mentioned philosophies are representative of a "philosophy from below," philosophies produced by the ruins of history, philosophies of historically oppressed peoples. It should be obvious that when one stands at the bottom of the ivory tower he or she sees differently to one who looks out from the upper windows. Therefore, one who stands at the bottom of the ivory tower will be preoccupied with a different set of questions to the one who looks out from the windows. For example, the question of other minds cannot possibly be a significant question for the oppressed. The ultimate question for the oppressed is "why are people stepping on me?"

As victims of racism, sexism, homophobia, classism, ageism and other forms of domination, members of historically oppressed groups have pushed philosophy in new directions and extended the boundaries of philosophical discourse so that their suffering may have a place in philosophical discourse. To this end, philosophers who are members of or who sympathize with oppressed groups have become preoccupied with the problem of rights and the issue of recognition. Philosophers such as Charles Taylor, Iris Young, and Axel Honneth have made the problem of recognition central to their projects. It is in this contemporary context that we may inquire about the relevance of Fichte's theory of rights and recognition. It is my position that while contemporary theories of rights and recognition may reveal the limits of Fichte's theory, it is also the case that there is much to be learned from his work. Indeed, Fichte's analysis of the relationship between self-consciousness, rights and community can provide us with a deeper understanding of the way in which past systems of domination may still be destructive of human community and individual self-development even after particular systems of domination appear to have been dismantled. In this chapter I will first define liberation philosophy by comparing it to its more recognized counterpart, liberation theology. I will then discuss the consequences of misrecognition and how this leads to certain false assumptions about rights. Then I will examine Fichte's theory of rights as relational and regulative. In section 5 I will discuss Fichte's theory in the context of contemporary struggles for recognition. Finally, I will suggest that Fichte's principle of forfeiture instills in oppressed groups the right to revolution.

2 What is Liberation Philosophy?

Like most philosophies, liberation philosophy is a response to a certain problem in the human condition. As philosophers such as Gabriel Marcel and Martin Heidegger knew, all philosophy is a response to a crisis. The task and method of liberation philosophy is best understood if the crisis which gave birth to it is distinguished from the crisis igniting more traditional philosophies.[1] Let's begin by comparing liberation philosophy to its counterpart, liberation theology.

One might claim that liberation theology stresses the primacy of practical reason as opposed to other theologies which tend to stress theoretical reason.[2] That is, liberation theology is preoccupied with praxis or, we may say, world transformative striving, or self-formative processes. The truth of religious texts, dogma, doctrine, and practices can only be revealed in the world-transformative praxis of the believer. Therefore, it is not enough to know the truth, it is more important to act. Like Fichte, most liberation theologians refuse to preoccupy themselves with questions about the existence of God and the afterlife. Truth is in praxis. The method of liberation theology is to read traditional texts from the perspective of the poor and oppressed.[3]

Such a reading sheds new light on the world-transformative power of these texts. New questions are asked and new solutions discovered. Unlike most academic theology such as neo-orthodox and liberal theology, liberation theology is not concerned about the crisis of knowledge but about the crisis of a meaningful life, the crisis of living a human life under dehumanizing conditions.

Liberation philosophy shares these concerns with liberation theology. Members of historically oppressed groups have begun to read the philosophical canon through different lenses and with different questions in mind. While liberation philosophy has epistemic concerns, its crisis is not an epistemological one. In his reflections of Ralph Ellison's *Invisible Man*, Charles Mills wrties:

> What are the problems that this individual faces? Is the problem global doubt? Not at all; such a doubt would never be possible, because the whole point of subordinate black experience, or the general experience of oppressed groups, is that the subordinated are in no position to doubt the existence of the world and other people, especially that of their oppressors. It could be said that only those most solidly attached to the world have the luxury of doubting its reality, whereas those whose attachment is more precarious, whose existence is dependent on the goodwill or ill temper of others, are those compelled to recognize that it exists.[4]

Mills' point is this; members of oppressed groups occupy a different social position than those who are not oppressed. The kinds of questions that the oppressed raise, philosophical or otherwise, are largely a function of their social position. As Mills goes on to claim, we are not merely autonomous epistemic agents. Rather, we are members of epistemic communities. I take Mills' claim to be consistent with the spirit of Fichte's philosophy. If personality is a function of intersubjectivity or community, then of course different kinds of communities will produce different kinds of subjects. It is the community wherein one lives, moves, and has his or her being that shapes one's practical and theoretical orientation. Hence, it should be clear that individuals who are members of historically oppressed groups will have a different theoretical and practical orientation to those who are from more privileged communities. The recent proliferation of literature on difference is the result of this awareness.

3 Between Rights and Recognition: Difference and Democratic Struggles

There are two approaches to the issue of difference that one might take. The first view focuses on the fact that there are cultural differences and the members of various cultures ought to be free to express themselves and participate in democratic processes. This approach is rather superficial and is captured by the recent injunction that we "celebrate diversity." This view is based on the notion that although we are different, we should be treated with equal respect. On the surface there is nothing wrong with this view. However, it is very limited in its ability to examine the ways in which oppression of certain social groups is perpetuated behind the backs of members of the dominant social group. I will focus on a second view, which asserts that certain groups of people continue to be excluded from democratic processes because of biological differences and further socially produced differences.[5]

The second view of difference is best explained by situating it in the movement known as the "politics of difference." In her article "Difference as a Resource for Democratic Communication" Iris Young defines the politics of difference as "social movements that make a political claim that groups suffer oppression or disadvantage on account of cultural or structural social positions with which they are associated."[6] She continues:

> The politics of difference arose from a frustration with exhortations that everyone should just be thought of as a unique individual person, that group ascriptions are arbitrary and accidental, that liberal politics should transcend such petty affiliations and create a public world of equal citizenship where no particularist differences matter to the allocation of benefits and opportunities. Oppressed groups found that this humanist ideology resulted in ignoring rather than transcending the real material consequences of social group difference, often forcing some people to devalue their own particular cultural styles and forms of life because they did not fit the allegedly neutral mainstream. Thus movements affirming group difference called for attending to rather than ignoring the consequences of such difference for issues of freedom and equality.[7]

The politics of difference is an attempt to remedy the well-meaning attempt by liberal political theorists to dismiss the effects of group membership on one's potential self-development. The liberal tradition entails the following tension, first, we are all unique individuals. This emphasis on individuality isolates the self-formative process of the individual from the social group wherein self-formation takes place. Second, liberals argue that fundamentally we are all the same. Hence, group identity is replaced by a universal, human identity.

The politics of difference does not oppose the ideals of liberal thought, it merely opposes the assumption that because we all ought to be equal, we in fact are. The inequalities that I am talking about here are not based on some essentialist notion of group properties, but rather, socially produced inequalities. This is what Charles Mills refers to as a social ontology. That is, people are indeed positioned differently in society. We are positioned in terms of race, class, sex, gender, religion etc. Social position does affect one's opportunities for self-development.

Pierre Bourdieu's analysis of social class and capital would be helpful here. Bourdieu writes:

> The primary differences, those which distinguish the major classes of conditions of existence, derive from the overall volume of capital, understood as the set of actually usable resources and powers – economic capital, cultural capital, and also social capital. The distribution of the different classes (and class fractions) thus runs from those who are best provided with both economic and cultural capital to those who are most deprived in both respects.[8]

Bourdieu interprets class or group difference in terms of usable resources. Therefore, group identity is not based on an essentialist notion of shared natural properties, but on the possession of usable resources, capital. Different groups possess different quantities of social capital (the quantity and quality of social relations, connections), economic capital (property, possessions), and cultural capital (cultural knowledge, education).[9] We can conclude then that some groups are not equal to others in terms of these three forms of capital.

What does this analysis of social inequalities have to do with rights? The liberal theory of rights is problematic because it entails assumptions about people and their capacity to participate in democratic processes without any consideration of social and material relations. It also has its foundation in the problematic claims that rights are the possessions of individuals, and that we are equal to the extent that as human beings we all possess an equal quantum of rights. Here, rights are taken to be metaphysical properties.

Following Iris Young (and Fichte) I think it better to think of rights as relationships rather than as possessions. Young argues:

> Rights are not fruitfully conceived as possessions. Rights are relationships, not things; they are institutionally defined rules specifying what people can do in relation to one another. Rights refer to doing more than having, to social relationships that enable or constrain action.[10]

This view of rights cannot be understood apart from a theory of recognition which seems to be absent from the traditional, liberal theory of rights.

Contemporary democratic struggles and the politics of difference are both of the same fabric, which Charles Taylor calls the "politics of recognition." Taylor writes:

> The thesis is that our identity is partly shaped by recognition or its absence, often by the *mis*recognition of others, and so a person or group of people can suffer real damage, real distortion, if the people or society around them mirror back to them a confining or demeaning or contemptible picture of themselves. Nonrecognition or misrecognition can inflict harm, can be a form of oppression, imprisoning someone in a false, distorted, and reduced mode of being.[11]

In her work on recognition, Jessica Benjamin speaks of harm that can be inflicted on an individual because of the absence of a "supportive social context." Taylor and Benjamin believe that without recognition or a supportive social context the individual cannot achieve the sense of well-being, necessary for human development.

The politics of recognition is driven by the problem of the absence of recognition in general and the failure of the dominant group to recognize the ways in which people have been socially disadvantaged. Social position may increase or decrease one's opportunities for self-development. We may say that rights are socially conditioned opportunities. Young writes:

> Being enabled or constrained refers more directly to the rules and practices that govern one's action, the way other people treat one in the context of specific social relations, and the broader structural possibilities produced by the confluence of a multitude of actions and practices. It makes no sense to speak of opportunities as themselves things possessed. Evaluating social justice according to whether persons have opportunities, therefore, must involve evaluating not a distributive outcome but the social structures that enable or constrain the individuals in relevant situations.[12]

Here I would like to extend Young's argument. It is still not clear from her position how rights fit into contemporary democratic struggles. While Young is right to claim that rights are not possessions, it is still not clear how they function as relationships. It would be helpful here to define rights as regulative ideas instead of constitutive properties. Rights are concepts whereby we orient ourselves in community with others. This is, essentially, the idea behind social contract theory. Democratic struggles occur when there is a contradiction in a society which purports to regulate itself according to democratic principles. Chantal Mouffe writes:

> People struggle for equality not because of some ontological postulate but because they have been constructed as subjects in a democratic tradition that puts those values at the center of social life. We can see the widening of social conflict as the extension of the democratic revolution into more and more spheres of life, into more social relations. All positions that have been constructed as relations of domination/subordination will be deconstructed because of the subversive character of democratic discourse.[13]

Democratic struggles are set in motion by a performative contradiction, whereby oppressed people are treated as subhuman and yet expected to identify with and support the values of the society that subordinates them. In oppressive societies, members of oppressed groups are recipients of a contradictory *aufforderung*. That is, the basic structure of society may be such that individuals are called into being as subjects while simultaneously having their subjectivity denied.

This contradictory interpellation or summons is the material of contemporary struggles for recognition. Is Fichte's theory of right relevant with respect to this problem? I think that this problem discloses the limits and the relevance of Fichte's theory at the same time. I will now try to develop this position.

In the remainder of this chapter I will reflect on Fichte's notion of right as a regulative idea. I will then discuss recent democratic struggles or struggles for recognition in light of Fichte's principle of forfeiture.

4 Beyond Liberalism: Rights, Community and Regulative Ideas

It is to Fichte's credit that his theory of right does not succumb to most of the contemporary criticisms of traditional, liberal theories of rights. Indeed, Fichte's theory breaks with traditional liberal theories in two important ways. First, rights are relational. Second, the first claim is based on Fichte's nonatomistic view of the subject. Fichte's rejection of the atomistic view of the human subject is at once a criticism of the so-called Cartesian subject. Such a subject is conceived as self-contained, independent, and autonomous. This atomistic view of the human subject implies that rights too are atomistic properties contained within each atomistic, self-enclosed subject. Fichte's great contribution to post-Cartesian philosophy is the construction of a more intersubjective view of the self-formative processes of the human subject.

This break from the so-called Cartesian view of the subject is evident in Fichte's 1794–95 presentation of his system. In the *Grundlage* Fichte shows that absolute self-identity is impossible for the finite human I. He shows this by deconstructing the notion of a pure or absolute I. That is, pure self-identity is unthinkable. Self-consciousness is such because it carries its "other" in it as that which co-constitutes its identity. Absolute or pure identity is deconstructed, that is, peeled open to reveal the necessary "other" which participates in the formation of the self.

Similarly, in the *Naturrechts*, Fichte's deduction of the concept of right is a form of deconstruction wherein the subject is made aware that the concept of right is not based on the possession of some metaphysical property. Rather, the concept is produced in relation with another being like the first subject. Here, rights are not possessions but they are instead produced by an agreement, however unstable, between two or more rational beings. To say that I have a right to X presupposes a possible interference by another with my acquisition of X. Further, when I say that I have a right to X this claim has content. That is, I claim to have a right to some determinate thing. However, consistent with Fichte's method since 1794, determinacy always requires indeterminacy. A determinate right to a determinate X has its origin in something originally indeterminate yet determinable. Here we encounter Fichte's double fiction.

After he has deduced the concept of right from self-consciousness Fichte analyzes the possibility of the application of the concept of right. He claims that "If reason is to be realized at all in the sensible world, it must be possible for rational beings to exist alongside one another as such, i.e., as free beings."[14] This is possible only if these free beings limit their freedom through the concept of the freedom of all others. Already we have before us a hypothetical situation. The community of free beings is not necessary, but if it is to exist then certain requirements must be met. Fichte begins his analysis of original right with the question "What is entailed by the idea that someone is free in general, or is a person?"[15] Fichte states:

> Since here we are considering the content of this idea as a condition of the possibility of the co-existence of free beings, such content is to be called *a right*; and for the same reason, the conditions of freedom and personality will be set forth here only insofar as they can be violated by physical force.

This right, or these rights, are contained in the mere concept of the person as such and are therefore called *original rights*. The doctrine of original rights arises through the mere analysis of the concept of personality insofar as the content of this concept *could* be, but – in accordance with the law of right – *ought* not to be, violated by the free action of others.[16]

Given Fichte's account of original right, only some version of social contract theory can secure such rights. Hence, Fichte formulates a contract theory of rights that is hypothetical like that of Hobbes. The law of self-limitation can be imposed on one only if one enters an agreement with other rational beings. The desired consequent is a community of free beings. The notions of original right and of community of free beings are both necessary fictions and regulative ideas. Susan Shell writes:

> Original or pre-communal rights (Fichte does not speak of natural rights) are a philosophic "fiction," since "man attains rights only in community with others." They are, however, a necessary fiction, for in order to come to a full comprehension of justice, which involves a mutual limitation of wills, we must first comprehend what is limited.[17]

Likewise, Gary Herbert claims:

> Fichte acknowledges that, "Original Rights are, therefore, a pure *fiction*, but a fiction necessary for the purpose of Science" (*The Science of Rights*, p. 160). So original rights (e.g., Hobbsian natural rights) do not exist, but we must assume that original rights do exist in order to put ourselves in a situation where we can demand that they be recognized, thereby bringing them into genuine, albeit communal existence. Rights, then, are the incredibly fragile products (and preconditions) of community consciousness. They presuppose the possibility that others exist who will, in response to our demand for recognition, voluntarily restrict their freedom.[18]

Both of the above passages highlight the hypothetical nature of Fichte's notion of original right. The demand that a subject exercise his/her efficacy in the world requires a concept of right. That is, the subject must be assured that he or she will be allowed to carry out a plan constructed by practical reason. The subject can exercise its efficacy in the world only if others agree to limit their freedom so that the subject can act.

Iris Young was right in her assertion that rights are not possessions but are relationships. Young makes this claim in the context of showing how rights are denied to oppressed groups because of their place within society. Oppression is not always the result of the intentions of individuals but it may be based on certain basic social structures. However, Young fails to explain in detail how rights as relationships come into existence. This is Fichte's major contribution to contemporary liberation philosophies. On Fichte's account we see that the concept of right is deeply intertwined with the concept of personality. While Fichte has disclosed for us the origin of right and explained the necessary conditions for human community, there is another side to this picture.

5 Contemporary Struggles for Recognition: The Other Side of Fichte's Coin

We have seen that, for Fichte, original right and community are regulative ideas. I take Fichte's account of the origin of right to be correct, that is, rights are relational. The concept of right implies the limitation of the freedom of another free rational being. However, those philosophers who do liberation philosophy are also concerned about the real state of humanity. That is, for all of our society's political rhetoric about human rights, a significantly large portion of the human race do not enjoy the benefit of equal rights. Fichte's theory of the origin of right is important here because it is he who systematically dismantles the liberal theory of rights. Fichte shows that rights are not metaphysical properties but relationships between free rational beings. If Fichte is right, then, we are in a better position to understand how oppression works behind the backs of intentional agents.

Here I will briefly depart from Fichte's text. Fichte's text gives us a view of one side of the coin. That is, Fichte weaves a hypothetical web, which is designed to deal with violations of the law of right. The other side of the coin is the real world in which groups of people suffer daily from oppression. Here I will offer a view which I think is consistent with the spirit of Fichte's theory.

In an earlier section of this chapter I briefly mentioned the views of Charles Taylor and Jessica Benjamin. Both Taylor and Benjamin believe that recognition is essential to human development. The absence of recognition produces real harm that restricts the individual's opportunities for growth and development. Working from this perspective we move beyond Fichte's analysis to the extent that Fichte does not offer us an account of the ways in which the formation of the self is paralyzed by *mis*recognition and oppressive social structures. Fichte tends to equate a violation of rights with restriction by physical force. However, recent theorists have argued that harm cannot be reduced to physical force. Any form of misrecognition can be harmful.

What is lacking in Fichte's account is an analysis of the formation of social structures, the formation of social groups in those structures, and power relations. The violation of the law of right is more complex than the intentional actions of an individual. To be fair to Fichte, he is aware of the fact that even those whom we have elected to protect us may violate our trust. But there is still no analysis of the struggle for recognition between social groups or of the role of power in those struggles.

The notion of misrecognition may best be described as disrespect or, in Jessica Benjamin's terms, the absence of a supportive social context. To be clear about what is missing in Fichte's account I will turn to the three types of disrespect outlined by Axel Honneth in his book *The Fragmented World of the Social*. The first type of disrespect is addressed by Fichte. This type of disrespect takes the form of physical force. In this case harm is done to one's body. Honneth writes:

> Those forms of practical maltreatment in which a person is forcibly deprived of any opportunity to dispose freely over his own body represent the most fundamental type of personal degradation. This is the case because every attempt to seize control of a person's body against his will, irrespective of the intention involved, causes a degree of humiliation which, by comparison to other forms of disrespect, has a more profoundly destructive impact on an individual's practical relationship to self.[19]

This type of disrespect is associated with slavery, rape and other forms of force applied to one's body by someone else.

The second form of disrespect is the structural exclusion of persons from the possession of rights enjoyed by others. I use the term "possession" loosely here because it is Honneth's term, but the notion of structural exclusion still implies that rights are relational. With respect to the second type of disrespect Honneth writes:

> We can construe the term "rights" to signify those individual claims which a person can legitimately expect society to fulfill, since, as a fully-fledged member of a community, he has an equal right to participate in its institutional order.[20]

Disrespect occurs when the person is systematically denied full and equal participation in the institutional order of society. This is the type of disrespect challenged by the civil rights movement in the US.

The third type of disrespect is not so easily recognized. Disrespect or, to put it boldly, oppression and its many forms are often camouflaged by what we call traditional values and norms. Honneth writes:

> If this hierarchy of societal values is structured so as to downgrade individual forms of life and convictions as being inferior or deficient, then it robs the

> subjects in question of every opportunity to accord social value to their abilities. Once confronted with an evaluation that downgrades certain patterns of self-realization, those who have opted for these patterns cannot relate to their mode of life as one which is invested with positive significance within their community.[21]

The outcome of this form of disrespect is a paralyzing self-image. The point here is that an individual's rights can be denied without the application of physical force. The first type of disrespect involves physical force. The second deals with overt practices of exclusion. For example, Jim Crow laws in the south were design to limit the participation of black people in American life. By law, the African-American was denied full citizenship. The third type of disrespect is not as visible as the first two. It involves the construction of a system of values which demeans the values of historically oppressed groups. For example, if an African-American professor knows very little about European art and music, his qualifications are likely to be questioned. However, the white professor feels no such pressure with respect to acquiring knowledge about African-American achievements. It is not important that white professors know anything about the blues or the emancipatory function of black spirituals. Such areas of knowledge are referred to as "group interests," whereas the former is the type of knowledge that all educated people should have. This hegemonic social structure does indeed paralyze the self-development of members of oppressed groups.

6 Fichte's Principle of Forfeiture: The Right to Revolution

We have seen above that there are several impediments to the existence of a community of free, rational beings. Simply put, not only individuals but entire groups can refuse to limit their freedom for the sake of others. For example, members of wealthy social groups are free to accumulate as much wealth as possible. However, if all members of a society are going to have an adequate quantity of the material resources necessary for not only the maintenance of life but also for further self-improvement and development, there must be a limit on the amount of material resources one individual or social group can amass. Indeed, such a refusal to limit one's freedom can be normalized by the dominant group.[22] Fichte argues that if an individual refuses to restrict his freedom for the sake of other free beings, he then loses his rights. That is, he forfeits his claim to have a right to exercise his efficacy in the world. This instills in the victim the right of coercion. Fichte argues:

> The quantity and the applicability of this law has been determinately stated. It holds in general only under the condition and in the event that a community, a reciprocal influence among free beings as such, is to exist without harm to their freedom. But since the end of this community itself is in turn conditioned by the behavior of the person with whom one wants to enter into community, the law's validity for the individual person is in turn conditioned by whether or not the other person subjects himself to the law. But if the other does not subject himself to the law, then the law holds precisely by not holding, and it entitles the one who has been treated contrary to right to treat the offender as he wills.[23]

This principle of forfeiture is stated in many different ways throughout the text. In another formulation of this principle Fichte states:

> This law is completely inapplicable to my behavior with respect to someone who has not given this law to himself, since the end for the sake of which I was supposed to respect the other person's original rights no longer exists.[24]

The end for the sake of which I am supposed to respect the other person's original right is that of a community of free beings. We have seen that such a community can exist only if all members agree to restrict their freedom for the sake of all other members. However, if a person does not keep this law then he or she forfeits their right to claim that others should respect their freedom.

Without going into the details of Fichte's solution to this problem, I want to take this opportunity to focus of the necessity on regulative principles such as "original right" and the "community of free beings" for dealing with contemporary issues of social injustice. An unjust state of affairs is one wherein the rights of an individual or social group are violated by another individual or social group, hence disrupting the equilibrium of rights in a community of free beings. The law of right is maintained in such a case because the violation of the original rights of an individual creates in the individual the right of coercion. Fichte claims that, "the right of coercion arises where the equilibrium of right has been violated."[25]

Fichte's ideal of a community of free beings becomes the criteria whereby we measure justice. However, with respect to contemporary society matters are quite complex. I think that Fichte has provided us with a way of thinking about rights that is quite correct. Nevertheless, more is needed for us to really understand the various ways in which rights are violated in our society. Although Fichte is aware of the fact that the state, which is supposed to secure the rights of its citizens, can be organized in an unjust way, his analysis of such possibilities is limited.

The task before us as people interested in bringing about the community of free beings described by Fichte is to disclose the way in which the basic structure of society violates the law of right. Therefore, I believe that Fichte's theory becomes more intelligible when read in conjunction with Marx. That is, Fichte discloses to us the foundation of right or the necessary conditions for the existence of rights and community. Marx discloses to us the real conditions whereby rights and community are destroyed. Liberation philosophy tends to focus on the impediments to an equilibrium of rights. However, this level of analysis is not possible without an adequate understanding of the necessary conditions for community, which is provided by Fichte.

7 Conclusion

We know that Fichte, like Marx, wanted to change the world. It is the task of the scholar to make the world more rational. In the "Vocation of the Scholar" the philosopher is viewed as a type of activist whose task is to educate people in such a way that we will be at harmony with ourselves and others. Fichte's philosophy is indeed a liberation philosophy to the extent that it is a philosophy of freedom. There are two senses of freedom in Fichte's philosophy. The first is freedom over nature. In this context it is the *anstoss* which limits our freedom. The second is freedom from oppression by other human beings. Here the limit to our freedom is at the same time a call to freedom. It is on the basis of an *aufforderung* that I am called to participate in a community of free beings. It is this latter context where contemporary liberation philosophies can claim Fichte as a precursor.[26]

Notes

1 The crisis that characterizes traditional philosophy (especially modern philosophy) is the crisis of knowledge. The primary concern here is with scientific knowledge and skepticism. For liberation philosophy the crisis is that of the domination of certain groups of human beings by others.

2 Theologies such as neo-orthodox theology and liberal theology are preoccupied with theoretical reason to the extent that they are concerned about avoiding theological skepticism by demonstrating the truth of religious beliefs. Such theologians often use the tools of philosophy and science in their arguments.

3 Privileging the perspective of the oppressed is not all that different from Rawls' maxim in principle where Rawls suggest that we evaluate the fairness of our institutions by the worst social conditions that they generate. See John Rawls, *A Theory of Justice* (Cambridge: Harvard University Press, 1999): 132–6.

4 Charles Mills, *Blackness Visible: Essays on Philosophy and Race* (Ithaca and London: Cornell University Press, 1998): 8.

5 I use the terms "democratic" and "democracy" in a very broad sense here. I am aware of Fichte's criticism of democracy (which I tend to disagree with). Nevertheless, my use of these terms in this paper is not contradictory to Fichte's position. I use these terms merely to signify freedom, equality, and participation in the decision processes that will affect one's life and opportunities for self-development.

6 Iris M. Young, "Difference as a Resource for Democratic Communication," in James Bohman and William Rehg (eds). *Deliberative Democracy: Essays on Reason and Politics* (Cambridge and London: The MIT Press, 1999): 383.

7 Ibid.: 386.

8 Pierre Bourdieu, *Distinction: A Social Critique of the Judgment of Taste*, trans, Richard Nice (Cambridge, MA: Harvard University Press, 1984): 114.

9 Axel Honneth, "The Fragmented World of Symbolic Forms: Reflections on Pierre Bourdieu's Sociology of Culture," in Charles Wright (eds), *The Fragmented World of the Social: Eessays in Social and Political Philosophy* (Albany: State Uuniversity of New York Press, 1995): 190.

10 Iris M. Young, *Justice and the Politics of Difference* (Princeton, New Jersey: Princeton University Press, 1990): 25.

11 Charles Taylor, "The Politics of Recognition," in Amy Gutmann (ed.), *Multiculturalism: Examining the Politics of Recognition* (Princeton, New Jersey: Princeton University Press, 1994): 25.

12 Iris M. Young, *Justice and the Politics of Difference*: 26.

13 Chantal Mouffe, "Hegemony and New Political Subjects: Toward a New Concept of Democracy," in Cary Nelson and Lawrence Grossberg (eds), *Marxism and the Interpretation of Culture* (Urbana and Chicago: University of Illinois Press, 1988): 95.

14 J.G. Fichte, *Foundations of Natural Right*, ed. Frederick Neuhouser, trans. Micheal Baur (Cambridge: Cambridge University Press, 2000): 85.

15 Ibid.: 87.

16 Ibid.

17 Susan Shell, "'A Determined Stand:' Freedom and Security in Fichte's *Science of Right*," *Polity*, 25 (1992): 106.

18 Gary B. Herbert, "Fichte's Deduction of Rights from Self-Consciousness," *Interpretation*, 25:2 (Winter 1998): 209.

19 Axel Honneth, "Integrity and Disrespect: Principles of a Conception of Morality Based on a Theory of Recognition," in *The Fragmented World of the Social*: 250.

20 Ibid.: 251.

21 Ibid.: 251–2.

22 Some good examples of this are the abstract concepts of "free competition," economic laws, equality, free market, etc., in capitalist societies. The notion of free competition has less to do with competition between members of the general public than with the freedom of capital to reproduce itself endlessly.

23 J.G. Fichte, *Foundations of Natural Right*: 84.

24 Ibid.: 88.

25 Ibid.: 109.

26 One obvious criticism that one might make of the position developed in this paper is that it entails a confusion between politics and political theory. That is, it may appear that I've confused Fichte's political theory with the politics of liberation. However, I am skeptical of such a distinction. This distinction may be best analyzed in terms of the distinction

between theory and practice. I would stress the unity of the two for the purpose of the present project. This is a problem for another paper.

For Product Safety Concerns and Information please contact our EU representative GPSR@taylorandfrancis.com
Taylor & Francis Verlag GmbH, Kaufingerstraße 24, 80331 München, Germany

www.ingramcontent.com/pod-product-compliance
Lightning Source LLC
LaVergne TN
LVHW011120300926
849160LV00008B/456

9781138252257